AF701449

## CIVIL RIGHTS IN AMERICAN LAW, HISTORY, AND POLITICS

*Civil Rights in American Law, History, and Politics* charts the ambiguous and contested meanings of civil rights in law and culture and confronts a variety of important questions about race in contemporary America. How important is civil rights in America's story of possibility and change? How has it transformed the very meaning of citizenship and identity in American culture? Why does the subject of race continue to haunt the American imagination and continue to play such a large role in political and legal debates? Do affirmative action and multiculturalism promise a way out of racial polarization, or do they sharpen and deepen it? Are there new and better ways to frame our commitment to equal justice? This book brings together the work of five distinguished scholars to critically assess the place of civil rights in the American story. It offers different ways of talking about civil rights and different frames through which we can address issues of civil rights in the future.

Austin Sarat is Associate Dean of the Faculty and William Nelson Cromwell Professor of Jurisprudence Political Science at Amherst College and Justice Hugo L. Black Senior Faculty Scholar at the University of Alabama School of Law. He is the author or editor of more than eighty books, including *The Road to Abolition?: The Future of Capital Punishment in the United States*; *The Killing State: Capital Punishment in Law, Politics, and Culture*; *When the State Kills: Capital Punishment and the American Condition*; *The Cultural Lives of Capital Punishment: Comparative Perspectives*; *Law, Violence, and the Possibility of Justice*; *Pain, Death, and the Law*; *Mercy on Trial: What It Means to Stop an Execution*; *When Law Fails: Making Sense of Miscarriages of Justice*; and the two-volume *Capital Punishment*. Sarat is the editor of the journal *Law, Culture and the Humanities and Studies in Law, Politics and Society*. He is currently writing a book entitled *Hollywood's Law: Film, Fatherhood, and the Legal Imagination*. His book *When Government Breaks the Law: Prosecuting the Bush Administration* was recognized as one of the best books of 2010 by the Huffington Post. In May 2008, Providence College awarded Sarat with an honorary degree in recognition of his pioneering work in the development of legal study in the liberal arts and his distinguished scholarship on capital punishment in the United States.

# Civil Rights in American Law, History, and Politics

Edited by

**Austin Sarat**

Amherst College

CAMBRIDGE
UNIVERSITY PRESS

**CAMBRIDGE**
**UNIVERSITY PRESS**

32 Avenue of the Americas, New York, NY 10013-2473, USA

Cambridge University Press is part of the University of Cambridge.

It furthers the University's mission by disseminating knowledge in the pursuit of education, learning, and research at the highest international levels of excellence.

www.cambridge.org
Information on this title: www.cambridge.org/9781107039292

© Austin Sarat 2014

This publication is in copyright. Subject to statutory exception and to the provisions of relevant collective licensing agreements, no reproduction of any part may take place without the written permission of Cambridge University Press.

First published 2014

*A catalog record for this publication is available from the British Library.*

*Library of Congress Cataloging in Publication Data*
Civil rights in American law, history, and politics / edited by Austin Sarat.
p. cm.
Includes bibliographical references and index.
ISBN 978-1-107-03929-2 (hardback)
1. Civil rights – United States. 2. Race discrimination – Law and legislation – United States.
3. African Americans – Civil rights. I. Sarat, Austin, editor of compilation.
KF4755.C58 2014
323.0973–dc23 2013036446

ISBN 978-1-107-03929-2 Hardback

Cambridge University Press has no responsibility for the persistence or accuracy of URLs for external or third-party Internet Web sites referred to in this publication and does not guarantee that any content on such Web sites is, or will remain, accurate or appropriate.

*To Ben, with gratitude for all he is*

# Contents

## Contributors

**Mark Brilliant** is Associate Professor of History and American Studies at the University of California, Berkeley.

**Devon W. Carbado** is Professor of Law at UCLA.

**Montré D. Carodine** is Associate Dean for Special Programs and Associate Professor of Law at the University of Alabama.

**Tanya Asim Cooper** is Assistant Professor of Clinical Legal Instruction and Director of the Domestic Violence Law Clinic at the University of Alabama.

**Richard Thompson Ford** is George E. Osborne Professor of Law at Stanford University.

**Steven H. Hobbs** is Tom Bevill Chairholder of Law at the University of Alabama.

**Ronald J. Krotoszynski, Jr.,** is John S. Stone Chairholder of Law and Director of Faculty Research at the University of Alabama.

**Grace Lee** is Associate Professor of Law at the University of Alabama.

**Rachel F. Moran** is the Dean and Michael J. Connell Distinguished Professor of Law at UCLA School of Law.

**Austin Sarat** is Associate Dean of the Faculty and William Nelson Cromwell Professor of Jurisprudence and Political Science at Amherst

College and Justice Hugo L. Black Visiting Senior Scholar at the School of Law at the University of Alabama.

**Susan Sturm** is the George M. Jaffin Professor of Law and Social Responsibility and the founding director of the Center for Institutional and Social Change at Columbia University.

**Fredrick E. Vars** is Associate Professor of Law at the University of Alabama.

# Acknowledgments

This volume is the product of a symposium held at the University of Alabama School of Law on March 29, 2013. I want to thank the colleagues, students, and staff who helped make it such a successful event. I am grateful for the financial support of the University of Alabama Law School Foundation. A special word of thanks to former Dean Ken Randall for his unstinting support, for sharing the vision of legal scholarship reflected in these pages, and for making me feel so at home at the law school.

This book is a product of the University of Alabama School of Law symposia series on "Law, Knowledge & Imagination." This series explores the ways law is known and imagined in a diverse array of disciplines, including political science, history, cultural studies, philosophy, and science. In addition, books produced through the Alabama symposia will explore various conjunctions of law, knowledge, and imagination as they play out in debates about theory and policy and will speak to venerable questions as well as contemporary issues.

# Introduction

## The Civil Rights Story/The American Story

**Austin Sarat**

To pursue the concept of racial entitlement – even for the most admirable and benign of purposes – is to reinforce and preserve for future mischief the way of thinking that produced race slavery, race privilege and race hatred. In the eyes of government, we are just one race here. It is American. – Justice Antonin Scalia

It never ceases to amaze me that the courts are so willing to assume that anything that is predominantly black must be inferior. . . . Because of their 'distinctive histories and traditions,' black schools can function as the center and symbol of black communities, and provide examples of independent black leadership, success, and achievement. – Justice Clarence Thomas

It is widely recognized that the idea of rights is central to America's national identity and its sense of itself.[1] So powerful is our attachment to rights that some scholars see the American story as powerfully intertwined with what they label a "myth of rights."[2] In this myth of rights perhaps nothing plays as important a role as the history of the mid-twentieth-century struggle for civil rights for African Americans. *Brown v. Board of Education* is, of course, the key moment in that struggle, and it has become one of America's "sacred texts," a decision to which almost everyone pays homage even when they act in ways incompatible with its central premises.[3] It is to the spirit of *Brown* that groups seeking recognition continuously appeal, a spirit that today plays a key role in the debate over gay marriage.[4]

*Civil Rights in American Law, History, and Politics* brings together the work of five distinguished scholars to critically assess the place of civil rights in the American story. This work includes examples of both the "old" and the "new" civil rights histories.[5] It uses the sources and analytics of both legal and social history. It takes law seriously on its own terms but defines "law" capaciously. It attempts to capture what happens before, after, behind, in front of, and with little relationship to the Supreme Court. It is thus less linear, more multiple. It highlights complexity and contingency. In doing so, it addresses the people, institutions, and legal and nonlegal arenas in which actors and arguments meet.[6]

*Civil Rights in American Law, History, and Politics* looks backward and forward, connecting the twentieth-century civil rights struggle with new perspectives on the meaning of equality post-*Brown*. It comes on the heels of yet another civil rights decision by the U.S. Supreme Court in which the Court sent a challenge to affirmative action back to the lower court for review on the basis of strict scrutiny and held that under strict scrutiny a university seeking to use affirmative action would have to demonstrate "before turning to racial classifications, that available, workable race neutral alternatives do not suffice."[7]

As this decision demonstrates, even as we celebrate and struggle over the meaning and reach of civil rights post-*Brown*, when it comes to race and racial issues, these are strange times, confused and confusing, for all Americans. This is especially true when the issue of race involves relations between African Americans and Caucasian Americans. It is especially true at a time when we celebrate the triumph of the black middle class[8] while demonizing young black males in our inner cities.[9] Almost seventy years after *Brown* put an end to segregation of the races by law, the question of whether Americans can live with racial differences, and how we can do so, is a very live one. Current debates about affirmative action, multiculturalism, and racial hate speech reveal persistent uncertainty and ambivalence about the place and meaning of race in American culture and the role of law in guaranteeing racial equality. Moreover, all sides in those debates claim to be the true heirs to *Brown*, even as they disagree vehemently about its meaning.[10]

What can we learn about the role of civil rights in the American story, one legitimately might ask, from the fact that two Justices of the Supreme Court, who in many other respects share similar social views, take radically divergent positions about what our country should aspire to in recognizing race and racial difference? One, Justice Scalia, advocates a kind of uniracialist ideal and sees the achievement of that ideal as central to our national identity, whereas the other, Justice Thomas, the only African American on the Court, speaks in the language of black pride, if not black nationalism. And these differences certainly could be multiplied if we examined a broader array of political views.

American uncertainties and ambivalence about race go at least as far back as Tocqueville's pained observations about the three races in America and their sad inability to live together as equals.[11] In the intervening two centuries they have not been resolved by civil war, legal prescription, mass protest, or inspiring leadership. Today conflict between blacks and whites, and conflict about black-white relations, is as vexing as it has ever been.[12] Race, as Gunner Myrdal reminded us, is the "American Dilemma."[13]

Uncertainty is particularly acute in the legal domain where, over the last six decades, courts and judges have struggled to come to terms with the meaning of the Constitution's guarantee of equal protection of the law. In that period the record of judicial interpretation and understanding of racial equality has taken the form of a back-and-forth movement in which first desegregation, then integration with its accompanying need for busing and affirmative action, and now color-blindness have been the prevailing ideologies.[14] At each turn courts have tried to come to terms with the following issues: Can or should the law see, or see through, the racial mosaic that is America? Is taking race into account to remedy the effects of past racial discrimination a form of racism or a path toward a more racially tolerant society? Can law lead us away from discrimination and racism, or is it hostage to prevailing sentiments and opinions?

*Civil Rights in American Law, History, and Politics* speaks to these questions. According to the authors whose work is assembled in this book, the significance of the twentieth-century civil rights movement involves more than even its remarkable willingness to say no to one of the great shames of American history. The struggle for civil rights was, in the last century, an occasion for the rebirth of America, a retelling of a story of struggle and liberation. It pointed the way for a new engagement with the problem of difference, of how men and women of different backgrounds and races might live together as equals.

But the idea of civil rights marked a radical departure in the style and substance of our law, and it had a profound impact on the way Americans thought about law's role in promoting social justice.[15] The drama of *Brown*, of an appeal to law to make good on its promises, has in the last six decades been repeatedly reenacted in courtrooms across the United States. And

*Brown*, even today, provides a powerful template and touchstone through which contemporary racial issues can be seen.

As is now widely recognized, until 1954 the project of establishing the American Constitution was radically incomplete. It was incomplete because, in both chattel slavery and then Jim Crow, the law systematically excluded people from participating fully, freely, and with dignity in America's major social and political institutions on the basis of their race. But *Brown* changed everything. "*Brown*," J. Harvie Wilkinson contends, "may be the most important political, social, and legal event in America's twentieth-century history. Its greatness lay in the enormity of the injustice it condemned, in the entrenched sentiment it challenged, in the immensity of law it both created and overthrew."[16] It stood for the proposition that "race is an impermissible basis for governmental decisions."[17] Yet it did not end the indignities that the law itself had heaped on African Americans. *Brown* was at once a turning point and a source of resistance, a point of pride and an object of vilification. Its legacy, like the legacy of all great historical events, is, even today, contested and uncertain.

Like Lincoln's Gettysburg Address, the text of *Brown* is marked by surprising brevity, but also by startling vision. It was, in Richard Kluger's words, "the turning point in America's willingness to face the consequences of centuries of racial discrimination."[18] It altered the course of constitutional history by sweeping away the legal and philosophical underpinnings of segregation, and, in so doing, took a giant step toward the realization of the vision of respect for persons that, from the beginning, has animated our Constitutional vision. Like Lincoln's Gettysburg Address, *Brown* reminds us, again in Kluger's words, that "[o]f the ideals that animated the American nation at its beginning none was more radiant or honored than the inherent equality of mankind. There was dignity in all human flesh, Americans proclaimed, and all must have a chance to strive and excel."[19]

As the then-editors of *The Yale Law Journal* put it in their celebration of the thirtieth anniversary of *Brown*, "No modern case has had a greater impact either on our day-to-day lives or on the structure of our government."[20] And what was true more than two decades ago is no less true today. Yet ours is a time of revision and mixed views about the civil rights movement and its legacy. Whereas some commentators have noted that it has not resulted in the elimination of racism in American society, others suggest that the civil rights movement in general and *Brown* in particular have been given too much credit for sparking racial progress. "[F]rom a long-range perspective," Michael Klarman argues, "racial change in America was inevitable owing to a variety of deep-seated social, political and economic forces. These impulses for racial change . . . would have undermined Jim Crow regardless of Supreme Court intervention."[21]

For scholars like Klarman, the victories of the civil rights movement stand not as a monument to law's ability to bring about social change, but instead as a monument to its failure to do so. In their view, whatever racial progress America has achieved cannot be traced back to *Brown*. "[C]ourts," Gerald Rosenberg contends,

> had virtually no effect on ending discrimination in the key fields of education, voting, transportation, accommodation and public places, and housing. Courageous and praiseworthy decisions were rendered, and nothing changed. . . . In terms of judicial effects, then, *Brown* and its progeny stand for the proposition that courts are impotent to produce significant social reform.[22]

And some scholars now say that the integrationist vision, which is most closely associated with *Brown*, is inadequate to deal with the continuing subordination of African Americans in contemporary American society.[23]

All told, the story of civil rights in America is far from a happy one. The legacy of that story is today seen in what Hazel Carby calls "political apartheid"[24] and in Carol Greenhouse's description of the "criminalization" of racial minorities.[25] And as the continuing controversy and confusion surrounding race all too dramatically reveal, the civil rights movement unsettled as much as it resolved; it opened up new avenues for contestation, new ideas about how Americans should think about race, new challenges for law.

While the chapters in this book look back on the civil rights movement to assess its legal and cultural significance, they also examine its contemporary meaning and hold on the future. They do so in a time of turmoil in the American debate about race. As Wilkinson argues, "America stands at a critical juncture with respect to its race relations – a juncture every bit as important as that which confronted the Supreme Court in 1954."[26] Where once the integrationist ideal and equal opportunity were the preeminent ideals of racial justice, today each is seriously contested. Today criticism of affirmative action as well as the development of black nationalism and multiculturalism undermine, or at least challenge, integration for hegemony in the story of racial progress.

*Civil Rights in American Law, History, and Politics* charts the ambiguous and contested meanings of civil rights in law and culture and confronts a variety of important questions about race in contemporary America. How important is civil rights in America's story of possibility and change? How has it transformed the very meaning of citizenship and identity in American culture? Why does the subject of race continue to haunt the American imagination and play such a large role in the political and legal debate? Do affirmative action and multiculturalism promise a way out of racial polarization, or do they sharpen and deepen it? Are there new and better ways to frame our commitment to equal justice?

Chapter 1, by Devon W. Carbado and Rachel Moran, considers the place of civil rights in the American story through a survey of major cases in U.S. legal history. They begin by examining the country's history of legalized slavery, rejection of the citizenship rights for black Americans in *Dred Scott*, and the abolition of slavery. They note that blacks were not the only group denied citizenship in American history. Mexicans, Chinese, and others have been viewed as racially inferior and unfit to participate in processes of governance.

Indeed, until relatively recently, the story of civil rights in America's law, history, and politics was as much one of denial as of extension of rights, of exclusion as of inclusion of groups. Law has played a key role in establishing caste-like systems in the United States. Carbado and Moran see this dynamic at work in cases such as *Pace v. Alabama*, which affirmed the constitutionality of laws banning interracial marriage. *Pace* held that policies that maintained "separate but equal" standards between races did not violate the Fourteenth Amendment. This line of argumentation was crucial for the decision in *Plessy v. Ferguson*. In *Plessy* the court ruled that a man who was one-eighth black and seven-eighths white could be denied seating in the whites-only train car because the segregated cars met the "separate but equal" standard.

The story of civil rights that centers on *Plessy* is one in which racialized persons tried to identify themselves as white in order to obtain a privileged position in America's racial caste system. They took up the Supreme Court's invitation to minorities to do what the authors describe as "litigate [their] racial identit[ies]." This invitation was central to the litigation in

*Hudgins v. Wrights*, in which three women had to prove to a Virginia court that they were descended from free Native Americans as opposed to black slaves. In *Lum v. Rice* Gong Lum refused to self-identify as either white or black and was thus denied entrance to an all-white school. The Supreme Court upheld that denial. Prior to this case, Takao Ozawa had applied for naturalization on the grounds that he could be considered white, because his light skin had allowed him to assimilate into white culture. Nonetheless, the court denied him naturalization rights.

Chapter 1 examines cases in which members of other minorities litigated their racial identities. Those cases involved Arab Americans, Native Americans, and Mexican Americans. Carbado and Moran point out that in some of those instances the social subordination resulted from race-based policies that considered race more openly than today's allegedly color-blind civil rights. Thus, as is now well known, in World War II, Japanese Americans were subject to special curfews and mandatory evacuation to internment camps, both of which actions were found constitutional.

But *Brown v. Board of Education* altered the civil rights story and opened avenues for challenging explicit racial classifications in several areas. For example, plaintiffs in two cases, *Perez v. Sharp* and *Loving v. Virginia*, successfully challenged antimiscegenation laws. Yet, Carbado and Moran argue, these cases were the first of many that advocated color-blindness in law while allowing for the continued existence of segregation in fact. This de jure versus de facto tension can be seen in the recent history of litigation surrounding affirmative action. In *Regents of the University of California v. Bakke*, the Supreme Court struck down universities' racial quota systems but ruled in favor of university affirmative action programs that reviewed candidates holistically and could be justified as contributing to a diverse student body. Yet in *Shaw v. Reno*, the Court ruled that creation of majority-minority districts, a tenet of the 1965 Civil Rights Act, was unconstitutional if the districts were drawn solely along racial lines. Similar to *Bakke*, the Court ruled that race could be taken into account when drawing the district lines, but that it could not be the sole factor in the decision.

In 2000, the Court struck down the voting process for the Office of Hawaiian Affairs, which is responsible for the interests of indigenous Hawaiians. The Court found the electoral process unconstitutional because only those descended from indigenous Hawaiians were allowed to vote. The case extended the color-blind approach beyond the traditional bounds of race as conceived in *Brown*. Carbado and Moran contend that this case, along with *Bakke* and *Reno*, exemplifies the Court's general trajectory toward color-blindness as the key element in the civil rights struggle.

Carbado and Moran see in the long sweep of American history an incorporation of civil rights into American law, history, and politics. We no longer require people to be white to avoid discrimination, but we live in a society, they note, in which race-based inequality coexists with color-blind policy and in which the Supreme Court's reluctance to consider cases from a race-conscious standpoint has limited its ability to stop the unequal treatment.

A similar point is made in Chapter 2. Here Montré Carodine describes the popular civil rights progress narrative. This narrative tells a story in which America has advanced beyond its years of racism and entered a post-racial, meritocratic society. Carodine argues that this narrative has been used to deny structural racism and avoid repairing a still racist America. Carodine seeks to illustrate the persistence of racial disadvantage in post-racial America by showing how race is used as character evidence in court.

Carodine describes what she calls a "black tax." This term applies to the added costs that come with being black. Sometimes the costs are purely social, but they can also be economic. The counterpart to the black tax is the recognition of whiteness as property, or something that confers value on its possessor. In the case of the 2012 shooting of Trayvon Martin by George Zimmerman, we see the black tax and white privilege at work. Carodine argues that police initially trusted Zimmerman because he was white and that Trayvon Martin's parents had to craft his image with extra care to avoid stories of his disciplinary trouble at school, because of his blackness. The case illustrates that, long after the storied success of the civil rights movement, people must still engage in the litigation of their race.

Carodine examines specific rules of evidence that bring about the litigation of one's race in court. The first rule she discusses is Rule 404. This rule works to prevent prior actions of the defendant from being raised as character evidence. However, the rule makes an exception for bad acts and allowed Zimmerman's defense to present Martin's school disciplinary record as character evidence against him, despite the fact that discipline in general likely falls unevenly on black children and adults. The uneven application of the law, followed by the further discrediting of defendants through the presentation of past convictions, allows for a cycle that leads to the mass imprisonment of the black (and Latino) populations. As the cycle deepens and the hopes for a fair trial worsen, minorities become more likely to take plea bargains that allow them to avoid the courtroom altogether, resulting in more minorities having criminal records.

Carodine's chapter concludes with an examination of evidence Rule 404(b), which has recently been used "in reverse" to vindicate misidentified minority defendants. In *United States v. Stevens*, a black defendant, who had been identified in an unfair manner, used the rule to show that a different person of similar appearance had committed a similar crime, and thus to shed doubt on his own guilt. Yet Carodine cautions that this rule only legitimizes the use of race in the courtroom. In her view, all racialized applications of evidence rules should be opposed. To make progress in seeing the dangers of racializing trials, Carodine notes that we must first acknowledge what the civil rights story with its emphasis on color-blindness now elides, namely the continuing salience of race and the dilemmas that its salience pose for people of color in the United States.

In Chapter 3, Mark Brilliant offers a different perspective on color-blindness and its place in the civil rights story from the one offered in the first two chapters. Unlike Carbado and Moran, Brilliant argues that the Supreme Court never pursued a wholly color-blind or race-conscious agenda. Brilliant rewrites a common narrative of the American civil rights movement. That narrative describes a shift in the tactics of the civil rights movement from the time of the New Deal and World War II to the more recent Cold War era. It describes a shift from race-conscious to race-blind action. Brilliant's chapter suggests that the distinction between race-conscious and race-blind action is, in reality, quite blurred. He argues that recent civil rights action has not been purely color-blind, and that America's civil rights policy has been both color-blind and color-conscious. He hopes that this recognition will blunt the effort by conservatives to paint all recent progress as resulting from commitment to color-blindness.

Brilliant's chapter examines the position of Thurgood Marshall in two Supreme Court cases. In *Hughes v. Superior Court*, the Progressive Citizens of America (PCA) and the National Association for the Advancement of Colored Persons (NAACP) demanded that Lucky Stores hire black workers in proportion to black patronage. After the stores refused, the PCA and the NAACP picketed Lucky Stores. A court ordered the picket to end, but the black leaders continued it. Eventually the Supreme Court upheld the lower court's order and found the hiring demanded by the PCA and NAACP to be illegal because hiring decisions could not be made on the basis of race. Marshall joined the decision. In *Bakke*, affirmative action was upheld only to support a diverse student body, as long as the evaluation was holistic and there were no racial quotas. This limited support of affirmative action was attacked by Marshall, who sided with the majority while also arguing that the decision was too limited.

Brilliant argues that Marshall's shift from *Hughes* to *Bakke* can be seen as moving from an embrace of color-blind principles to those of color-consciousness, but he warns against embracing this simplified narrative. He notes that most civil rights efforts mix color-blindness and color-consciousness, and he sees Marshall's change between the two cases as just one example of that mix.

The bulk of the chapter carries this argument forward by discussing California's Fair Employment Practice Act, which was passed in 1959 and established the Fair Employment Practice Commission (FEPC) to enforce the law. This law made discrimination in hiring decisions on the basis of race, religion, ethnicity, or nationality illegal. Brilliant shows that in its enforcement decisions the FEPC did not simply prevent race from being considered in hiring, but it also consistently investigated the racial composition of companies' employees. When the composition was notably unbalanced, the FEPC would require employers to achieve more racial balance. By doing so, the FEPC mixed color-blind and color-conscious civil rights policy.

Brilliant's chapter uses the examples of Marshall and California's FEPC to argue that to really understand the place of civil rights in America's law, history, and politics, we need to go below the surface of macro trends to capture individual and local action. When we do, we see a more complex story than the kind Carbado and Moran or Carodine tells. This more complex story reveals ambiguities and uncertainties in America's understanding and embrace of civil rights.

Susan Sturm in Chapter 4 argues that the current approach to civil rights law, usually involving legal compliance and individual litigants, is an unnecessarily limited one for achieving progress. She offers a broader "collective impact" approach as better suited to the realities of racial inequality in American life. Like Carbado and Moran, Sturm believes that compliance-based color-blindness as the dominant policy approach to inequality is an insufficient means by which to address deep structural inequalities. Sturm examines what the compliance frame looks like in the case of antidiscrimination action. She discusses the main actors (such as civil rights lawyers), the role of government agencies (such as the Equal Employment Opportunity Commission), the primary strategies used to act (such as processing of complaints or monitoring), the leverage points, and the metrics used to measure success. When applied to antidiscrimination efforts, the compliance frame acts to disrupt differential treatment of legally recognized groups. The approach is limited by what the law recognizes as significant and by what can be feasibly achieved by a court.

Strum describes the collective impact framework by offering the example of Rutgers University's efforts to diversify its student body. Rutgers administrators were concerned that the university accepted too few students from New Jersey's inner cities. Affirmative action programs were being used to the extent allowed by law, and poor students were getting the kind of equal treatment that regulatory agencies required. This frustration led to the development of "Rutgers Future Scholars," a program that combined the efforts of leaders in government, communities, corporations, schools, and many other areas to increase Rutgers' accessibility to inner-city students.

Collective impact of the kind Rutgers embraced focuses on institutional change, which is achieved by involving many groups in a shared mission. The goal is to achieve equal opportunity and, in the process, "full participation." Full participation requires active reduction of inequality in institutions. Sturm notes that full participation allows actors to move forward and work on projects people agree about without needing to define the exact nature of the goal or the language used to explain the project.

Sturm's chapter rightly notes the key role of litigation-based civil rights action in contemporary American law and politics. Like Carbado and Moran and Carodine, she worries that antidiscrimination litigation often leaves existing structures of inequality intact. Compliance with antidiscrimination norms cannot accomplish enough on its own, and it often feeds what Richard Thompson Ford in Chapter 5 describes as an inaccurate progress narrative. Strum suggests that the civil rights story needs to embody a larger commitment to change in society and its institutions, one in which full participation is the goal.

In the closing chapter of the book, Ford contends that civil rights in American law, history, and politics is enfolded in a larger "progress myth." This "Whiggish" understanding of history is applied on too small a scale and actually blinds people to the kinds of problems with past policy noted by Carbado and Moran, Carodine, and Strum.

Ford defines progress as something more than incremental improvement. He is not clear about where the line falls, but he notes quite plausibly that progress should not be seen as the simple accumulation of small improvements. What worries him is that when these improvements begin to be called progress, we blind ourselves to the trade-offs that underlie most legal decisions.

Ford examines the effect of the progress myth on two issues in civil rights law: (1) the elimination of quotas in favor of holistic consideration to promote diversity and (2) the expansion of antidiscrimination criteria following passage of the 1964 Civil Rights Act.

The elimination of quotas in university affirmative action policy is often seen as representing progress in civil rights law. Yet Ford points to clear advantages of a quota-based system: it is cheaper than individualized, holistic review; it is a more certain route toward integration; and the current holistic review causes students to emphasize their "diversity" in ways that undermine the very goals of integration. Post-*Bakke*, there were complaints that the individualized "Harvard Plan" for admissions was too expensive for most universities. These complaints are forgotten as liberals and conservatives alike fit civil rights law into the progress myth.

Ford sees many problems with *Bakke*'s emphasis on "diversity." First, it equates racial difference with ethnic difference, thus underplaying the unique set of disadvantages black students have had to overcome. It tends to ignore and underplay continuing injustice. Finally, it denies the socializing element of education. Encouraging diversity denies this function, thus entrenching the cultural deficit of discriminated-against minorities.

On the problem of trade-offs and costs of civil rights policies, Ford turns to the Age Discrimination and Employment Act (ADEA) of 1967. The ADEA was meant to stop employment discrimination against elderly workers. Unfortunately, the law contributed to an increase in unemployment of older workers. By making employers fearful of a future wrongful termination suits, the law created a disincentive to hire unemployed older workers. Despite such problems, the ADEA has been enfolded into the civil rights progress myth, with the result that it has become harder to address structural inequalities.

Like Sturm, Ford worries that merely extending rights does not afford adequate protection for minority groups. Also like Sturm, Ford worries that extending rights is a way to avoid correcting the worst injustices. In the final analysis, the way we talk about civil rights in American law, history, and politics may offer consolation at the price of real progress and may help America avoid addressing real injustices that continue to characterize race relations.

While offering diverse perspectives, the works collected here are united in offering a complex view of the place of civil rights in American law, history, and politics. These essays ask us to think about the price of the progress we have achieved using the civil rights frame. They offer different ways of talking about civil rights and different frames through which we can address issues of civil rights in the future.

## Notes

1. Gary Jacobsohn, "Rights and American Constitutional Identity," 43 *Polity* (2011), 409.
2. Stuart Scheingold, *The Politics of Rights: Lawyers, Public Policy and Political Change*, 2nd ed. Ann Arbor: University of Michigan Press, 2004.
3. See Adam Liptak, "Brown v. Board of Education, Second Round," *New York Times*, December 10, 2006. Retrieved from http://www.nytimes.com/2006/12/10/weekinreview/10liptak.html?pagewanted=all&_r=0. As Liptak writes, "If there is a sacred text in the American legal canon, it is the Supreme Court's 1954 decision in Brown v. Board of Education. It is the court's one undisputed triumph, and no Supreme Court nominee who expressed doubt about the decision would ever be confirmed. Who can argue, after all, with the wisdom of putting an end to state-sanctioned racial segregation in the public schools?

   "But, as an extraordinary two-hour Supreme Court argument last week demonstrated, the meaning and legacy of Brown remain up for grabs. The court was considering whether school systems in Seattle and Louisville, Ky., could take account of students' races to ensure racial balance."

   "During the argument, two sets of justices managed, with equal vehemence, to invoke Brown – while understanding it to require precisely opposite things."

4. Martha Minow, "Same Sex Marriage and Brown v. Board of Education," *Balkinization*, August 10, 2010. Retrieved from http://balkin.blogspot.com/2010/08/same-sex-marriage-and-brown-v-board-of.html.
5. See Risa Goluboff, "Lawyers, Law, and the New Civil Rights History," 126 *Harvard Law Review* (2013), 2318.
6. *Id.*, 2319.
7. See *Fisher v. University of Texas*, No. 11–345, June 24, 2013, at 11.
8. A. J. Robinson, "The Two Nations of Black America," *Frontline*, February 1997. Retrieved from http://www.pbs.org/wgbh/pages/frontline/shows/race/economics/analysis.html. Robinson states: "The Black middle class is not only larger than ever, but [that] it is the fastest growing and largest segment within the Black community."
9. Tricia Rose, "Rap Music and the Demonization of Young Black Males," *USA Today*, May 1994. Retrieved from http://www.questia.com/read/1G1-15282517/rap-music-and-the-demonization-of-young-black-males.
10. See Martha Minow, *In* Brown's *Wake: Legacies of America's Educational Landmark*. New York: Oxford University Press, 2010.
11. Alexis de Tocqueville, *Democracy in America*, Henry Reeves, trans. Boston: John Allyn, 1976, ch. 18.
12. See Stephen Grant Meyer, *As Long as They Don't Move Next Door: Segregation and Racial Conflict in American Neighborhoods*. New York: Rowman & Littlefield, 2001.
13. Gunnar Myrdal, *An American Dilemma: The Negro Problem and Modern Democracy*. New York: Harper, 1944.
14. Kimberle Williams Crenshaw, "Race, Reform, and Retrenchment: Transformation and Legitimation in Antidiscrimination Law," 101 *Harvard Law Review* (1988), 1331.
15. What follows was first developed in Austin Sarat, "The Continuing Contest about Race in American Law and Culture: On Reading the Meaning of *Brown*," in Austin Sarat, ed., *Race, Law, and Culture: Reflections on* Brown v. Board of Education. New York: Oxford University Press, 1997. See also Myriam Gilles and Risa Goluboff, eds., *Civil Rights Stories*. New York: Foundation Press, 2007.
16. J. Harvie Wilkinson, *From* Brown *to* Bakke*: The Supreme Court and School Integration: 1954–1978*. New York: Oxford University Press, 1979, 6.
17. Charles Black, "The Lawfulness of the Segregation Decision," 89 *Yale Law Journal* (1960), 421.
18. Richard Kluger, *Simple Justice*. New York: Knopf, 1975, 8.
19. *Id.*, ix.
20. See 93 *Yale Law Journal* (1984), 981.
21. Michael Klarman, "*Brown*, Racial Change, and the Civil Rights Movement," 80 *Virginia Law Review* (1994), 10.
22. Gerald Rosenberg, *The Hollow Hope: Can Courts Bring About Social Change?* Chicago: University of Chicago Press, 1991, ch. 1.

23. See, for example, Drew Days, "*Brown* Blues: Rethinking the Integrationist Ideal," 34 *William and Mary Law Review* (1992), 53.
24. Hazel Carby, "Can the Tactics of Cultural Integration Counter the Persistence of Political Apartheid? Or, the Multicultural Wars, Part Two," in Austin Sarat, ed., *Race, Law, and Culture: Reflections on* Brown v. Board of Education. New York: Oxford University Press, 1997, 221.
25. Carol Greenhouse, "A Federal Life: *Brown* and the Nationalization of the Life Story," in Austin Sarat, ed., *Race, Law, and Culture: Reflections on* Brown v. Board of Education. New York: Oxford University Press, 1997, 184.
26. J. Harvie Wilkinson, "The Law of Civil Rights and the Dangers of Separatism in Multicultural America," 47 *Stanford Law Review* (1995), 993.

# 1

## Race Law Cases in the American Story

Devon W. Carbado and Rachel F. Moran

It is difficult to think of "Civil rights in the American story" and not have African Americans in mind.[1] Indeed, it is fair to say that African Americans have long functioned as the quintessential subjects around whom to frame civil rights interventions. This helps to explain the prevalence of analogies to race (or, more accurately, analogies to the African-American experience) in a range of civil rights debates, including gay marriage discourses that circulated the phrase, "Gay is the New Black."[2] These comparisons seek to trade on (and sometimes displace) the extent to which the African-American experience anchors our understanding of civil rights in the American story.

We think it makes sense that African-American encounters with American democracy have profoundly shaped our conceptions of civil rights. At the same time, our understanding of civil rights in the American story is decidedly incomplete to the extent that it is framed exclusively with reference to African Americans. This narrow focus forecloses the articulation of other civil rights narratives that have helped to form the American story. This chapter brings these narratives into sharp relief. We do so not by marginalizing the African-American experience, but by situating that experience in the context of a broader story about race, law, and American national identity. In this respect, the civil rights in the American story we will tell is one in which both race and law play crucial roles. In fact, race and law have interacted to produce some of the most dramatic stories about civil rights violations, civil rights reform, and civil rights retrenchment.

In pursuing this project, we mean not only to explore the leading cases, but also to investigate their relationship to other decisions that came before and after. By looking beyond the most salient decisions, the chapter will demonstrate how dominant accounts of civil right in the American story elide the significance of some racial and ethnic groups, reify race, and obscure ongoing questions about the meaning and relevance of race vis-à-vis American identity. By moving beyond the accepted racial canon of civil rights cases, we hope to achieve considerable diversity in coverage. Our engagement will cover blacks, Latinos, Asian Americans, Native Americans, and whites. Moreover, we will take up decisions not just from the United States Supreme Court, but also from state courts and lower federal courts. This will enable us to identify some "hidden gems"; decisions that arguably deserve greater attention than they have so far received in scholarly treatments of race, civil rights, and the American story.

The disputes underlying the cases we will analyze cover a range of contexts, including education, employment, housing, criminal law, marriage, and family law. Our aim is to show how some of the simplest aspects of everyday life became bound up in and manifestations of what Gunnar Myrdal famously called the "American dilemma."[3] Consistent with the storytelling theme of this book, we will describe the cases that constitute our archive not simply as legal events, but as narratives – narratives about hope and pessimism, power and marginalization, resistance and acquiescence, slavery and freedom, defeat and triumph, and life and death – in short, narratives about civil rights in the American story.

We have organized this chapter into four parts: "Birth of a Nation: Formal Citizenship and Sovereignty," "Separate and Unequal: Classification and Caste," "Our Constitution is Color-Blind: The Doctrine of Race Neutrality," and "With All Deliberate Speed: Race-Conscious Remedies." Notwithstanding that our treatment of the cases we explicate is decidedly summary, our hope is that our analysis will demonstrate the ways in which the narrative of civil rights in the American story has always been a multiracial phenomenon – from the very birth of our nation.

## Birth of a Nation: Formal Citizenship and Sovereignty

After the heady rhetoric of the Declaration of Independence sparked a successful revolution, the fledgling United States of America embarked on the hard work of nation-building. The drafters of the Constitution took a sober second look at the rhetoric of radical egalitarianism in the Declaration, and they blinked. The adoption of the Constitution in 1787 and its ratification one year later depended on a compromise – one that integrated slavery into the very fabric of American democracy. But this was not the end of the role race would play in forging our country's identity. In short order, in 1790, Congress further entrenched slavery and adopted an immigration law that restricted naturalization to whites. In 1793, Congress passed the Fugitive Slave Act, which allowed slaveholders to turn to federal courts for assistance in recapturing runaways who had fled to free states. Eventually, Congress moved to adopt whites-only voting rules in every territory except Illinois.[4] These actions demonstrated that race was far from a superficial wound on the body politic; in fact, race played a constitutive role in defining that body politic.

For many, the United States Supreme Court's 1857 decision in *Dred Scott v. Sandford*[5] is the paradigmatic anti-canonical case that illustrates the courts at their worst in dealing with questions of race, citizenship, and sovereignty.[6] There, the Court nullified the Missouri Compromise of 1820, a federal law that struck a fragile balance between slave states and free states. The Compromise permitted slavery to persist, but prohibited its expansion to territories newly acquired through the Louisiana Purchase. The Court, in a splintered decision that spawned nine separate opinions, found that the Compromise violated a constitutional right to own slaves.[7]

In the process, the justices rejected Dred Scott's claim that although once a slave, he had become free by residing in territories where slavery was prohibited. The justices found that Dred Scott, as "a negro, whose ancestors were imported into this country, and sold as slaves . . . [could not] become a member of the political community formed and brought into existence by the Constitution of the United States."[8] As a result, he was not entitled to the rights, privileges, and immunities that it guaranteed. As a black man, whether slave or free, Dred Scott existed beyond the boundaries of formal federal citizenship. The opinion made clear that the Constitution aspired to build a white nation. In reaching this conclusion, the Court hoped to end the relentless political struggle between pro-and anti-slavery factions as the nation expanded westward. Yet, instead of protecting the nation-building project by according constitutional protection to slaveholder rights, the *Dred Scott* decision pushed the country toward a profound political rupture, one that would ultimately lead to a bloody Civil War.[9]

The drama of *Dred Scott* has rightly earned a place in the anti-canon of race law, but the decision should not blind us to the manifold ways in which race has influenced the nation-building project. Indeed, almost ten years before Chief Justice Roger Taney decided *Dred Scott*, America ended its war with Mexico. Mexico had long been on America's expansionist agenda. As early as 1787, "Benjamin Franklin had identified Mexico . . . as [a] target for further expansion."[10] It was not until the 1840s, however, that America's expansionist agenda, or Manifest Destiny, took hold. As Laura Gomez notes, "[f]or many, Manifest Destiny conjures up a moment of national triumph before the dark years of conflict over slavery that culminated in the Civil War."[11] Gomez rightly argues that this conception of Manifest Destiny obscures that it was "a cluster of ideas that relied on racism to justify a war of aggression against Mexico."[12]

President James Polk played a significant role in effectuating this war. In 1845, Polk succeeded in annexing Texas.[13] Although the 1836 Treaty of Velasco had secured Texas's independence from Mexico, it was not yet part of the United States.[14] That incorporation would have to wait until March 1, 1845, when President-elect Polk succeeded in inspiring Congress to admit Texas to the Union.[15] Polk's postinaugural efforts to purchase California from Mexico were not so successful.[16] He came to realize that the only other way he could possess this vast region was by war – and, more particularly, a war in which Mexico was the perceived aggressor.[17] Thus, in 1845, America's investment in and commitment to waging a war against Mexico was firmly in place. War itself would come the following year. In March of 1846, President Polk moved American troops into the disputed territory between Nueces River and the Rio Grande, thus precipitating a conflict with Mexican troops. "Mexico has . . . shed American blood upon American soil," Polk told the Congress on May 11, 1846.[18] This affront, he suggested, demanded a decisive response. He asked Congress for a declaration of war, which he shortly got.[19]

As historian Rodolfo Acuña has observed, "The poorly equipped and led Mexican army had little chance against the expansion-minded Anglos."[20] Within two years, the war was over. The Treaty of Guadalupe Hidalgo, which remains under-studied in American law schools despite its crucial role in understanding the Mexican-American experience, transferred ownership of California and other Southwest territories to the United States.

At best, the treaty conferred formal citizenship on the Mexicans who remained in newly acquired American territory after the war. These Mexicans found themselves on the other side of a border they did not cross. Whereas conquest and expansionism had brought them into the United States, white supremacy kept them trapped inside the box of formal citizenship. Deemed racially inferior, they were considered unfit for the exercise of any real rights.

But even this extension of formal citizenship was highly contestable. Polk wanted the property (Mexico) without the people (Mexicans). Formal citizenship was the racial price he had to pay for his territorial ambitions. This political compromise meant that Mexicans themselves would have the citizenship rights that Chief Justice Taney could not imagine extending to blacks. At the same time, because Mexicans were not perceived to be of pure "Anglo-Saxon" racial stock, but instead were viewed as an impure and racially mixed group, they experienced the Jim Crow color line of separate and unequal before it was formally articulated as such in the South. As Laura Gomez observes, Mexican Americans became white by law but nonwhite by social practice.[21] This liminal status was a direct result of the ideology and practice of Manifest Destiny.

Nor were Mexicans the only nonwhite group whose "American" identity was forged at the interstices of conquest and American expansionism. At the outset, the United States had to grapple with the problem of treaties that accorded Native American tribes semi-sovereign status.[22] The tribes were something of an anomaly in a nation that equated whiteness with fitness for citizenship and self-governance. The heavy hand of the law might require that the treaties be honored, but the heavier hand of the politics of nation-building relegated tribes to a position of inferiority as nonwhites. The "peculiar" position that Native Americans found themselves in did not escape Chief Justice Taney in *Dred Scott*.[23] Indeed, he drew on it to distinguish Native Americans from people of African descent. Taney reasoned that "although they [Native Americans] were uncivilized, they were yet a free and independent people, associated together in nations or tribes, and governed by their own laws."[24]

According to Taney, America treated Native Americans as foreign governments, "as much so as if an ocean had separated the red man from the white."[25] This was not so, he maintained, with respect to Africans. In effect, "Taney extraterritorialize[d] Indians (people who were actually here) and intraterritorialize[d] blacks (people who had in fact been separated from white inhabitants by an ocean)."[26] He did this to suggest that whereas Native Americans were naturalizable, blacks were not. Taney acknowledged that "it has been found necessary, for their own sake as well as our own, to regard them as in a state of pupilage,"[27] but maintained that Native Americans – as subjects of foreign governments – could, unlike blacks, become American citizens.

The notion of Native Americans as at once sovereign, uncivilized, and "in a state of pupilage" permeates the case law on Native Americans. Consider, for example, the Cherokee cases,[28] which are rarely discussed in the context of narratives about civil rights in the American story. The Cherokee Nation was primarily concentrated in Georgia, a state that was becoming aggressively hostile to the tribe when the federal government did not completely remove all Native Americans from the state under the Georgia Compact of 1802. Georgia, a state in which slavery and hence presumptions of racial inferiority were deeply entrenched, increasingly extended its laws into Cherokee lands. The Cherokee Nation soon realized that the only way its members could regain their rights under treaties with the United States was through the United States Supreme Court. Rennard Strickland has argued that the status of Native Americans as both sovereign and inferior influenced the United States Supreme Court's resolution of the conflict.[29] His claim is that the racialization of the Cherokee people left them vulnerable to marginalization and exile. Eventually, the tribe was forcibly removed from its homeland, decimated, and divided by internal feuding.

Whereas the Cherokee cases figure marginally, if at all, in discourses about civil rights in the American story, *Dred Scott* occupies a central place. Most scholars treat *Dred Scott* as an egregious departure from American law and values. *t* In fact, the case built on the tragic consequences of earlier decisions that denied blacks due-process protections in the name of federal power. The most salient example of this is *Prigg v. Pennsylvania*, the first pronouncement on slavery by the U.S. Supreme Court.[30] In that case, Justice Joseph Story upheld the Fugitive Slave Act of 1842, despite his personal reservations about slavery. Margaret Morgan, the subject of the case, was a black woman whose parents, although never formally emancipated, lived in freedom on their owner's estate in Maryland, a slave-holding state. Morgan married an emancipated black man from Pennsylvania, with whom she raised six children. The couple initially resided in Maryland, but eventually moved to Pennsylvania, where they lived happily until Morgan and her children were seized, enslaved, and forcibly taken back to Maryland by the son-in-law of her parents' deceased owner. Justice Story believed that respect for federal power and the preservation of comity among slave states and free states were essential to the nation-building project. As a result, he read the Fugitive Slave Act to provide that the federal government had the sole power to regulate the recapture of runaway slaves. The price for this display of unity was borne by blacks, who even when free could not fully protect themselves from being kidnapped and enslaved by a master who claimed them as his property. As Ronald Sullivan argues, this price was palatable because of pervasive beliefs in the racial inferiority of blacks; beliefs that Story undoubtedly shared, whatever his views on slavery.[31]

Even though the notion of black inferiority lived on after the Civil War and the end of slavery, this ideology had to contend with the Reconstruction Amendments, which, among other things, conferred formal citizenship on blacks.[32] In particular, the Fourteenth Amendment expressly repudiated the logic of *Dred Scott* and earlier cases such as *Prigg*. But formal citizenship for blacks did not necessarily mean formal citizenship for other nonwhites – even those who were born on American soil. Notwithstanding the Fourteenth Amendment's language that "[a]ll persons born or naturalized in the United States, and subject to the jurisdiction thereof, are citizens of the United States,"[33] there was a very real question about whether this language applied to the Chinese, who by the end of the nineteenth century were already perceived to be irreducibly foreign and thus incapable of being folded into the nation-state. Situating the Chinese in the context of a discussion about nationhood is crucial, given cases like *United States v. Wong Kim Ark*.[34] The presumptively permanent foreign status of Chinese people was inscribed in a federal statute: the 1790 naturalization law that restricted naturalization to whites. Wong Kim Ark did not dispute his status as a nonwhite person; he was, therefore, unnaturalizable under the 1790 statute. The question was whether the Fourteenth Amendment accorded him citizenship as a function of his birth in the United States.

Wong Kim Ark's civil rights challenge pitted a federal statute against a constitutional provision. The naturalization law equated an ascribed characteristic – race – with presumptive unfitness for citizenship. The Constitution equated another ascribed trait – place of birth – with presumptive fitness. As a person of Chinese descent born in the United States, Wong Kim Ark brought these conflicting claims into sharp relief. Was he fit by birth or unfit by race? Ultimately, the Court held in 1898 that Wong was an American citizen, yet his race continued to make his citizenship suspect – a subject of speculation by immigration officers who required extensive documentation whenever he sought to reenter the United States after traveling abroad. Although home might have been where Wong's heart was, home was never a place for his race. To put the point slightly differently, and to borrow from Gloria Anzaldua, after acquiring formal citizenship, Wong Kim Ark was "at home, a stranger."[35] He became "not quite, not American,"[36] "foreign in a domestic sense."

The phrase "foreign in a domestic sense" comes from *Downes v. Bidwell*,[37] another marginalized case in our understanding of civil rights in the American story. As the United States became a colonial empire at the very moment in which it was constituting itself as a post-slavery nation-state, race played a critical role in determining how newly acquired territory would be incorporated. This question of incorporation was never just about places; it was also always about people. Before the Civil War, Congress and the states battled over the future of slavery on the assumption that all territories were on the path to statehood. Later, however, a model emerged in which some areas could remain perpetually dependent possessions with only limited sovereignty.[38] As Pedro Malavet has argued, *Downes v. Bidwell* facilitated such an arrangement for Puerto Rico by relegating the newly acquired territory to the status of an insular possession – "foreign in a domestic sense"[39] – rather than a site of self-determination.[40] This structural arrangement rendered the residents of unincorporated territories such as Puerto Rico second-class citizens, both inside and outside the borders of America's national identity. Meanwhile, on the mainland, a similar dynamic was at play. It, too, was producing second-class citizens – but through a formal system of racial classification and caste.

## Separate and Unequal: Classification and Caste

Given how centrally race has figured in the construction of national identity, no one should be surprised that race also plays a central role in defining personal identity. Understanding this role is crucial to understanding the place of civil rights in the American story. Far from being a superficial matter of skin color, race often has determined individuals' life chances. Even after the Civil War and the Reconstruction Amendments, Jim Crow segregation left blacks separate and unequal by law.[41] Two Supreme Court cases in particular facilitated the official use of racial classifications to both police the color line and create a deeply subordinating caste system: *Pace v. Alabama*[42] and *Plessy v. Ferguson*.[43]

In *Pace*, the Court confronted a challenge to an antimiscegenation law that banned marriage between blacks and whites. The state of Alabama argued that the law did not violate the equality guarantees in the Fourteenth Amendment because members of each race faced equivalent penalties for crossing the color line. The justices agreed, noting that the regulation of marriage was primarily a state concern and that the punishment was directed at the offense rather than a particular race.[44] The decision led to a proliferation of bans on interracial marriage, and fourteen years later, the Court extended its "separate but equal" analysis to uphold segregation in public places in *Plessy*.[45]

In *Plessy*, a man who was "of mixed Caucasian and African descent in the proportion of seven-eighths Caucasian and one-eighth African blood"[46] unsuccessfully challenged his expulsion from a whites-only train car as a violation of the constitutional rights secured to blacks under the Reconstruction Amendments. Part of the Court's analysis employed the same racial logic as *Pace*. According to Justice Henry Billings Brown's majority opinion, Plessy failed to demonstrate an equal protection violation because the Louisiana law in question separated blacks from whites and whites from blacks. In other words, as a formal matter, the law treated blacks and whites the same, so there was no constitutional problem.

Plessy's counsel advanced a second argument for overturning the law: The lawyers questioned the propriety of a statute that delegated to private railway companies the power to determine who was black and who was white. In arguing the case before the United States Supreme Court, attorney Albion Tourgee, a noted advocate for racial equality, contended that whiteness was a valuable form of property and that railway employees were able to deprive individuals of that property without due process of law.[47] It is precisely this argument to which Cheryl Harris turns in grounding her theory of whiteness as property. As Harris notes, Plessy's claim was that extensive race mixture meant that it was often difficult, if not impossible, to determine racial identity. Tourgee pushed this argument to show the contingency of racial determinations: "Why not count everyone as white in whom is visible any trace of white blood?" he queried. "There is but one reason to wit, the domination of the white race."[48]

In part, the Court neatly sidestepped this novel question by concluding that the issue of racial identity was a question of state law and that at any rate, Plessy had not formally challenged his classification in the earlier proceedings.[49] But the Court also partially engaged Plessy's whiteness as a property argument, observing that "we are unable to see how this statute deprives him of, or in any way affects his right to" a property interest in whiteness.[50] The Court reasoned that "[i]f he be a white man and assigned to a colored coach, he may have his action for damages against the company for being deprived of this so called 'property.' Upon the other hand, if he be a colored man and be so assigned, he has been deprived of no property."[51] The Court was inviting Plessy to litigate his racial identity.

This invitation was not necessarily disingenuous. Even in the context of slavery, there are a significant number of cases in which people litigated their race. *Hudgins v. Wrights*[52] is but one example of this juridical dynamic. How courts resolved these cases could mean the difference between freedom and bondage. Whereas a court's determination that a litigant was black or African always resulted in bondage, whiteness was not the only identity upon which one could ground a claim to freedom. Indeed, in *Hudgins*, the possibility of freedom was predicated upon Native American – not white – identity. Decided by the Supreme Court of Appeals of Virginia in 1806, *Hudgins* involved the legal battle of three women to prove that they were free citizens, not slaves. This determination rested on whether they were proved to have descended from a free American-Indian woman, as they claimed, or an enslaved black woman, as the alleged slaveholder claimed. At one time it had been legal to enslave American Indians, but when the government of Virginia began to find it lucrative to increase trade between whites and American Indians, their enslavement was prohibited. As enslavement of blacks was still perfectly legal, the ability to distinguish one's self as descending from American Indians was critical to many people's freedom.

As Angela Onwachi-Willig has argued, the court's opinion reveals the enormous role that hair and phenotype can play in determining an individual's race.[53] Yet, the fact that the case was decided in the context of slavery raises a question about its relevance today. Do we read this case only for the historical exegesis it provides or do we read it as well for its contemporary relevance? Asked more pointedly, do people continue to litigate their race? If so, how difficult are these cases to resolve and what is at stake? To the extent that neither slavery nor Jim Crow legislation is a part of the contemporary legal landscape, one might think that the problems engendered by racial classification have disappeared. On the contrary, the dilemmas and difficulties of categorizing people by race persist today, bedeviling both antidiscrimination law and efforts on the part of the federal government to count individuals for purposes of the U.S. census. Were Homer Plessy alive today, there would be a real question not only about how to count him, but about how he would count himself on the census.

Because of the centrality of *Plessy* as an anti-canonical case about African Americans, we sometimes ignore the significance of the case for other racial groups, particularly Asian Americans. Yet, *Plessy* profoundly affected the lives of people of Asian descent. Largely, it was with a simple citation to *Plessy* that the Supreme Court in *Gong Lum v. Rice* rejected a claim brought by Martha Gong Lum that her exclusion from a white-only high school violated equal protection.[54] Significantly, the relevant Mississippi constitutional provision did not specifically mention the "yellow race" – one of the preferred terms, along with "Oriental," for Asian Americans – but only "white and colored races." Martha Gong Lum thus had to decide on which side of the color line she belonged. In effect, her answer was neither; more particularly, she refused to identify herself as either white or colored.[55]

Only a few years earlier, Takao Ozawa found himself in a similar racial predicament.[56] However, this time the legal regime was not a state constitutional provision, but a federal statute. As noted earlier, in 1790, Congress had limited naturalization to free white persons. Congress amended this statute in the context of Reconstruction so that "aliens of African nativity and . . . persons of African descent" also were eligible for naturalization.[57]

Like Martha Gong Lum, Ozawa had to decide whether he could find a path to citizenship as a white person or one of African descent. How would Ozawa situate himself? Ozawa argued that he was white. For the most part, he based his claim on his success in assimilating to an American way of life and on the lightness of his skin. But, as Carbado has argued elsewhere, Ozawa also advanced a more radical claim that reflected his skepticism about the utility of whiteness as a category.[58] As Ozawa explained in his brief, "there is not an absolutely white person existing on this earth."[59] Like Plessy, Ozawa found that the Court was unreceptive to his efforts to complicate racial identity. His petition for naturalization was denied, and eventually, other Asian-origin groups would encounter similar barriers. Even when anthropologists considered some groups, such as Asian Indians, to be Caucasian, the justices relied on a widespread common belief that these groups were in fact nonwhite.[60] In doing so, the Court cemented their place on the wrong side of the color line.

Importantly, people of Asian descent were not the only group who asserted whiteness to acquire citizenship. "Middle Easterners" did so as well.[61] As John Tehranian notes, "[t]he results of these cases were mixed."[62] Courts sometimes considered Middle Easterners white, as in *Ex parte Mohriez*, where a federal district court invoked "the sciences of algebra and medicine, the population and the architecture of Spain and of Sicily, the very words of the English language," to conclude that a man of Arab descent was white.[63] However, most often, courts reached the opposite conclusion, as in *In re Ahmed Hassan*.[64] In that case, the court focused on skin color, religion and assimilability to conclude that Ahmed Hassan was unnaturalizable.

> Apart from the dark skin of the Arabs, it is well known that they are a part of the Mohammedan world and that a wide gulf separates their culture from that of the predominately Christian peoples of Europe. It cannot be expected that as a class they would readily intermarry with our population and be assimilated into our civilization.[65]

Like Ozawa, Ahmed Hassan found himself on the nonwhite/nonblack side of the color line, a racial position from which even formal citizenship was unattainable.

The question of situating individuals along the color line did not always involve racial categorization – whether, for example, a person is yellow or white. Sometimes the question was whether a person or group belongs on the color line at all. This is precisely the issue in *Morton v. Mancari*.[66] The case presents another dilemma of federal classification: How to deal with the identity of Native Americans in determining the permissibility of federal affirmative action programs. Tribes have been the subject of special legislation based on a history of conquest and treaties that accorded them semi-sovereign status. At the same time, and as our discussion of the

Cherokee cases reveals, Native Americans have been racialized, and their racial inferiority often has been used as a justification to divest them of their land and their rights. Today, the tendency to treat tribes as either racial or political has significant consequences. The Court has become increasingly unreceptive to programs such as affirmative action that weigh race in allocating jobs or government contracts. Therefore, if Native American tribes have a purely racial identity, programs directed at their needs are suspect. If, however, the tribes are political entities, the programs are simply part of a complex and ongoing negotiation about the tribes' relationship as dependent sovereigns of the federal government.

Carole Goldberg has argued that serendipity played an important role in the framing of this key case in Native American law.[67] Carla Mancari was a non-Indian employee at a Bureau of Indian Affairs school, who challenged policies that were designed to advance the hiring and promotion of Indians. During the litigation, a lawyer advocating on behalf of these policies, by happenstance, had a conversation that led him to appreciate the distinction between Indian identity as racial or political. The result was a victory in the United Supreme Court that preserved the Bureau of Indian Affairs policies, even as the justices rejected other affirmative action programs.[68]

Mexican Americans experienced a similar victory in 1954 in *Hernandez v. Texas*.[69] As in *Morton v. Mancari*, the Supreme Court did not employ an explicitly racial analysis. Decided shortly before *Brown v. Board of Education*,[70] the landmark case that struck down school desegregation laws, *Hernandez* addressed the systematic exclusion of Mexican Americans from grand juries in Texas. As Ian Haney Lopez and Michael A. Olivas have argued, there were important differences between *Brown* and *Hernandez*.[71] *Brown* was a highly controversial case targeting Jim Crow segregation and was very much in the public eye, whereas *Hernandez*, which invoked the same principles but for a different racial group, was virtually unknown and unrepresented in the media. Moreover, whereas *Brown* was backed by many prominent groups with substantial funding and support, the lawyers for Hernandez had to scrape together the funds even to afford the Supreme Court filing fee and the trip to Washington, DC. Finally, *Brown* treated African Americans as a distinct racial group; *Hernandez* did not do so with respect to Mexican Americans.[72]

Notwithstanding these differences, the *Hernandez* Court, like the *Brown* Court, found wrongful discrimination. *Hernandez*'s ruling in this respect made the opinion "the first civil rights decision of the Warren Court."[73] Yet, the case figures only marginally in our understanding of civil rights in the American story. In extending Fourteenth Amendment protection to Mexican Americans, the Court did not characterize Mexican Americans as a distinct, nonwhite group. Indeed, lawyers on both sides of the litigation argued that Mexican Americans were white. This agreement "precluded a racial analysis for what was otherwise evidently a racial case."[74] According to Haney Lopez and Olivas, one positive aspect of the Court's refusal to treat Mexican Americans as a distinct and nonwhite race was that it forced the Court to adopt an anti-subordination approach; one that focused on hierarchy and social stratification, and not simply on formal racial classifications.[75] In this sense, *Hernandez* helped to make clear that caste is often accomplished by, but does not require, formal classifications. This insight has largely disappeared into a contemporary normative claim that our Constitution is color-blind. Contrary to the lessons of history, today's Court treats race neutrality as a complete cure for discrimination, despite clear evidence of ongoing racial inequality.

## Our Constitution is Color-Blind: The Doctrine of Race Neutrality

No discussion about race and civil rights in the American story would be complete without an engagement with color-blindness or the doctrine of race neutrality. Justice John Marshall Harlan's dissent in *Plessy* is most often cited for this principle. According to Harlan, "Our Constitution is color-blind, and neither knows nor tolerates classes among citizens."[76] Although this was an important and radical position for Justice Harlan to stake out, it did not bespeak a commitment to social equality across the color line. Two passages in Justice Harlan's dissent make this clear. In one passage, Harlan observed that "[t]he white race deems itself to be the dominant race in this country. And so it is, in prestige, in achievements, in education, in wealth, and in power. So, I doubt not, it will continue to be for all time, if it remains true to its great heritage."[77] After reading this passage, one has to remind oneself that Justice Harlan was arguing against, not for, racial segregation. In short, "[w]hile in Harlan's view, the law should be employed neither to separate the races nor to create a dominant race, he [was] comfortable with a society within which there [was] . . . racial dominance."[78]

Further along in his dissent, and again ostensibly in the spirit of antiracism, Justice Harlan invoked the specter of the Chinese to question the constitutionality of the "separate but equal" doctrine. Again, he relied on images of racial inferiority even as he questioned segregation by law. As he wrote, "There is a race so different from our own that we do not permit those belonging to it to become citizens of the United States. Persons belonging to it are, with few exceptions, absolutely excluded from our country. I allude to the Chinese race. But by the statute in question, a Chinaman can ride in the same passenger coach with white citizens of the United States."[79] Here, Harlan's color-blind constitutionalism coexisted comfortably with the notion of the Chinese as being unfit for citizenship. In fact, Harlan's dissent traded on the unnaturalizability of the Chinese. Because Justice Harlan was arguing only against state-sanctioned racial segregation, these passages reinforcing images of racial inferiority remain obscure, and his vision of color-blindness has become politically and constitutionally ascendant.

Indeed, *Brown v. Board of Education*[80] is often celebrated as the realization of Harlan's vision. In part, this is because *Brown* overruled *Plessy*, but it is also because of the manner in which *Brown* did so. In *Brown*, Chief Justice Earl Warren, writing for a unanimous Court, struck down laws mandating racial segregation in the public schools. The Court rejected *Plessy*'s "separate but equal" doctrine by finding that "[s]eparate educational facilities are inherently unequal."[81] Regardless of whether tangible resources like facilities, books, and teacher qualifications in black and white schools could be equalized, segregation by law inflicted irreparable, intangible harms on school children that would "affect their hearts and minds in a way unlikely ever to be undone."[82] Some scholars have read this language to suggest that racial classifications per se are unconstitutional, and that the Constitution requires race neutrality. *Brown* did not expressly articulate this race-neutral principle, but that is one of the most common ways in which the case is interpreted.

Significantly, in delegitimizing the racial classification at issue in *Brown*, Chief Justice Warren had more to draw on than Harlan's dissent. Only ten years earlier, the Court had decided another racial classification case, *Korematsu v. United States*.[83] In *Korematsu*, the Court confronted the internment of Japanese and Japanese-American residents who allegedly posed a threat to national security.[84] Much as in *Brown*, there was no dispute about whether there was a racial classification. The question was whether the racial classification was constitutional. In the context of answering that question, *Korematsu* declared that "all legal restrictions which curtail the civil rights of a single racial group" are constitutionally suspect.[85] This heightened standard of review, or what we now refer to as "strict scrutiny," did little to help people of Japanese descent. The Court upheld the internment practices, leaving open the question of how vigorous the Court would be in striking down invidious racial classifications. This outcome might help to explain why *Korematsu* played no role at all in the *Brown* litigation. In compartmentalizing an inconvenient precedent, the Court could draw a formal distinction between *Korematsu*, which was litigated under the due-process clause of the Fifth Amendment, and *Brown*, which was litigated under the Equal Protection Clause of the Fourteenth Amendment.

Although many believe that *Korematsu* was the first case to apply a nascent interaction of strict scrutiny to a racial classification, *Hirabayashi v. United States*,[86] which was decided one year earlier, in fact deserves that distinction. Gordon Hirabayashi was born and raised in a small Christian farming cooperative south of Seattle, Washington. When, at age twenty-four, he was ordered to evacuate, he took a moral stand against the mandate, despite his mother's deep desire to keep the family together. Rather than comply, he turned himself in to the Federal Bureau of Investigation explaining the constitutional and moral bases for his civil disobedience. Because Hirabayashi admitted to violating curfew and exclusion orders, his trial was short and his conviction assured. The judge granted his request to serve a ninety-day sentence for each offense, a longer sentence than initially given. The appeal was certified to the Supreme Court, bypassing Ninth Circuit review, and the American Civil Liberties Union took over Hirabayashi's defense.

According to Jerry Kang, in deciding the case, the Court avoided the issue of Japanese internment entirely by "segmenting" the case; it focused only on the conviction for a curfew violation and not on the violation of the exclusion order.[87] The question presented to the justices became: In the context of war, was the military's promulgation of curfew orders lawful? Phrasing the issue this way allowed the Court to avoid the issue of the constitutionality of internment. As Kang observes, the Supreme Court reproduced this avoidance strategy in *Korematsu*, focusing on evacuation rather than detention – a focus that, once again, makes it easier for the Court to legitimize the internment apparatus.[88]

If the internment cases were an abject lesson in the limits of law as an instrument of racial justice during wartime, then *Perez v. Sharp*[89] shows how the postwar promise of equality could transform legal doctrine. In *Perez*, a black man and a Mexican-American woman, who was classified as white, challenged California's ban on interracial marriage. At the time of their challenge, the United States Supreme Court had upheld an Alabama antimiscegenation statute in *Pace*, and the decision was still good law. Moreover, *Brown v. Board of Education* had yet to be decided. In the following decade, when *Brown* (and a series of cases issued shortly thereafter) dismantled the doctrine of "separate but equal" in public life, none of the opinions reached interracial intimacy. Indeed, based on the thinking that "one bombshell at a time is enough,"[90] the justices refused to hear cases challenging bans on interracial marriage.

By 1967, however, the Court felt confident enough to issue another decision striking down the legacy of segregation. In *Loving v. Virginia*,[91] Chief Justice Earl Warren wrote for a unanimous Court in holding that antimiscegenation laws violated equal protection because they were designed to promote white supremacy. With one exception, the Justices also found that the statutes infringed on due process by burdening a fundamental freedom: the right to marry.[92]

But none of this would help Andrea Perez and Sylvester Davis in 1947. Indeed, as Robin Lenhardt has argued, at the time of the *Perez* litigation, California was one of thirty states with antimiscegenation laws.[93] When Perez and Davis took their case to the state courts, they were represented by a lawyer who decided, in contrast to most such challengers, to attack the fundamental basis of California's laws. He argued that the law violated the couple's freedom of religion, hoping that the California Supreme Court would exercise its original jurisdiction to hear the case without its ever going through the normal trial process. Although the court was in fact persuaded to take the case, religion did not figure in the analysis. For Justice Roger Traynor, the case involved "the right to marry . . . the person of one's choice." According to Lenhardt, this characterization enabled Traynor to elucidate a color-blind understanding of race – that it is biologically irrelevant. With *Perez* as a part of its jurisprudence, the California Supreme

Court became the first and only state high court since Reconstruction to invalidate an antimiscegenation law.[94]

An important part of Lenhardt's engagement with *Perez* is her suggestion that the case offers important civil rights lessons that go well beyond those in *Loving*. For one thing, Justice Roger Traynor's majority opinion in *Perez* was far more skeptical of the legitimacy of racial categories than was Chief Justice Warren's opinion in *Loving*. Traynor's doubts reflected a heightened awareness of the dangers of an ideology of racial inferiority, the very philosophy that Americans had confronted in the war against Nazism. By contrast, in 1967, racial classifications had become necessary to implement desegregation decrees, and Warren was simply willing to take them for granted.[95] For another, *Perez* has become a centrally important precedent in the contemporary same-sex marriage movement because Justice Traynor spent considerable time addressing the right to marry. By contrast, Chief Justice Warren relegated this issue to a couple of paragraphs at the end of the *Loving* opinion. To preserve a unified Court, Warren had to downplay this holding as a way to mollify colleagues who worried about recognizing rights not set forth explicitly in the Constitution. Traynor presumably had no hope of a unanimous decision in *Perez*, and so was free to develop an account of the unique role that intimate associations play in forming an individual's identity. Explicitly rejecting the "separate but equal" doctrine in the context of marriage, Traynor noted that "the essence of the right to marry is freedom to join in marriage with the person of one's choice[.]"[96] The antimiscegenation law violated this right because a person's chosen partner could be "irreplaceable,"[97] yet irretrievably unavailable by reason of race. Traynor's opinion drew together themes of equality and freedom in ways that are missing in both *Brown* and *Loving*.

Even as *Brown* and *Loving* assumed iconic status, the two decisions revealed some unresolved tensions in the Court's canon of color-blindness. After *Brown*, the Court had insisted on desegregation plans that used race to eliminate past discrimination "root and branch"[98] in school districts. Busing became the most conspicuous and contentious example of judicial reliance on color-conscious remedies.[99] *Loving*, by contrast, at least in part, espoused a norm of color-blindness, but the Court did not contemplate "a state-run interracial dating service."[100] On the contrary, the fundamental right to marry meant that government officials had to respect personal choices, even if high rates of same-race marriage persisted after *Loving*. As a result, *Loving* became "the first modern civil rights decision to treat colorblindness and segregation as compatible concepts."[101]

The juxtaposition of the two cases revealed a fundamental dilemma: How could the Court's formal commitment to color-blindness be reconciled with the ongoing need for race-conscious remedies? In the area of school desegregation, the Court eventually retreated from busing orders. As school desegregation litigation moved to the North and West, the justices limited the scope of relief in urban school districts marked by segregation and poverty. The Court exempted nearby suburban districts, typically with affluent, white student bodies, from busing orders, unless there was proof that these districts had intentionally promoted interdistrict segregation.[102] Such evidence was hard to come by, and so schools remained racially identifiable.[103] Even in the South, the federal courts increasingly found that school districts were unitary because they had eliminated the vestiges of past discrimination.[104] When desegregation remedies drew to a close, schools often became resegregated.[105]

The Court's retreat was not limited to school desegregation. Affirmative action was highly controversial because color-conscious policies could be adopted in the absence of an official finding of past discrimination. These programs seemed to fly in the face of the principle of color-blindness because they were adopted voluntarily, rather than in response to sanctions for constitutional wrongdoing. *Richmond v. J. A. Croson Co.* highlights this dynamic.[106] The case began when J. A. Croson Company filed a lawsuit against the City of Richmond because Richmond denied Croson's bid for a plumbing contract. The city refused the bid because the company failed to comply with the Minority Business Utilization Plan (the "MBUP"), the municipal initiative that required contractors to reserve at least 30 percent of subcontracts for Minority Business Enterprises. Croson claimed that the MBUP violated the Fourteenth Amendment's Equal Protection Clause.

This case sparked bitter division among the justices. As Reggie Oh and Tom Ross have argued, the conflicting opinions in *Croson* relied on distinct narratives that depicted affirmative action either as "simple racial politics"[107] or a modest concession to the ongoing realities of societal racism.[108] The majority of the justices considered the program a product of the black city council's pork-barrel politics and applied a rigorous, strict scrutiny test to invalidate the set-aside plan. The dissenting justices saw the initiative as a benign remedy to overcome the legacy of unequal access in the construction industry and would have applied a less stringent, intermediate standard of review to uphold the program.

Oh and Ross argue that in this polarizing debate, none of the justices fully appreciated the structural obstacles to full inclusion for nonwhites in metropolitan areas. This was true, they argue, even with respect to Justice Thurgood Marshall, one of the most liberal justices ever to sit on the Court and at that time, the only African American. Marshall's opinion was deeply contextual, particularly when compared to the more abstract narratives of the other justices, but nonetheless was limited in that it remained situated within the boundaries of the city of Richmond. According to Ross and Oh, by expanding the geographical scope to include the suburbs outside of the city, the Court's narrative would have become more about the "continuing political and socioeconomic powerlessness of African Americans"[109] as white flight both created the city's black majority and caused the city's economy to decline abruptly. The Court's commitment to color-blindness, they argue, made this complex racial narrative difficult to tell.[110]

The hold of color-blindness on American law transcends the equal protection doctrine. Consider, for example, *Whren v. United States*,[111] a critical Fourth Amendment case. In *Whren*, police officers stopped a car, purportedly for a traffic violation, conducted a search, and found narcotics. The defendants contended that the stop was a pretext and that they had been victims of racial profiling. That profiling allegedly violated the Fourteenth Amendment, but what the defendants wanted was relief under the Fourth Amendment, which forbids unreasonable searches and seizures. If the Court concluded that the search or seizure was unreasonable, any evidence acquired as a result would be inadmissible in court. Whren argued that the narcotics seized during the search should not be allowed into evidence because the police officer's decision to perform the traffic stop was based on race. Without the incriminating drugs, Whren's conviction would be overturned.

Kevin Johnson has argued that, consistent with the logic of color-blindness, the Court ignored the racial elements of the case, among them the fact that at least one of the officers was white and that the defendant and his passenger were black.[112] More profoundly, the Court, in a unanimous opinion, rejected the argument that a racial profiling claim of the sort Whren advanced could be the basis for invoking remedies under the Fourth Amendment.[113] As a result, the most meaningful relief for illicit racial profiling was not available to defendants, even if they could surmount the evidentiary challenges of proving discrimination. The Court's decision in *Whren* meant that racial profiling must be addressed in the political rather than the judicial arena. In the meantime, officers were given a license to make racial distinctions that were justified as part of the war on drugs. These distinctions, like other racialized aspects of the criminal justice process, seemed not to run afoul of the notion that our Constitution is color-blind.[114] This reliance on racial distinctions, on the one hand, and the denial of race-conscious remedies, on the other, is a more general problem vis-à-vis civil rights in the American story. One consequence of this dilemma is that civil rights has never proceeded "with all deliberate speed."[115]

## With All Deliberate Speed: Race-Conscious Remedies

The roots of the dilemma over race-conscious remedies can be found in *Brown* itself. Despite the fact that the Court spoke with a single voice, the school desegregation mandate could not be implemented without the support of Congress and the executive branch. The following year, in *Brown II*, the Court found that school integration would proceed with "all deliberate speed."[116] As it turned out, there was far more deliberation than speed. For the next decade, the Court maintained a studied detachment in the face of Southern resistance. Only when Congress passed the Civil Rights Act of 1964, which endorsed a principle of nondiscrimination on the basis of race, did the Court begin vigorous efforts to enforce the integrationist ideal set forth in *Brown*. At the same time, state governments and the federal government began to take "affirmative" steps to improve the school and workplace opportunities for people of color. This is the context in which affirmative action was born – not in the courts, but in the crucible of politics.

As our discussion of *Croson* demonstrates, the Supreme Court has had little difficulty in striking down affirmative action programs. Recall that in *Croson*, the Court applied strict scrutiny, the most stringent level of judicial review, to conclude that the city of Richmond's set-asides in government contracting were unconstitutional. As a formal matter, the case centered on the conduct of a city government. Still, there was no doubt that the Court's approach applied to both state and municipal affirmative action programs. All would be subject to strict scrutiny. But what about affirmative action programs promulgated by the federal government? Should the same level of scrutiny apply to them? Later in *Adarand Constructors v. Pena*,[117] the Court answered that question in the affirmative, despite Congress's special role in implementing norms of equality under the Fourteenth Amendment. The Court insisted that color-blindness required that all race-based classifications, whether hostile or benign, at whatever level of government, be subject to strict scrutiny; a test that (at least after *Korematsu*) increasingly seemed to be "strict in theory and fatal in fact."[118]

Despite this commitment to color-blindness, in *Regents of the University of California v. Bakke*,[119] the justices made clear that race-based affirmative action admissions regimes are not per se unconstitutional. There, Allan Bakke, an applicant to medical school, challenged the University of California at Davis's policy of setting aside seats in the entering class for underrepresented minority students. He alleged that this reverse discrimination violated the Equal Protection Clause as well as the nondiscrimination principle set forth in Title VI of the Civil Rights Act. Four justices agreed with Bakke, concluding that any use of race triggered strict scrutiny and that Davis had not offered a compelling justification for its program.[120] Four other justices sided with Davis, finding that a lower level of judicial review should apply to affirmative action because it was designed to rectify inequality; under this intermediate test, the Davis plan passed muster.[121] With the justices split four to four, Justice Lewis Powell cast the deciding vote. He concluded that affirmative action in higher education could be justified by a university's compelling interest in diversity. By diversity, he meant an "atmosphere which is most conducive to speculation, experiment, and creation"[122] that was generated by bringing together students with different backgrounds and perspectives. Diversity included not just race, but other characteristics that shaped a person's world view.[123] Powell therefore insisted on individualized review of applicants with race treated as one factor among others. He cited the undergraduate admissions program at Harvard as one that could survive strict scrutiny. By contrast, Davis's set-aside program resembled a group-based quota, so Powell found it unconstitutional.[124]

For almost eighteen years, the question of affirmative action's constitutional status in college and university admissions seemed reasonably settled. In 1996, however, the Fifth Circuit Court of Appeals in *Hopwood v. Texas*[125] posed a direct challenge to the regime that *Bakke* had established. The court of appeals ruled that the Supreme Court had never held that diversity was a compelling state interest for affirmative action; only Justice Powell's lone opinion articulated that position. *Hopwood* turned the affirmative action world upside down. Colleges and universities had thoroughly internalized the *Bakke* holding in revamping their admissions processes. What were they to do now?

In 2003, the Supreme Court weighed in. When Barbara Grutter was waitlisted and denied admission, she brought suit alleging unconstitutional reverse discrimination at the University of Michigan's law school. When the Court granted certiorari in the case, no one knew where the decision would fall. It was less than clear whether the Court would place affirmative action on surer constitutional footing or whether, instead, it would delegitimize the policy altogether. Ultimately, the Court upheld affirmative action that relied on holistic review of applicants in *Grutter v. Bollinger*,[126] a decision upholding the law school admissions program at the University of Michigan. In rejecting Grutter's claim, Justice O'Connor not only reaffirmed Powell's diversity rationale, but also linked it to core democratic values. Because elite institutions such as Michigan's law school were pathways to leadership, O'Connor found that access was important to preserve a sense that groups from all walks of life have a fair chance to participate in shaping our nation's destiny.[127] Moreover, she concluded that the law school had treated applicants as individuals with race weighed as but one factor in admission; in seeking a critical mass of underrepresented students, Michigan pursued an aspiration, not a quota.[128]

As one of us (Moran) has argued, O'Connor's majority opinion, although an important victory, is part of a jurisprudence of fragmentation that has seriously weakened the Court's authority in matters of civil rights and affirmative action.[129] The Court's ruling was anything but a resolution of the controversy surrounding affirmative action. Indeed, after *Grutter*, the electorate in Michigan passed a referendum that banned consideration of race in public decision making.[130] As a result, the law school could no longer use the affirmative action program it had fought so hard to defend.

That the Court could not have hoped to resolve the contestation over affirmative action was evident from the very nature of the *Grutter* litigation itself. For one thing, a record number of organizations and institutions filed amicus briefs in this case, including Fortune 500 corporations and a group of retired generals, who argued that affirmative action was necessary to promote the national security of the United States. For another, there was intense controversy about the terms upon which the case should be argued. The student-intervenors unsuccessfully sought to redefine the litigation as an epic struggle over racial subordination, rather than a referendum on *Bakke*. Once the case was heard by the Supreme Court, the student-intervenors were not even allowed to participate in oral argument.

According to Moran, the foregoing controversies, combined with the deep divisions among the justices, suggest that the future of affirmative action remains up for grabs.[131] The Supreme Court's most recent decision, *Fisher v. Texas*,[132] bears this out. On the one hand, the Court affirmed diversity's status as a compelling state interest. On the other hand, the Court found that the lower court's review of the University of Texas's admissions process had been unduly deferential and remanded the case so that the lower court could determine whether the university offered sufficient evidence on the need for race-based admissions. How the lower court will resolve these issues remains an open question. Moreover, however that court rules, likely there will continue to be state-by-state contestations about the permissible scope of affirmative action. As in California and Michigan, both states in which popular referenda banned the use of race in public college and university admissions, people will speak with their votes.

At the very least, this is worrisome. Historically, voting has been both a racialized opportunity and a site for racialized retrenchment. This is precisely why Congress both passed the Voting Rights Act of 1965[133] and facilitated the creation of majority/minority districts.[134] Yet, such districts have engendered significant pushback on the ground that they violate the principle of color-blindness. *Shaw v. Reno*[135] is perhaps the clearest expression of this point.

In *Shaw*, the plaintiffs challenged two majority-black districts in North Carolina created to satisfy the Act's requirements as products of racial gerrymandering. Dan Tokaji has argued that *Shaw* pitted the Justice

Department's interpretation of voting rights law as color-conscious by congressional design against the Supreme Court's interpretation of the Equal Protection Clause as color-blind in cases like *Croson* and *Adarand*.[136] Ultimately, the Court rejected bizarrely shaped districts that highlighted race as the primary factor in how boundaries were drawn. However, the justices did leave room for race to play some role because it was closely correlated with political behavior in North Carolina. In short, the Court demanded that remedies under the Voting Rights Act be narrowly tailored, but the justices refused to find that the Act's mere invocation of race was unconstitutional. The Court recognized that the Act had become intricately entwined with notions of democratic legitimacy and fair play. As a result, the justices were understandably reluctant to undermine a law that had so dramatically altered the concept of "We, the People."

At the same time, the Court was clear that concerns about color-blindness do not disappear in the voting-rights context. According to the Court, "[r]acial classifications of any sort pose the risk of lasting harm to our society."[137] Thus, we should strive to make race irrelevant; we should strive to make it unnameable; and we should strive not to see it. To some extent, these ideas are reflected in the most recent Supreme Court case on the Voting Rights Acts, *Shelby County v. Holder*.[138] *Shelby* litigated the constitutionality of section 5 of the Voting Rights Act. That provision required states with a history of racial discrimination in the context of voting to seek approval from the federal government before changing any aspect of their electoral process. The Supreme Court ruled that this "preclearance" process was no longer necessary.[139]

Central to the Court's conclusion was the view that rampant, systemic discrimination in voting no longer infects America's electoral processes.[140] "Problems remain . . . but there is no denying that, due to the Voting Rights Act, our Nation has made great strides."[141] From the Court's perspective, because we largely live in a color-blind society, the race-conscious orientation of section 5 was problematic. although this is a somewhat weaker articulation of color-blindness than the Court invoked in *Shaw*, it nevertheless builds on the general suspicion with which the Court approaches race-conscious remediation. Three relatively recent cases will illustrate what we mean.

In 2007, in *Parents Involved in Community Schools v. Seattle School District*,[142] the Court ruled that school boards could not strive to achieve or maintain racial integration through race-conscious student assignments because such approaches violate the notion that our Constitution is color-blind. Two years later, in *Ricci v. Destefano*,[143] the Court similarly limited the scope of race-conscious remedies. In that case, to avoid disparate impact liability under Title VII of the Civil Rights Act of 1964, the city of New Haven had set aside the results of a test administered by the New Haven Fire Department because African Americans and Latinos had lower scores than whites. The Court concluded that "whatever the City's ultimate aim – however well intentioned or benevolent it might have seemed – the City made its employment decision because of race."[144]

The Court employed a very similar logic in yet another context, this one affecting a special-purpose election designed to safeguard the interests of native Hawaiians. In *Rice v. Cayetano*,[145] a wealthy white rancher challenged the process used to elect board members for the Office of Hawaiian Affairs (OHA). The OHA was designed to be a "receptacle for reparations"[146] that would better the lives of indigenous Hawaiians. To facilitate self-determination, only individuals of Hawaiian ancestry were permitted to vote for board members. As a result, Rice's request for a ballot was denied and he filed suit, alleging that the voting restriction violated his civil rights.

According to Eric Yamamoto and Catherine Corpus Betts, the Supreme Court wrongly rejected the OHA's electoral limit.[147] In their view, the justices failed to recognize the special history and claims of indigenous peoples. By ignoring the impact of colonization on native Hawaiians, the Court was able to use the rhetoric of color-blindness not to avoid race, but to invoke it. Rather than viewing Native Hawaiians as members of an indigenous group and a once-sovereign nation whose government the United States illegally overthrew, the Court framed Native Hawaiians as a racial group. Thus, unlike both the district court and the Ninth Circuit Court of Appeals, the Supreme Court did not conceive of OHA as facilitating a relationship of trust between the Native Hawaiians and the United States. After explicitly inserting race into the case, the Court ruled that OHA's voting regime was reverse discrimination. Yamamoto and Betts suggest that, in the end, *Rice* is a case both about collective memory and about the power to name and describe one's own reality. The Native Hawaiians became a race by law, not by self-definition.

The issue of race by self-definition is particularly salient for Middle Easterners, across religious identity. As noted earlier, in the context of seeking naturalization, people of Middle Eastern descent argued that they were white. Sometimes this argument carried the day; most often it did not. As a formal matter, inside and outside the domain of "science," Middle Easterners today are classified as Caucasian or white. The question is whether, in terms of self-definition, they should embrace or reject that classification. How one answers this question has important race-conscious remedial implications. Only in 1987 did the Supreme Court make clear that although Middle Easterners are classified as white, they still can sue for racial discrimination.[148] Implicit in the Court's reasoning was the notion that Middle Easterners could be racially vulnerable. Our national response to the terrorist attack of September 11, 2001 has confirmed that assumption.

As Leti Volpp observes, "September 11 facilitated the consolidation of a new category that groups together persons who appear 'Middle Eastern, Arab, or Muslim.'"[149] Although one can query whether this identity is new, its particular consolidation in the wake of September 11 has, as Muneer Ahmad notes, rendered people who are perceived to be Middle Eastern, Arab, or Muslim vulnerable to state and private violence.[150] How should Middle Easterners respond to this? Should they affirmatively assert a Middle Eastern racial identity? More than that, should they draw on the consolidation of this racial identity to seek race-conscious remedies such as affirmative action in the political and legal arenas? The answer is not obviously yes, and not only because of concerns of essentialism and the reification of identity categories, but also because people of Middle Eastern descent are differentially vulnerable to discrimination. Those who "look white" and work their identities[151] to obscure their Middle Eastern origins might experience "short-run freedom from discrimination."[152] Put another way, there is an incentive for Middle Easterners who have what John Tehranian refers to as "assimilatory choices"[153] to exercise them. Hair can function as one such option. For example, to some Americans, facial hair on a Middle Eastern man signifies a terrorist. As a result of the potential for this signification, Tehranian "do[es] not go to the airport without shaving first. It is covering, plain and simple, and a rational survival strategy. [He] prefer[s] the close shave to the close full-body-cavity search."[154]

In a completely different remedial context, Renee Rogers confronted an analogous problem.[155] That is, similar to Tehranian, she had to decide whether to allow her hair to make her vulnerable to discrimination. Paulette M. Caldwell has written compellingly about this case.[156] As she notes, Rogers worked for American Airlines and was reprimanded for wearing a braided hairstyle on the job in violation of her employer's grooming code. For the most part, under employment discrimination law, female plaintiffs of color have had to choose between defining their injuries as either racial discrimination or gender discrimination. Yet, Caldwell argues, the prohibition on braids discriminated against Rogers as an African-American woman, who was uniquely burdened in ways that did not affect her black male or white female colleagues. She faced what Kimberle Crenshaw refers to as intersectional discrimination; that is, discrimination on the basis of more than one axis of difference.[157] To be fully protected by law, Rogers did not want to be compartmentalized into either a race or gender identity. As Caldwell notes, the *Rogers* court enforced that compartmentalization nonetheless, refusing to analyze the case in intersectional terms.

Although most intersectionality theorists have focused on employment discrimination claims like the one in *Rogers*, Caldwell shows that this approach is relevant to other areas of the law such as jury selection. Currently, the Constitution prevents prosecutors from striking jurors on the basis of race or gender.[158] Drawing on a controversial article in the *New Yorker*,[159] Caldwell argues that some prosecutors fear that African-American women will become irrational holdouts in criminal cases. To avoid a hung jury, these prosecutors strike black women in disproportionate numbers based on prejudice and stereotyping. Yet, their exclusion from juries will not be remedied so long as black men (who can stand in for race) and white women (who can stand in for gender) are selected as jurors. Caldwell contends that intersectionality should apply here as well to protect against the compound and complex interaction of race and gender bias. She argues that, to a considerable extent, courts continue to be intersectionally blind.

This is partially a reflection of concerns about the proverbial slippery slope. As one court put it, "[t]he prospect of the creation of new classes of protected minorities [like black women], governed only by the mathematical principles of permutation and combination, clearly raises the prospect of opening the hackneyed Pandora's box."[160] But there is a normative concern as well. Intersectionality forces courts to be mindful of more differences than those associated with either race or gender in isolation. This more-textured jurisprudence makes clear the ways in which race is linked to other dimensions of subordination and so reveals the limits of formal race neutrality. Understood in this way, intersectionality threatens the very possibility of color-blindness and exposes its inadequacy. This helps to explain why one court refers to it as a "super-remedy"[161] that is outside the legitimate boundaries of both gender- and race-conscious remedies.

Intersectionality claims are even more problematic for courts when they involve sexual orientation. Under Title VII, sexual orientation as such is not a protected identity category. What this means concretely is that employers may legally discriminate on that basis – at least under federal law. One implication is that employers can invoke what one might call the "sexual orientation defense" to a plaintiff's claim of discrimination, whether intersectional or not. To understand how this might work, imagine that an employee is a black lesbian. Her employer knows this and terminates her, not because she violated a grooming policy, but because she did not get along with other employees and was not collegial. To the extent that the fired employee brings a discrimination suit based on race or gender or both, her employer can respond that it did indeed discriminate, but that discrimination was based on sexual orientation, not race or gender or a combination of the two. This sexual orientation defense is perfectly consistent with Title VII's antidiscrimination mandate.[162] In this sense, gays and lesbians of color are disadvantaged not only because they cannot include their sexual orientation in an intersectional claim of discrimination, but also because their sexual identity can function as a defense to discrimination claims based on aspects of their identities – like race and gender – that are protected statuses under the law.

Renee Rogers may or may not have known this, but her case opened the window not only on the specific problem of intersectionality, but the more general problem of color-blindness. Color-blindness was designed to undo the formal classification schemes that arose to enforce a racial caste system. This explains its constitutional genesis in Justice Harlan's *Plessy* dissent. Yet, the simple elimination of these categories alone will not address all the ways in which race can be institutionally entrenched. American Airlines did not prohibit black women from wearing braids; it prohibited all women from wearing braids. But as Caldwell notes, this seeming neutrality was deeply gendered and raced. Bo Derek notwithstanding, the identity of white women is not linked to the all-braided hairstyle that American Airlines' grooming policy prohibited. *Rogers* thus helps to illuminate a lesson the *Plessy* dissent teaches: that color-blindness and inequality can comfortably coexist. Race-conscious remedies are therefore necessary at times.

## Conclusion

Race is deeply embedded in the American body politic, a constitutive part of the American story. Yet, judges and policymakers continue to articulate color-blindness as the cure. This makes little sense. Color-blindness emerged in response to the formal classification schemes that the federal and state governments promulgated to enforce a racial caste system. The simple elimination of these categories alone cannot address the ways in which race has been entrenched in the very structure of our democracy. Racism is part of our history. As one of us (Carbado) has noted, "[o]ur sense of ourselves as Americans, of others as Americans, and of the nation is itself, is inextricably linked to racism."[163] Race-conscious remedies are modest means of both addressing this problem and promoting democratic legitimacy. This is one of the important lessons civil rights in the American story can teach us.

## Notes

1. An earlier version of this chapter appears as "The Story of Law and American Racial Consciousness: Building a Canon One Case at a Time," 76 *UMKC Law Review* (Spring 2008), 851–883 and as the introduction to Devon W. Carbado and Rachel F. Moran, eds., *Race Law Stories*. New York: Foundation, 2008.
2. See Michael Joseph Gross, "Gay is the New Black?" *The Advocate*, November 19, 2008. Retrieved from http://www.advocate.com/news/2008/11/16/gay-new-black.
3. Gunnar Myrdal, *An American Dilemma: The Negro Problem and Modern Democracy*. New York: Harper, 1944.
4. Philip A. Klinkner and Rogers Smith, *The Unsteady March: The Rise and Decline of Racial Equality in America*, paperback ed. Chicago: University of Chicago Press, 1999, pp. 28–29.
5. *Dred Scott v. Sanford*, 60 U.S. (19 How.) 393 (1857).
6. Christopher L. Eisgruber, "The Story of *Dred Scott*: Originalism's Forgotten Past," in *Constitutional Law Stories*, ed. Michael C. Dorf (New York: Foundation 2004), 151–152.
7. Ibid., 157.

8. *Dred Scott*, 60 U.S. (19 How.) 403 (opinion of Chief Justice Taney).
9. Eisgruber, "The Story of *Dred Scott*. . . ." 174–178; Xi Wang, "The *Dred Scott* Case (1857)," in Annette Gordon Reed, ed. *Race on Trial: Law and Justice in American History*. Oxford: Oxford University Press, 2002, p. 26.
10. Juan Perea et al., *Race and Races*. St. Paul, MN: Thomson/West, 2007, p. 258.
11. Laura E. Gomez, *Manifest Destinies: The Making of the Mexican American Race*. New York: New York University Press, 2007, p. 3.
12. Ibid.
13. Polk had not yet been inaugurated on the first of March when Congress passed the Joint Resolution reflecting his commitment. Joint Resolution for Annexing Texas to the United States, H.R.J. Res. 8, 28th Cong. (1845). However, his position on the matter and his political efforts are reflected in his presidential inaugural address, which he delivered four days later. See James K. Polk, Inaugural Address, March 4, 1845, accessed November 13, 2013. Retrieved from http://www.inaugural.senate.gov/swearing-in/address/address-by-james-k-polk-1845.
14. Treaties of Velasco, Republic of Texas/Mexico, May 14, 1836.
15. See Joint Resolution for Annexing Texas to the United States, H.R.J. Res. 8, 28th Cong. (1845).
16. Gene M. Brack, "Mexican Opinion, American Racism, and the War of 1846," *Western Historical Quarterly* 1, no. 2 (1970), 161; "James K. Polk-Biography," The White House, accessed June 19, 2013. Retrieved from http://whitehouse.gov/about/presidents/jamespolk/
17. The White House, "James K. Polk-Biography."
18. James K. Polk, Message on War with Mexico, May 11, 1846, accessed November 13, 2013. Retrieved from http://www.presidency.ucsb.edu/ws/?pid=67907.
19. Ibid.; The White House, "James K. Polk-Biography."
20. Rodolfo Acuña, *Occupied America: A History of Chicanos*. New York: Harper, 1988, p. 13.
21. Gomez, "Manifest Destinies," p. 4.
22. Judith Resnick, "Dependent Sovereigns: Tribes, States and the Federal Courts," 56 *University of Chicago Law Review* (1989), 671–759.
23. Cf. Kenneth Stampp, *The Peculiar Institution: Slavery in the Ante-Bellum South*. New York: Vintage Books, 1989.
24. *Dred Scott v. Sandford*, 403.
25. Ibid., 404.
26. Devon W. Carbado, "Racial Naturalization," 57 *American Quarterly* (2005), 644.
27. *Dred Scott v. Sandford*, 403–404.
28. *Cherokee Nation v. Georgia*, 30 U.S. (5 Pet.) 1 (1831); *Worcester v. Georgia*, 31 U.S. (6 Pet.) 515 (1832).
29. See Rennard Strickland, "The Tribal Struggle for Indian Sovereignty: The Story of the *Cherokee Cases*," in Devon W. Carbado and Rachel F. Moran, eds., *Race Law Stories*. New York: Foundation, 2008, pp. 37–57.
30. *Prigg v. Pennsylvania*, 41 U.S. (16 Pet.) 539 (1842).

31. See Ronald S. Sullivan Jr., "Classical Racialism, Justice Story, and Margaret Morgan's Journey form Freedom to Slavery: The Story of *Prigg v. Pennyslvania*," in Devon W. Carbado and Rachel F. Moran, eds., *Race Law Stories*. New York: Foundation, 2008, pp. 59–87.
32. U.S. Const. amends. XII, IV, XV.
33. U.S. Const. amend. XIV, §1.
34. *United States v. Wong Kim Ark*, 169 U.S. 649 (1898).
35. Carbado, "Racial Naturalization," 639 (drawing on Gloria Anzaldua to advance a theory of racial naturalization).
36. Ibid.
37. *Downes v. Bidwell*, 182 U.S. 244 (1901).
38. Efren Rivera Ramos, "The Legal Construction of American Colonialism: The Insular Cases (1901–1922), 65 *Revista Juridica Universidad de Puerto Rico* (1996), 236–239.
39. *Downes v. Bidwell*, 341.
40. See Pedro A. Malavet, "'The Constitution Follows the Flag . . . but Doesn't Quite Catch Up with It': The Story of *Downes v. Bidwell*," in Devon W. Carbado and Rachel F. Moran, eds., *Race Law Stories*, New York: Foundation, 2008, pp. 111–146.
41. See C. Vann Woodward, *The Strange Career of Jim Crow*, commemorative ed. New York: Oxford University Press, 2002.
42. *Pace v. Alabama*, 106 U.S. 583 (1882).
43. *Plessy v. Ferguson*, 163 U.S. 537 (1896). For accounts of the *Plessy* case, see Cheryl I. Harris, "The Story of *Plessy v. Ferguson*: The Death and Resurrection of Racial Formalism," in Michael C. Dorf, ed., *Constitutional Law Stories*, New York: Foundation 2004, p. 181; Thomas J. Davis, "Race, Identity, and the Law: *Plessy v. Ferguson* (1896)," in Annette Gordon Reed, ed. *Race on Trial: Law and Justice in American History*. Oxford: Oxford University Press, 2002, p. 61.
44. *Pace v. Alabama*, 585.
45. Rachel F. Moran, *Interracial Intimacy: The Regulation of Race and Romance*. Chicago: University of Chicago Press, 2001, pp. 80–81.
46. Petition for Writs of Prohibition and Certiorari at 1, *Plessy v. Ferguson*, 163 U.S. 537 (1986) (No. 15,248).
47. Cheryl I. Harris develops this claim in her article "Whiteness as Property," 106 *Harvard Law Review* (1993), 1707–1791.
48. Brief for Plaintiff in Error at 11, *Plessy v. Ferguson*, 163 U.S. 537 (1896) (No. 15,248).
49. *Plessy v. Ferguson*, 549.
50. Ibid.
51. Ibid.
52. *Hudgins v. Wrights*, 11 Va. (1 Hen. and M.) 134 (1806).
53. See Angela Onwuachi-Willig, "Multiracialism and the Social Construction of Race: The Story of *Hudgins v. Wrights*," in Devon W. Carbado and Rachel F. Moran, eds., *Race Law Stories*. New York: Foundation, 2008, pp. 147–173.
54. *Gong Lum v. Rice*, 275 U.S. 78 (1927).

55. Sora Han argues that Gong Lum's claim shifted the racial lens from a black/white paradigm to a black/nonblack paradigm, further entrenching the notion of blackness as the identity categorization to avoid. See Sora Y. Han, "The Politics of Race in Asian American Jurisprudence," 11 *Asian Pacific American Law Journal* (2006), 2–24.
56. *Ozawa v. United States*, 260 U.S. 178 (1922).
57. 8 U.S.C. §359 (1875), amended by 8 U.S. C. §1422 (1952).
58. See Devon W. Carbado, "Yellow by Law: The Story of *Ozawa v. United States*," in Devon W. Carbado and Rachel F. Moran eds., *Race Law Stories*. New York: Foundation, 2008, pp. 175–235.
59. Takao Ozawa, "Naturalization of a Japanese Subject: A Brief in re Ozawa Case Now Pending in the Supreme Court of U.S.A." Brief printed for private circulation, October 1922 (on file with author), p. 15.
60. *United States v. Thind*, 261 U.S. 204 (1923).
61. We put this term in quotes here to signal our recognition that it is from a Western gaze that people became Middle Easterners. We deploy it nonetheless – and throughout the remainder of the introduction without quotes – because it continues to be a cognizable racial category both ascriptively and self-definitionally. See John Tehranian, "Compulsory Whiteness: Towards a Middle Eastern Legal Scholarship," 82 *Indiana Law Journal* (2007), 11.
62. Ibid.
63. Ex parte Mohriez, 54 F. Supp. 941, 942 (D. Mass. 1944).
64. In regard to Ahmed Hassan, 48 F. Supp. 843 (D. Mass. 1942).
65. Ibid., 845.
66. *Morton v. Mancari*, 417 U.S. 535 (1974).
67. See Carole E. Goldberg, "What's Race Got to Do with It? The Story of *Morton v. Mancari*," in Devon W. Carbado and Rachel F. Moran, eds., *Race Law Stories*. New York: Foundation, 2008, pp. 237–272.
68. Ibid.
69. *Hernandez v. Texas*, 347 U.S. 475 (1954).
70. *Brown v. Board of Education*, 347 U.S. 483 (1954).
71. See Ian Haney López and Michael A. Olivas, "Jim Crow, Mexican Americans, and the Anti-Subordination Constitution: The Story of *Hernandez v. Texas*," in Devon W. Carbado and Rachel F. Moran, eds., *Race Law Stories*. New York: Foundation, 2008, pp. 273–310.
72. See Ibid.
73. Ibid., 273.
74. Ibid., 301.
75. Ibid., 301–306.
76. *Plessy v. Ferguson*, 537, 539 (Justice Harlan, dissenting).
77. Ibid.
78. Carbado, "Racial Naturalization," 647. For an extended critique of Justice Harlan's dissent, see Devon W. Carbado, "Race to the Bottom," 49 *UCLA Law Review* (2002), 1283–1312.

79. *Plessy v. Ferguson*, 561 (Justice Harlan, dissenting). Gabriel Chin was one of the first to note the racial problems of Harlan's dissent. See Gabriel J. Chin, "The Plessy Myth: Justice Harlan and the Chinese Cases," 82 *Iowa Law Review* (1996), 151–182.
80. *Brown v. Board of Education*, 347 U.S. 483 (1954). The literature of *Brown* is vast. Among the many accounts are: Richard Kluger, *Simple Justice: The History of* Brown v. Board of Education *and Black America's Struggle for Equality*. New York: Alfred A. Knopf, 1975; Charles Ogletree, *All Deliberate Speed: Reflections on the First Half-Century of* Brown v. Board of Education. New York: W. W. Norton, 2004; Leland Ware, "The Story of *Brown v. Board of Education*: The Long Road to Racial Equality," in Michael A. Olivas and Ronna Greff Schneider, eds., *Education Law Stories*. New York: Foundation, 2008, p. 19; Risa L. Goluboff, "*Brown v. Board of Education* and the Lost Promise of Civil Rights," in Risa L. Goluboff and Myriam E. Gilles, eds., *Civil Rights Stories*. New York: Foundation, 2007, p. 25; Mark Tushnet, "*Brown v. Board of Education* (1954)," in Annette Gordon Reed, ed. *Race on Trial: Law and Justice in American History*. New York: Oxford University Press, 2002, p. 25.
81. *Brown v. Board of Education*, 484.
82. Ibid., 494.
83. *Korematsu v. United States*, 323 U.S. 214 (1944). For accounts of this case, see Neil Gotanda, "The Story of Korematsu: The Japanese-American Cases," in Michael C. Dorf, ed., *Constitutional Law Stories*. New York: Foundation 2004, p. 249; Roger Daniels, "*Korematsu v. United States* revisited," in Annette Gordon Reed, ed., *Race on Trial: Law and Justice in American History*. New York: Oxford University Press, 2002, p. 139.
84. This is not entirely accurate in the sense that the Court never actually addressed the internment of Japanese Americans as such. See Jerry Kang, "Denying Prejudice: Internment, Redress, and Denial," 51 *UCLA Law Review* (2004), 933–1013.
85. *Korematsu v. United States*, 216.
86. *Hirabayashi v. United States*, 320 U.S. 81 (1943).
87. Jerry Kang, "Dodging Responsibility: The Story of *Hirabayashi v. United States*," in Devon W. Carbado and Rachel F. Moran, ed., *Race Law Stories*. New York: Foundation, 2008, pp. 319–320.
88. Ibid., 326–328.
89. *Perez v. Sharp*, 198 P.2d 17 (Cal. 1948).
90. Walter F. Murphy, *Elements of Judicial Strategy*. Chicago: University of Chicago Press, 1964, p. 193.
91. *Loving v. Virginia*, 388 U.S. 1 (1967). For an account of the *Loving* case, see Peter Wallenstein, "Interracial Marriage on Trial: *Loving v. Virginia* (1967)," in Annette Gordon Reed, ed., *Race on Trial: Law and Justice in American History*. New York: Oxford University Press, 2002, p. 177; Robert A. Pratt, "The Case of Mr. and Mrs. Loving: Reflections on the Fortieth Anniversary of *Loving v. Virginia*," in Carol Singer, ed., *Family Law Stories*. New York: Foundation, 2007, p. 7.
92. Moran, "Interracial Intimacy," 98.

93. See R. A. Lenhardt, "Forgotten Lessons on Race, Law, and Marriage: The Story of *Perez v. Sharp*," in Devon W. Carbado and Rachel F. Moran, eds., *Race Law Stories*. New York: Foundation, 2008, pp. 343–379.
94. Moran, "Interracial Intimacy," 84.
95. Ibid., 98–99.
96. *Perez v. Sharp*, 20–21.
97. Ibid., 25.
98. *Green v. County School Board*, 391 U.S. 430, 437–438 (1968); *Swann v. Charlotte-Mecklenburg Board of Education*, 402 U.S. 1, 15 (1971).
99. Gary Orfield, *Must We Bus? Segregated Schools and National Policy*. Washington: Brookings Institute, 1978.
100. Moran, "Interracial Intimacy," 8.
101. Rachel F. Moran, "Loving and the Legacy of Unintended Consequences," 2007 *Wisconsin Law Review* (2007), 262.
102. *Milliken v. Bradley*, 418 U.S. 717 (1974).
103. Gary Orfield, "Turning Back to Segregation," in Gary Orfield and Susan E. Eaton, eds., *Dismantling Desegregation: The Quiet Reversal of* Brown v. Board of Education. New York: New Press, 1996, pp. 10–13.
104. *Freeman v. Pitts*, 503 U.S. 467 (1992) (Atlanta, Georgia); see also *Board of Education v. Dowell*, 498 U.S. 237 (1991) (Oklahoma City, Oklahoma).
105. Orfield, "Must We Bus?" 14–22; Gary Orfield, "The Growth of Segregation: African Americans, Latinos, and Unequal Education," in Gary Orfield and Susan E. Eaton, eds. *Dismantling Desegregation: The Quiet Reversal of* Brown v. Board of Education. New York: New Press, 1996, p. 53.
106. *City of Richmond v. J. A. Croson Co.*, 488 U.S. 469 (1989).
107. Ibid., 493–494, 510 (plurality opinion of Justice O'Connor).
108. See Reginald Oh and Thomas Ross, "Judicial Opinions as Racial Narratives: The Story of *Richmond v. Croson*," in Devon W. Carbado and Rachel F. Moran, eds., *Race Law Stories*. New York: Foundation, 2008, pp. 386–417.
109. Ibid., 409.
110. Ibid., 415–417.
111. *Whren v. United States*, 517 U.S. 806 (1996).
112. Kevin R. Johnson, "The Song Remains the Same: The Story of *Whren v. United States*," in Devon W. Carbado and Rachel F. Moran, eds., *Race Law Stories*. New York: Foundation, 2008, p. 435.
113. *Whren v. United States*, 811–813.
114. See Devon W. Carbado, "(E)racing the Fourth Amendment," 100 *Michigan Law Review* (2002), 946–1044.
115. *Brown v. Board of Education II*, 349 U.S. 294 (1955).
116. Ibid.
117. *Adarand Constructors v. Pena*, 515 U.S. 200 (1995).
118. Gerald Gunter, "The Supreme Court, 1971 Term–Foreword: In Search of Evolving Doctrine on a Changing Court: A Model for New Equal Protection," 86

*Harvard Law Review* (1972), 8. But see Adam Winkler, "The Federal Government as a Constitutional Niche in Affirmative Action Cases," 54 *UCLA Law Review* (2007), 1931–1961 (suggesting that there is a meaningful survival rate for strict scrutiny cases).

119. *Regents of the University of California v Bakke*, 438 U.S. 265 (1978).
120. Ibid., 418 (opinion of Justice Stevens).
121. Ibid., 336–340 (opinion of Justice Brennan).
122. Ibid., 312 (opinion of Justice Powell) (citing *Sweezy v. New Hampshire*, 354 U.S. 234, 236 (1957)).
123. For a conception of what we might mean by the expression "racial diversity," see Devon W. Carbado and Mitu Gulati, "What Exactly is Racial Diversity?" 91 *California Law Review* (2003), 1149–1165.
124. *Bakke*, 315–324 (opinion of Justice Powell).
125. *Hopwood v. Texas*, 78 F. 3d 932 (5th Cir. 1996).
126. *Grutter v. Bollinger*, 539 U.S. 306 (2003).
127. Ibid., 332.
128. Ibid., 334–339.
129. See Rachel F. Moran, "The Heirs of *Brown*: The Story of *Grutter v. Bollinger*," in Devon W. Carbado and Rachel F. Moran, eds., *Race Law Stories*. New York: Foundation, 2008, pp. 451–496.
130. Proposal 2 (November 7, 2006) (codified at Mich. Const. art I, §26).
131. See Moran, "The Heirs of *Brown*," 451–496.
132. *Fisher v. University of Texas*, 133 S. Ct. 2411 (2013).
133. Voting Rights Act of 1965, 42 U.S.C. §§1971 et seq.
134. See ibid., §1973(b). The 1982 amendment to the act relaxed the burden of proof for minorities challenging voting dilution. Cf. *City of Mobile v. Bolden*, 446 U.S. 55 (1980) (holding that claims of vote dilution require proof of "discriminatory purpose").
135. *Shaw v. Reno*, 509 U.S. 630 (1993).
136. See Daniel P. Tokaji, "Representation and Raceblindness: The Story of *Shaw v. Reno*," in Devon W. Carbado and Rachel F. Moran, eds., *Race Law Stories*. New York: Foundation, 2008, pp. 497–540.
137. *Shaw v. Reno*, 657.
138. *Shelby County v. Holder*, 133 S. Ct. 2612 (2013).
139. Ibid., 2630–2631.
140. Ibid., 2626.
141. Ibid.
142. *Parents Involved in Community Schools v. Seattle School District*, 551 U.S. 701 (2007).
143. *Ricci v. Destefano*, 557 U.S. 557 (2009).
144. Ibid., 579–580.
145. *Rice v. Cayetano*, 528 U.S. 495 (2000).
146. Hawaii Revised Statutes §10–13 (1993).

147. See Eric K. Yamamoto and Catherine Corpus Betts, "Disfiguring Civil Rights to Deny Indigenous Hawaiian Self-Determination: The Story of *Rice v. Cayetano*," in Devon W. Carbado and Rachel F. Moran, eds., *Race Law Stories*. New York: Foundation, 2008, pp. 541–570.
148. See *Saint Francis College v. Al-Khazraji*, 481 U.S. 604 (1987).
149. Leti Volpp, "The Citizen and the Terrorist," 49 *UCLA Law Review* (2002), 1575–1576.
150. Muneer Ahmad, "A Rage Shared by Law: Poster September 11 Racial Violence as Crimes of Passion," 92 *California Law Review* (2004), 1259–1330.
151. See Devon Carbado and Mitu Gulati, "Working Identity," 85 *Cornell Law Review* (2000), 1259–1308.
152. Tehranian, "Compulsory Whiteness," 18.
153. Ibid.; for a general discussion of different kinds of passing strategies, see Carbado and Gulati, "Working Identity," 1259–1308. See Kenji Yoshiro, "Covering," 111 *Yale Law Journal* (2002), 769–939 (employing the language of covering to describe the same phenomenon).
154. Tehranian, "Compulsory Whiteness," 20.
155. *Rogers v. American Airlines*, 527 F.Supp. 229 (S.D.N.Y. 1981).
156. See Paulette M. Caldwell, "Intersectional Bias and the Courts: The Story of *Rogers v. American Airlines*," in Devon W. Carbado and Rachel F. Moran, eds., *Race Law Stories*. New York: Foundation, 2008, 571–600.
157. Kimberlé Crenshaw, "Demarginalizing the Intersection of Race and Sex: A Black Feminist Critique of Antidiscrimination Doctrine, Feminist Theory and Antiracist Politics," 1989 *University of Chicago Legal Forum* (1989): 139–167. See Angela P. Harris, "Race and Essentialism in Feminist Legal Theory," 42 *Stanford Law Review* (1990), 581–615.
158. *Batson v. Kentucky*, 476 U.S. 79 (1986) (race); *J. E. B. v. Alabama*, 511 U.S. 127 (1994) (gender).
159. Jeffrey Rosen, "One Angry Woman: Why Are Hung Juries on the Rise?" *New Yorker*, February 24/March 3, 1997, 48.
160. *Degraffenreid v. General Motors*, 413 F. Supp. 142, 145 (E. D. Mo. 1976).
161. Ibid., 143.
162. See Anthony E. Varona and Jeffrey M. Monks, "En/gendering Equality: Seeking Relief under Title VII Against Employment Discrimination Based on Sexual Orientation," 67 *William & Mary Journal of Women & Law* (2000), 67–132. This intersectional problem also marginalizes gays and lesbians in antiracist and gay rights discourses. See Devon W. Carbado, "Black Rights, Gay Rights, Civil Rights," 47 *UCLA Law Review* (2000), 1467–1519.
163. Carbado, "Racial Naturalization," 651.

# Commentary on Chapter 1
# Race Law Cases in the American Story: *Adoptive Couple v. Baby Girl*

Grace Soyon Lee

In "Race Law Cases in the American Story," Devon Carbado and Rachel Moran argue that "our understanding of civil rights in the American story is decidedly incomplete to the extent that it is framed exclusively with reference to African Americans."[1] They then work to remedy that deficit by illustrating how cases involving nonblack litigants enhance our understanding of the ways in which American legal history has been influenced by race. They note that the legal treatment of Native Americans presents a particularly unique challenge because

> [t]he tendency to treat tribes as either racial or political has significant consequences. The Court has become increasingly unreceptive to programs like affirmative action that weigh race in allocating jobs or government contracts. Therefore, if Native American tribes have a purely racial identity, programs directed at their needs are suspect. If, however, the tribes are political entities, the programs are simply part of a complex and ongoing negotiation about the tribes' relationship as dependent sovereigns of the federal government.[2]

As an example of the law's struggle over how to classify Native Americans, Carbado and Moran cite the case *Morton v. Mancari*,[3] in which a class of non-Indian employees at the Bureau of Indian Affairs unsuccessfully challenged affirmative action policies regarding the hiring and promotion of Native Americans. In finding that the policies did not constitute invidious racial discrimination in violation of the Due Process Clause of the Fifth Amendment, the United States Supreme Court discussed "the unique legal status of Indian tribes under federal law and upon the plenary power of Congress, based on a history of treaties and the assumption of a 'guardian-ward' status, to legislate on behalf of federally recognized Indian tribes."[4] As a result, the Court demonstrated a willingness to preserve policies based on Native American identity within the Bureau of Indian Affairs, even as they rejected other affirmative action programs.[5]

The United States Supreme Court recently decided another case involving the treatment of Native Americans, this time in the emotion-laden areas of family and adoption law. In the case *Adoptive Couple v. Baby Girl*,[6] the Court reversed the South Carolina Supreme Court's decision to uphold a family court decision denying the adoption of a Native American child by a non-Native American family and awarding custody to the biological father, who is a member of the Cherokee Nation. This decision, when viewed in conjunction with the dissent, sheds further light on the issue of whether Native Americans are considered racial or political entities under the law.

## African Americans and Interracial Adoption

*Adoptive Couple v. Baby Girl* touches on the politically and emotionally charged issue of interracial adoption, an issue that courts and legislatures have grappled with before, primarily when dealing with white couples who are interested in adopting black children. As Rachel Moran points out in a previous work, courts move away from their general stance of color-blindness when dealing with interracial adoption, as

> they typically treat race as relevant in assessing the "best interest of the child." These color-conscious placement decisions have reflected a societal judgment that same-race families are not only statistically commonplace but normatively desirable. Race is pertinent because agencies try to replicate 'naturally occurring' biological families. The vast majority of these families are racially homogeneous. In addition, race matters because it is linked to social and cultural differences that affect a parent's competency to raise a child. A white adoptive parent in a white neighborhood may not be prepared to meet the psychological needs of a black child, for example.[7]

As a result, "[a]lthough the ideal of colorblindness is well entrenched in civil rights rhetoric, the role of race in child placement policy has been hotly debated."[8] Congress attempted to resolve some of the debate over interracial adoption through the Multiethnic Placement Act (MEPA), passed in 1994, which prohibits federally funded adoption agencies from making placement decisions solely on the basis of race, although it does allow agencies to consider a child's race in conjunction with other factors to the extent it is deemed relevant to the determination of the child's best interest.[9] Subsequent amendments to MEPA further solidified the position that "[g]eneralizations based on race, national origin, and ethnicity were forbidden in the adoption process," although "agencies could consider the attitudes and preferences of prospective parents to decide whether placement was in a child's best interest."[10] Moran notes that, despite Congressional attempts to provide a unified policy through MEPA, "[s]hifts in the official interpretation of federal adoption policy left colorblindness a contested and uncertain principle despite recent congressional action."[11]

Unsurprisingly, MEPA and its amendments have been criticized for impeding the adoption of black children in the name of "cultural competency" and racial continuity.[12] For example, Randall Kennedy argues that any suggestion that black parents are more suitable for black children than white parents will have a "chilling" effect on interracial adoption that exacerbates existing prejudices and makes such adoptions "sources of unfairness and oppression that should be erased."[13] On the other side of the debate, Moran argues that, although race as a biological construct should play no role in the area of adoption,

> race may matter, even when its biological significance is rebutted. Race marks important social and cultural boundaries that can hardly be ignored in determining a child's best interest . . . The child's racial designation can influence how adoptive parents understand their responsibilities. Prospective parents already have well-developed notions about race that can empower or stigmatize a child. In addition, a racial designation can be a proxy for future social experiences, both positive and negative, for which the child needs to be prepared . . . For all of these reasons, the social and cultural implications of race are undeniably relevant to placement policy.[14]

On the one hand, in enacting MEPA and its amendments, Congress clearly did not want to place primacy on the physical characteristics of race, which had historically been used to justify invidious forms of racial discrimination. On the other hand, they felt the need to acknowledge the continued pervasiveness of racial discrimination today, as well as the legitimate cultural and historical components of racial identity. This tension between the desire to downplay the physical aspects of race and the need to respect its non-physical aspects came even more sharply into focus under The Indian Child Welfare Act.

## The Indian Child Welfare Act

The Indian Child Welfare Act (ICWA) applies to an "Indian child" who is the subject of a child custody proceeding, which includes placement of the child with an adoptive family.[15] An Indian child under the act is "an unmarried person less than eighteen years old who is either a member, or eligible for membership, of an Indian tribe."[16] The very definition of Indian child under the ICWA is the result of combining several different factors: "the federal government's definition of 'tribe' and its insistence on membership criteria for the dissemination of federal benefits, the tribes' coerced acquiescence in that system and their frequent use of blood quanta for defining membership, and the fluctuating social and cultural value to an individual of assuming the identity of 'Indian.'"[17]

Federal legislation like the ICWA is ostensibly aimed at Native Americans "as members of quasi-sovereign tribal entities" rather than "as a discrete racial group."[18] However, critics allege that, by giving Native American bloodlines primacy over religion, culture, and social ties, the ICWA "may serve indirectly to reinforce biological notions of race."[19] For example, Randall Kennedy called the ICWA "ill conceived and counterproductive" and argued that "[t]he policy and its purported justifications decrease the likelihood that needy children will find adoptive homes, popularize hurtful superstitions, and reinforce claims that unfairly stigmatize substantial numbers of non-Indian adoptive parents."[20]

Without directly addressing these critiques, the Supreme Court's recent decision in *Adoptive Couple v. Baby Girl* chips away at the scope of the ICWA and therefore presents a step away from the primacy of tribal sovereignty over the freedom of non-Indian adoptive parents to adopt Indian children.

### Adoptive Couple v. Baby Girl

In *Adoptive Couple v. Baby Girl*, a Native American child ("Baby Girl") was born to a non-Native American mother and a father who is a member of the Cherokee Nation.[21] Baby Girl's biological parents, who were engaged at the time of her conception, broke up prior to her birth and had minimal contact with each other after their breakup.[22]

Approximately three months prior to the birth, Baby Girl's mother contacted a non-Native American couple who agreed to adopt Baby Girl; she then contacted Baby Girl's father via text, asking him whether he would prefer to provide financial support or relinquish his parental rights.[23] Baby Girl's father responded (also via text) that he would relinquish his rights.[24] Although an attempt was made to verify Baby Girl's Native American heritage as part of the adoption proceedings, these attempts failed owing to various bureaucratic errors (and some possible subterfuge on the part of Baby Girl's mother).[25] Upon learning of the pending adoption, Baby Girl's father protested and sought custody of Baby Girl; the family court denied the prospective adoptive parents' petition for adoption and granted custody to Baby Girl's father.[26] The prospective adoptive parents then appealed to the South Carolina Supreme Court.[27]

In upholding the family court's decision to deny the prospective adoptive parents' petition and grant custody to Baby Girl's father, the South Carolina Supreme Court first determined that the Indian Child Welfare Act applied to the case because of Baby Girl's status as an Indian child.[28] They then found that Baby Girl's father has standing to invoke the protection of the ICWA despite his initial text message relinquishing his rights because he later acknowledged his paternity in court proceedings.[29] Because Baby Girl's father did not consent to Baby Girl's adoption under the ICWA and because Baby Girl's prospective adoptive parents could not show beyond a reasonable doubt that granting him custody "would result in serious emotional or physical harm to Baby Girl," the South Carolina Supreme Court upheld the family court's denial of the adoption and transfer of custody to Baby Girl's father.

In making its determination, the South Carolina Supreme Court noted that "the child's relationship with his or her tribe is an important consideration, as the ICWA is 'based on the fundamental assumption that it is in the

Indian child's best interest that its relationship to the tribe be protected."[30] They also noted that, "in transferring custody to Father and his family, Baby Girl's familial and tribal ties may be established and maintained in furtherance of the clear purpose of the ICWA, which is to preserve American Indian culture by retaining its children within the tribe."[31] A very vehement dissent argued that "Congress did not intend the Indian Child Welfare Act to be applied in derogation of the child's best interests and welfare" and that "Congress intended ICWA-controlled cases to be decided based on a preference for placement with an Indian family, not an irrebuttable presumption mandating an Indian family placement."[32]

The Supreme Court overturned the South Carolina court's decision, holding that the ICWA "does not apply when, as here, the relevant parent never had custody of the child."[33] The Court further held "that §1912(d) – which conditions involuntary termination of parental rights with respect to an Indian child on a showing that remedial efforts have been made to prevent the 'breakup of the Indian family' – is inapplicable when, as here, the parent abandoned the Indian child before birth and never had custody of the child."[34] Finally, the Court held "that §1915(a), which provides placement preferences for the adoption of Indian children, does not bar a non-Indian family like Adoptive Couple from adopting an Indian child when no other eligible candidates have sought to adopt the child."[35]

In a vigorous dissent, Justice Sotomayor, along with Justices Ginsburg and Kagan, argued that the South Carolina Supreme Court's decision should have been affirmed.[36] The dissent took particular issue with the majority's description of the goals of the ICWA, arguing that they ignored one of the primary goals of the ICWA, which is to "'promote the stability and security of Indian . . . families,' in part by countering the ternd of plaing 'an alarmingly high percentage of [Indian] children . . . in non-Indian foster and adoptive homes and institutions."[37]

## The Racial Implications of the ICWA and Baby Girl

In the same way that cases like *Morton* highlighted the ways in which Native Americans were viewed differently from other races under employment law, *Baby Girl* illustrates how the debate over Native American identity draws on not only the physical aspects of race, but the cultural, historical, and political dimensions as well. The differences between the treatment of African Americans and Native Americans under family law can be seen by contrasting MEPA, which expressly limits the use of race as a factor when placing children in adoptive families, with the ICWA, which not only allows, but mandates consideration of a Native American child's heritage when making such placements.[38] As noted by Solangel Moldanado, "MEPA pretends that race, color, and ethnicity do not or should not matter while ICWA strongly suggests that attempts to ignore racial, cultural, and ethnic differences will have detrimental effects on children."[39] Although some have argued that the black community should have the same authority over its members as Indian tribes, such concerns failed to hold sway with the drafters of MEPA and its subsequent amendments.[40]

Moran observes that, to the extent statutes like MEPA take a color-blind approach to adoption, they "assume that race is a biological irrelevancy, a trivial artifact of ancestry and appearance."[41] The issue becomes more complicated, however, when dealing with the adoption of Native American children by white families, and Moran argues that the "ICWA reflects a fear that white parents see Indian children as phenotypically similar enough to be adopted and absorbed into white society."[42] Whereas critics of the ICWA argue that it emphasizes physical "blood quantum" requirements over the social, cultural, and political aspects of racial identity, its defenders argue that such requirements are necessary because the social ties that previously connected Native Americans to their tribes have been artificially disrupted.[43]

The majority of the Supreme Court in *Baby Girl* argued that the ICWA was intended only to prevent "the unwarranted *removal* of Indian families due to the cultural insensitivity and biases of social workers and state courts."[44] It also noted that, to the extent that the ICWA mandates preference be given to a child's extended family, tribe, and other Indian families, such "preferences are inapplicable in cases where no alternative party has formally sought to adopt the child."[45] By negating the need for preferences based on tribal membership when a child is not in the immediate care of an Indian parent, the majority clearly sided with those critics of the ICWA who fear that the Act places too much importance on "blood quantum" requirements.[46]

The dissent countered that the ICWA's goals included not just protecting the interests of Indian parents by preventing the dissolution of currently intact Indian families but also protecting the interests of Indian tribes by restricting "placement of Indian children in homes with no connection to the tribe, whether or not those children were initially in the custody of an Indian parent."[47] According to the dissent, in enacting the ICWA,

> Congress recognized that "there is no resource that is more vital to the continued existence and integrity of Indian tribes than their children," and it found that this resource was threatened. State authorities insufficiently sensitive to "the essential tribal relations of Indian people and the cultural and social standards prevailing in Indian communities and families" were breaking up Indian families and moving Indian children to non-Indian homes and institutions. As §1901(4) makes clear, and as this Court recognized in *Mississippi Band of Choctaw Indians v. Holyfield*, adoptive placements of Indian children with non-Indian families contributed significantly to the overall problem.[48]

By arguing for "uniform federal standards for child custody proceedings involving Indian children and their biological parents," the dissent seemed to side more with the proponents of the ICWA, emphasizing that Indian tribes are both "independent political entities" and racially cohesive.[49]

Even though *Baby Girl* presented a unique opportunity for the Court to clarify notions of Indian identity as a matter of race or politics, the extent of the disagreement between the majority and the dissent on both the goals and the scope of the ICWA, as well as each side's reluctance to explicitly address the issue head-on,[50] belie how controversial the location of Indian identity along (or outside of) the color line continues to be.

## Notes

1. Devon W. Carbado and Rachel F. Moran, "Race Law Cases in the American Story," in Austin Sarat, ed., Civil Rights in the American Story. Cambridge: Cambridge University Press, 2013, p. 1.
2. Id., p. 18.
3. 417 U.S. 535 (1974).
4. Id., 551.
5. Carbado and Moran, "Race Law Cases in the American Story," p. 18 (citing Carole Goldberg).
6. 398 S.C. 625 (2012), *overruled by* 133 S. Ct. 2552 (2013).

7. Rachel Moran, *Interracial Intimacy*. Chicago: University of Chicago Press, 2001, p. 126.
8. Id., 127.
9. Id., 133 ("An agency, or entity, that receives federal assistance and is involved in adoption or foster care placements may not . . . delay or deny the placement of a child for adoption or into foster care, or otherwise discriminate in making a placement decision, solely because of the race, color or national origin of the adoptive or foster parent, or the child, involved").
10. Id., 134.
11. Id., 144. See also Randall Kennedy, *Interracial Intimacies*. New York: Pantheon, 2003, p. 400. ("The [Inter-Ethnic Adoption Amendment to MEPA] has yet to halt entirely the practice of race matching.")
12. Kennedy, *Interracial Intimacies*, 446.
13. Id.
14. Id., 145–146.
15. Michelle L. Lehmann, "Comment: The Indian Child Welfare Act of 1978: Does It Apply to the Adoption of an Illegitimate Indian Child?" 38 *Catholic University Law Review* (1989), pp. 511–518.
16. Id.
17. Barbara Ann Atwood, "Flashpoints under the Indian Child Welfare Act: Toward a New Understanding of State Court Resistance," 51 *Emory Law Journal* (2002), 587–607.
18. Solangel Maldonado, "Race, Culture, and Adoption: Lessons from *Mississippi Band of Choctaw Indians v. Holyfield*," Columbia Journal of Law and Gender (2008): 26 (quoting Morton v. Mancari, 417 U.S. 535, 554 (1974)).
19. Id.
20. Kennedy, Interracial Intimacies 480.
21. *Adoptive Couple v. Baby Girl*, 398 S.C. 625, 632 (2012). Although the majority argued that Baby Girl's "[f]ather's family has a deeply embedded relationship with the Cherokee Nation" (654, n. 28), the dissent found that "[t]here is scant evidence that Father ever established significant social or cultural ties with Cherokee Nation" (669, n. 46).
22. Id., 630.
23. Id., 631.
24. Id. Baby Girl's father later claimed that he did not know that Baby Girl's mother was planning to place her up for adoption and that he would not have relinquished his rights had he known of her plans.
25. Id., 632.
26. Id., 636.
27. Id.
28. Id., 637. The court also determined that it had jurisdiction over the case, despite the fact that Baby Girl was born in Oklahama, because the Oklahoma court declined to exercise jurisdiction over the case. Id., 643.

29. Id., 644.
30. Id., 653 – quoting *Mississippi Band of Choctaw Indians v. Holyfield*, 490 U.S. 30, 50 n.24 (1989). See also Atwood, "Flashpoints under the Indian Child Welfare Act," 621 ("tensions come into play when state judges question the legal, social and cultural meaning of Indian identity and the propriety of assigning a single identity to children . . . To the extent that the Act is founded on categories that essentialize Indian children, the tensions are inevitable").
31. Id., 655 (citing Holyfield, 490 U.S. 37).
32. Id., 658.
33. 133 S.Ct. 2552, 2557 (2013).
34. Id.
35. Id. In a concurring opinion, Justice Thomas argued that "[b]ecause adoption proceedings like this one involve neither 'commerce' nor 'Indian tribes,' there is simply no constitional basis for Congress' assertion of authority over such proceedings." Id., 2571. Justice Breyer also concurred with the majority opinion, stating that, "while I agree that the better reading of the statute is, as the majority concludes, to exclude most [absentee Indian fathers], I also understand the risk that, from a policy perspective, the Court's interpretation could prove to exclude too many." Id., 2571.
36. Id., 2572. Justice Scalia joined Justice Sotomayor's dissent in part, arguing that "there is no reason that 'continued' [custody] must refer to custody in the past rather than custody in the future" and adding that the majority opinion "needlessly demeans the rights of parenthood."
37. Id., 2583.
38. Maldonado, "Race, Culture, and Adoption," 36–37.
39. Id., 42.
40. Kennedy, Interracial Intimacies," 437 (citing Cynthia G. Hawkins-Leon, "The Indian Child Welfare Act and the African American Tribe: Facing the Adoption Crisis," *Brandeis Journal of Family Law* 36 (1998), 201).
41. Moran, *Interracial Intimacy*, 138.
42. Id., 140.
43. Id., 140.
44. 133 S.Ct., 2561.
45. Id., 2564.
46. This point is not lost on the dissent, which criticizes the majority's "repeated, analytically unnecessary references to the fact that Baby Girl is 3/256 by ancestry." Id. at 2584.
47. Id., 2584.
48. Id., 2573.
49. Id., 2585 ("I am particularly averse to [second-guessing tribal decisions on membership] when the Federal Government requires Indian tribes, as a prerequisite for

official recognition, to make 'descen[t] from a historical Indian tribe' a condition of membership").

50. At the end of its opinion, the majority obliquely suggests that a contrary result "would raise Equal Protection concerns," Id., 2565, a suggestion that is greeted by the dissent with derision. Id., 2584.

2

# Race Is Evidence

## (Mis)Characterizing Blackness in the American Civil Rights Story

Montré D. Carodine

### Introduction

Race is an intractable part of not just the American civil rights story, but the American story. Race has a grip on the American experience, although, ironically, many try to avoid discussions revolving around race and the implications that race has on every facet of our lives. There seems to be a pervading mainstream sentiment that it is time to move on from that ugly chapter in American history in which overt, invidious racism was legally sanctioned. With the formalization of racial equality, many believe that we have turned a corner with respect to race relations. But at the same time, reality has a way of reminding us – especially people of color – that racial inequality, although not formally tolerated, is a persistent part of the American story.

In light of the great degree of pride that Americans take with respect to racial progress, we are challenged in this symposium "to inquire about the place of civil rights in America's post-*Brown v. Board of Education* story." Specifically, we are to consider, among others, these questions: "How important has the story of civil rights 'progress' been in the last half century? What have been the most important counter-narratives? What issues, e.g. affirmative action, immigration, have posed the greatest challenges to America's embrace of the narrative of progress in civil rights?"[1]

We are certainly in the midst of a myriad of celebrations of civil rights progress – celebrations commemorating various notable events during the height of the civil rights movement.[2] These types of celebrations are somewhat disconcerting to the extent that they suggest that American society has "arrived" with respect to equality and racial progress. Moreover, it is disquieting that the message that we have arrived has also given way to a commercialization of the civil rights discourse. In what is likely the result of strategizing and consultations with public-relations experts, some institutions and localities that were once violently hostile to the very thought of treating black citizens with the same dignity and respect as their fellow white citizens now seem eager to embrace their sad history and brag about the changes that they were forced to make (as if they did so willingly and now somehow deserve to be rewarded and to have special attention bestowed upon them). Although I do think that it is important to commemorate what are undoubtedly landmark achievements in this country, the tone of such observations should be less celebratory and self-congratulatory and more reflective on the progress yet to be realized and the extent to which in some ways we have regressed as a society.

This essay addresses the issue that, in my view, serves as the greatest counter-narrative to the story of "progress" in America with respect to race and civil rights: the criminalization of blackness. It has largely been done through a characterization (or *mis*characterization) of what it means to be black. This mischaracterization has historical roots in the institution of slavery, stood as a major obstacle in the struggle for formal equality during the civil rights movement, and has persisted – and in some ways, intensified – since the achievement of formal equality under the law. One need only look to prison statistics in the post-civil rights era. We should find it difficult to pat ourselves on the back and to celebrate "progress" in the fight for racial equality when statistics show that one in three black males have or will be imprisoned, jailed, placed on probation, or paroled at some point in their lifetimes. Indeed, according to Marc Mauer of the Sentencing Project, "[n]early one in three (32%) black males in the age group 20–29 is under some form of criminal justice supervision *on any given day* – either in prison or jail, or on probation or parole."[3] In a 2003 special report, the Bureau of Justice statistics stated that "[a]bout 1 in 3 black males, 1 in 6 Hispanic males, and 1 in 17 white males are expected to go to prison during their lifetime, if current incarceration rates remain unchanged."[4]

The over-incarceration of the black male – and increasingly Hispanic males as well – is a moral and social crisis that threatens to undo most of the much-celebrated civil rights progress in this country. How can we claim progress when there are more black people imprisoned than there were slaves? In fact, with today's prison industrial complex, blacks are imprisoned and are forced to labor for nearly nothing in terms of wages.[5] Corporations are being enriched as a result of mass incarceration.[6] Is this progress? Sure, there have been discrete improvements, as Professor Ford notes in his essay, but like him, I find myself questioning the notion of progress that has been romanticized in the civil rights rhetoric.

As an evidence professor, I often view issues through the lens of evidentiary rules and concepts. The rules that govern the way in which we arrive at legally recognized truths are useful because they reflect our values as a society. Therefore, I find that viewing race from an evidentiary standpoint is particularly useful conceptually. It is also very practical given the racial disparities in the criminal justice system today – race is literally on trial almost daily in this country. In this essay, I will consider the intersection of race and the judicial process in criminal cases against the backdrop of some of the most important evidentiary rules that govern that process – the character evidence rules. To state it succinctly, race is one form of character evidence in the criminal justice system.

What distinguishes my approach to the issue of race and criminal justice is that I look to a source of law that is probably *facially* one of the most neutral and broadly applicable – the rules of evidence. They have an impact not only on cases that go to trial, but also on cases that do not because they facilitate settlement or plea bargains (and, in the criminal case, they often have an impact on whether someone is ever criminally charged in the first place). Despite their broad applicability, race scholars largely have overlooked them when addressing inequality in the criminal process. The rules of evidence do not frequently come up in discussions of the civil rights agenda, which is somewhat baffling given the heavy use of judicial process during the height of the civil rights movement. Of course, the common law evidentiary rules were not codified in the federal system until the 1970s (and many states followed suit), which may explain the lack of historical emphasis. At any rate, the rules are vitally important in that they govern what the trier of fact can consider in deciding a case. Moreover, as I mentioned earlier, they often reflect our societal values – including society's biases against disfavored groups. Feminists have sought reforms through changes in the evidentiary rules – such as the rape shield statute and with special domestic violence evidentiary rules, for example. Civil rights activists and race scholars should take note.

This essay is a part of my larger agenda to make the case – through various rules of evidence and procedure, criminal cases, and narratives – that race itself is suspected, pursued, arrested, convicted, and even exonerated in our judicial system. Race is evidence.

## "Show Me Your Papers"

In many ways, denying the existence of racism is the new racism.[7] Yet, race continues to permeate every aspect of daily life in America. Before I delve into the specific ways in which race equates to evidence in the law, I want to talk about the modern realities of race in our society. Today, it is fashionable to point to the election and reelection of Barack Obama as the ultimate evidence of racial progress in this country – that America has reached a post-racial era. Ironically, the battle for basic respect and legitimacy that he has had to fight since rising to the top of American politics belies that notion of post-racialism.

The level of disrespect for his authority, particularly during his first term, seems unprecedented. From the cringe-worthy "you lie!" moment during his health care speech before Congress in 2009[8] to the bizarre "birther" movement, the president's very legitimacy is under constant attack.[9] Many minorities, myself included, understand what it is like to have your legitimacy challenged on an almost daily basis, although obviously not to such a degree and on a national scale as the resident. For people of color in this country, race evidences a prima facie illegitimacy that must constantly be disproven if one is to have any hope whatsoever of being successful. Just as President Obama literally was forced to show his papers – his-long form birth certificate – we people of color must show our papers in a variety of ways, whether it is our driver's license to a police officer who had no probable cause to stop us on the freeway or the contents of our shopping bag to a suspicious clerk on our way out of a department store.

In many ways, the law legitimizes this presumption of illegitimacy. Take, for example, the harsh immigration laws that some states have passed recently. The harshest of those laws was what the Alabama legislature passed in 2011.[10] The law essentially placed a stamp of illegitimacy on every person who "looked" like they did not "belong." Everyone who engaged in any business dealings – or frankly, in dealings whatsoever – with persons who looked "foreign" would be prudent to demand that those persons "show their papers." This included utility companies and municipalities that provide residential utility services, driver's license bureaus, and all employers, included ordinary homeowners hiring workers to provide home maintenance and improvement services.[11]

## The Relevance of Race

Rule 401 of the Federal Rules of Evidence deems evidence to be relevant if "it has any tendency to make a fact more or less probable than it would be without the evidence" and "the fact is of consequence in determining the action."[12] Under this definition, race both currently and historically has evidentiary value and significance.[13]

Historically, under the law, blacks were considered inferior and morally corrupt, bad actors for whom the institution of slavery and the harsh penalties of the criminal justice system, even for the pettiest of crimes, were deemed justified and necessary to maintain social order and the economic structure that benefitted whites. During the slavery era, race in and of itself was of consequence to the determination of a person's status as a slave or a free person. In other words, a person's color – or the perception thereof – was so powerful in terms of its evidentiary status that it could take away a person's inherent freedom. In almost every jurisdiction in the United States, one could legally *presume* – upon encountering a person who was "evidently" black – that he or she was a slave.

As with today's "show me your papers" culture that presumes illegitimacy, the presumption of slave status could be disproven; that is, it was rebuttable. For example, in *Gentry v. McMinnis*, a Kentucky court discussed the evidentiary value of a person's race: "[A] black or mulatto complexion is prima facie evidence that the person of such color is a slave . . . [B]eing a white person, or having less than a fourth of African blood, is prima facie evidence of freedom."[14] Furthermore, the *McMinnis* court stated succinctly "[a]ll negroes are deemed slaves; all whites and Indians free, *when their color is the only evidence*."[15] The issue in the case involved the status of a woman (the defendant) whom the plaintiff tried to claim as his slave.[16] The appellate court hailed as superior evidence the defendant's appearance to the jury, stating that "the jury had a right to regard the evidence of their own eyes, on inspection in court; and therefore . . . [the trial court] did right in telling [the jury] that, if they should, on their own view, believe that she was not a white woman, then prima facie, or in the absence of any opposing evidence, she was a slave."[17] The court called the testimony of others about the woman's race "an inferior grade of evidence."[18]

Race (or the apparent race) of a person even determined how the burden of proof was allocated in "suits for freedom."[19] In *Hudgins v. Wright*, one judge stated that "[a]ll white persons are and ever have been free in this country. If one *evidently* white, be notwithstanding claimed as a slave, the proof lies on the party claiming to make the other his slave."[20] In the same case, another judge stated the law as follows:

> In the case of a person visibly appearing to be a negro, the presumption is, in this country, that he is a slave, and it is incumbent on him to make out his right to freedom: but in the case of a person visibly appearing to be a [W]hite man, or an Indian, the presumption is that he is free, and it is necessary for his adversary to shew [sic] that he is a slave.[21]

Applying the evidentiary concept of relevance, the person's apparent blackness had a tendency to make it more probable that he was a slave.

Moreover, unless there was evidence to the contrary, he was indeed a slave under the law. Beyond the issue of slave status, race was widely used in the criminal justice system to determine the length and severity of penalties.[22] There were separate court systems – civil and criminal – for blacks and whites. Blacks, simply by virtue of their blackness, received far harsher penalties than whites for many crimes.[23] Indeed, in the infamous southern "black codes," blacks were specifically targeted in the criminalization of behavior disproportionately engaged in by former slaves.[24] Furthermore, certain crimes were only criminal if committed by a black person, such as possessing weapons or selling alcohol.[25] Furthermore, a number of offenses were designated capital offenses if the defendant was black, so a black person could receive the death penalty if found guilty, whereas a white person would not.[26] Race was a direct substitute for evidence on material issues in some cases. In post-Civil War rape prosecutions, for example, where the accused was black and the alleged victim was white, evidence that the accused was black was actually considered probative evidence of his intent.[27] It was also not uncommon for prosecutors to openly appeal to juror's racial prejudices and biases in court.[28]

We still see some examples of such open use of race and evidence, as in a case that recently made headlines when Justice Sonia Sotomayor took the unusual step of issuing an opinion, even though the Court had denied certiorari. In that case, the prosecutor had used a racist and stereotypical line of questioning that painted Latinos as likely drug dealers, stating: "You've got African–Americans, you've got Hispanics, you've got a bag full of money. Does that tell you – a light bulb doesn't go off in your head and say, This is a drug deal?" Justice Sotomayor, in a scathing opinion joined (only) by Justice Breyer, wrote: "It is deeply disappointing to see a representative of the United States resort to this base tactic more than a decade into the 21st century. Such conduct diminishes the dignity of our criminal justice system and undermines respect for the rule of law. We expect the Government to seek justice, not to fan the flames of fear and prejudice."[29]

In the examples that I have highlighted above, the connection between blackness and evidentiary concept of relevance is that blackness was thought to predict bad character, just as whiteness was thought to be presumptive of good character. Thus, the law formally considered race to be character evidence. Using blackness as evidence of bad character was necessary because of the moral depravity of slavery and the Jim Crow regime. As Professor William Carter, Jr. notes, the equating of race and criminality was "crucial" to the institution of slavery. According to Professor Carter, the "myth of blacks' inherent, criminal propensity (and, particularly, violent criminality) was key to dehumanizing the enslaved as 'beasts' or chattel over whom brutal control was both needed and justified." The slave codes, and the post-Civil War black codes "enshrined the connection between skin color and criminality into law." Moreover, these laws legitimized the black-as-criminal stereotype and appealed to white fear and were touted as "necessary to ensure white safety."[30]

Despite the attempts by some to characterize slavery as "not that bad," it was a cruel, dehumanizing institution, as was Jim Crow. So, to justify their enslavement of blacks and the harsher treatment of blacks in the criminal justice system, white slave owners and legislators actually constructed what I call a "mischaracterization" of blacks by racializing Africans and then inventing and perpetuating multiple negative stereotypes about them. Among other things, blacks were characterized as being lazy, lascivious, unclean, dishonest, ignorant, violent, and even barbaric. The underlying message with respect to these stereotypes about blacks was the notion of black inferiority. Blacks were cast as the "other" in society. To maintain social control over blacks, whites again used their mischaracterization of blacks not only to justify harsher punishments for slaves and free blacks in the criminal justice system, but also in the broader American society.

The *Calhoun* case notwithstanding, the law generally does not tolerate, for the most part, *formal* racism and its mischaracterization of blacks. Overt racism is not fashionable or politically correct. A person who openly touts negative (and sometimes positive) views about someone based on race will most likely be ostracized swiftly. At the same time, ironically, the existence (or persistence) of institutionalized racism is vehemently denied even as it occurs right before our eyes. And anyone who challenges actions and institutions as racist faces a potential backlash. It is silly, however, to think that so many years of formal bigotry in society and the law, which was reflective of society's values, would leave no vestiges of discrimination.

Despite racism deniers' attempts to shout down protests against racism, it is incumbent upon scholars and commentators to continue to expose institutional racism, particularly in the law. Race still has significant meaning in today's society and in the law. Denying this reality does not negate that fact. Instead, racism denial exacerbates the frustrations of those who are subjected to the consequences of the negative evidentiary value that their race carries. These denials add more costs to being a person of color in America.

## The Tax Metaphor

I will diverge here and discuss two other important "race as" metaphors that inform my conceptualization of race as evidence. Minorities have often observed (and accepted) that there is a "black tax," or an added cost or burden of being a person of color in America. University of Southern California Law Professor Jody Armour has written much about the so-called black tax, particularly in his seminal work *Negrophobia and Reasonable Racism: The Hidden Costs of Being Black in America*.[31] As Professor Armour defines it, "[t]he Black tax is the price Black people pay in their encounters with Whites (and some Blacks) because of Black stereotypes."[32] The tax causes minorities very real financial and social disadvantages daily.

Coined in the early 1950s, the term black tax described the higher housing prices that West Indians paid for housing in Britain. The term was also used to describe the tax that South African blacks were forced to pay. More recently, the *New York Times* published an article on the "Ghetto Tax," another name for the black tax.[33] A study featured in the *Times* article discussed showed that "poor urban residents frequently pay hundreds if not thousands of dollars a year in extra costs for everyday necessities."[34] For example, the article noted that "[d]rivers from low-income neighborhoods of New York, Hartford and Baltimore, insuring identical cars and with the same driving records as those from middle-class neighborhoods, paid $400 more on average for a year's insurance."[35] The article also noted that "rent to own" stores, notorious for inflating prices on appliances and furniture, primarily prey upon poor people – their "main customers."[36] Poor people, who are disproportionately minorities in this country, pay more for car loans and for check cashing services.

Tax Professor Dorothy Brown has argued that the housing market "penalizes integration" and that "[t]he higher the percentage of blacks in the neighborhood, the less the home is worth, even when researchers control for age, social class, household structure, and geography."[37] Homes in wealthy minority neighborhoods are worth less than homes in wealthy white neighborhoods.[38] And homes in poor white neighborhoods are worth more than homes in poor minority neighborhoods. Most telling is that it is the actual presence of blacks (not crime statistics or school quality) that was determinative. Professor Brown's bottom line is that blacks do not benefit financially from homeownership in the same way that whites do. In some of Professor Brown's other work, which focuses on the intersection of race and tax issues, she has shown how some blacks literally pay more in taxes than similarly situated whites.[39] Thus, the tax code actually perpetuates the black tax.

Sports writer Jarrett Bell recently made headlines by arguing that there is a black tax charged to black quarterbacks in the National Football League (NFL). He pointed to the discovery of a scouting report on University of West Virginia quarterback Geno Smith, which "contain[ed] damning proclamations" by a football draft analyst about Smith, allegations that are apparently unfounded.[40] Some of those proclamations were what some have called code words. The analyst said that Smith was "not a student of the game" and that he "operated almost exclusively from the gun." He also said that Smith was "not committed or focused," and had a "marginal work ethic."[41] Moreover, he claimed that Smith "interviewed poorly" and "did not show an understanding of concepts on the white board."[42] The analyst certainly comes off as attacking Smith's intellect, work ethic, and speaking ability. Although his critique is (somewhat) carefully worded, he is essentially calling Smith lazy, dumb, and inarticulate – typical stereotypes of blacks.[43] Jarrett wrote, "Even in 2013, it's apparent that conditions remain in this society where analysis and opinions are seemingly clouded by racial bias. It's easy to slap a stereotypical label on a minority –from quarterbacks to the blue-collar men on the street – without the benefit of the doubt."[44]

In his book, *Negrophobia and Reasonable Racism*, Professor Armour also highlights the existence of the black tax within our criminal justice system. "Like a tax, racial discrimination is persistent [and] pervasive . . . And just as the state stands behind the collection of the general taxes, Blacks often have good cause to view state representatives such as police and judicial officers as IRS agents for the Black tax."[45] Examples of the black tax, according to Professor Armour, include "profile stops of Blacks by drug enforcement officers" and "Blacks being stopped and interrogated by police for walking or jogging through 'White' neighborhoods." The tax metaphor is an apt one, as "[t]axation [is often viewed] as a regular and unpleasant interaction between state and citizen."[46] I would submit, however, that the tax is perpetuated in the financial sector, in the criminal justice system, and elsewhere only because there is an evidentiary value attached to race.

The black tax is nothing more than a reflection, or result of, the use of blackness as "bad" character evidence. With respect to housing or other purchases, blacks are penalized or "taxed" for bad character through higher interest rates. Similarly, in the employment setting, blacks are penalized or taxed by having to work harder than their white colleagues and peers for the same benefits. And in the criminal context, they are penalized and taxed by a hostile judicial system that has made them the very face of criminality.

A part of the black tax that is often overlooked is its corollary, which I will refer to as the "white credit." The assessment of the black tax, be it through blacks being charged higher interest rates or having to work "twice as hard," provides whites with undeserved and unearned benefits because of their lighter skin color.

In the context of the criminal justice system, the white credit is particularly beneficial. White drivers, who do not have to concern themselves with the burdens of racial profiling and baseless traffic stops, enjoy an undeserved benefit. White criminal defendants enjoy an undeserved benefit from being white because the face of crime in America is decidedly black. Indeed, the system often punishes blacks more harshly than whites who have committed the same acts.

## The Property Metaphor

The idea of white credit is consistent with the theory of whiteness as a property right. Professor Cheryl Harris has written extensively about whiteness as property, noting in particular that historically, "[w]hite identity conferred tangible and economically valuable benefits and was jealously guarded as a valued possession." Moreover, she argues that in today's society, "[w]hen the law recognizes, either implicitly or explicitly, the settled expectations of whites built on the privileges and benefits produced by white supremacy, it acknowledges and reinforces a property interest in whiteness that reproduces Black subordination."[47] The privileged status of whites in the criminal justice system is an example of the law's reinforcement of whiteness as property.

The white credit, however, is a dangerous phenomenon, particularly in the criminal justice system. It masks criminality and lulls white communities into a false sense of security. As I am writing this chapter, the country is still reeling over the tragic and unspeakable shooting and merciless slaughter of twenty innocent elementary children and six adults entrusted with their care in Newtown, Connecticut.[48] As a parent of a small child around the same age as the kids who were slaughtered, I hesitate to even write about this in the context of a race discussion. But race really is evidence, in every sense of the word, and it is important to see it in a case as tragic as this one.

I have been struck by how many people have expressed shock that something could happen in a "place like this" and that a "nice kid" could do something so heinous. I wonder what the discussion would be like if the perpetrator had been a black kid and if nearly all of the victims were black. I do not doubt that there would have been similar outrage. Think back to the bombing of the Birmingham church that killed those precious little black girls and convicted the conscience of the nation. But if the Connecticut shooter had been black and in a black neighborhood, would the nation have been surprised that such violence could occur? It is doubtful because blackness and violence are synonymous.

Something is considered "off" or abnormal when this type of act occurs in a white community and the perpetrator is white. The discussion has quickly turned to a debate on gun control *and* mental illness. It is rare that the mental health of a black perpetrator of a violent act is discussed. Contrast the discussion of the Connecticut massacre with the much-less outraged discussion, to the extent that there really barely is one, over then senseless violence that continues to take place in urban areas such as Chicago and New Orleans. One weekend in 2012, Chicago in particular had an astounding 26 murders, and there were around 506 total for that year.[49] The conversations are very different when young white kids commit violent acts as opposed to young black kids. But President Obama was correct in his remarks following the Newtown shooting, in which he referenced the "street corner in Chicago" in the same breath as the school in Newtown and the movie theater in Aurora, Colorado. These are all "our" neighborhoods. Criminality does not have just one color. Unfortunately, the way that we use race as evidence in this country misleads us into thinking that it does.

## Recognizing Race as Evidence

It is my position that, as a general matter, laws governing trial process should be structured in a way that openly acknowledges the evidentiary value of race while simultaneously working to diminish that value to the extent that it is unfairly prejudicial and impedes truth seeking. The rules currently operate in the opposite manner. They do not acknowledge the evidentiary value of race, but at the same time often operate in a manner that perpetuates and increases the probative value and prejudicial effect of race. The black tax and white credit affect the manner in which jurors and prosecutors independently view black defendants and are also camouflaged in the rules of evidence that filter what the jury hears about the case (and what cases even make it to a jury or to trial). This is true particularly in criminal cases.

The evidence rules, which at face value appear to be race neutral, often instead operate in a racially biased manner, giving race substantial evidentiary value. The rules reinforce the "show me your papers" mentality that has dogged President Obama since day one of his presidency. As President Obama's experience on the national stage has shown, it is very difficult to overcome a presumption of illegitimacy that is institutionally ingrained. Even with irrefutable proof of legitimacy, that presumption persists and even becomes conclusive.

## Character Counts

Some of the most important rules of evidence pertain to character. Indeed, much of what consumes a trial and much of what leads up to a trial revolves around the issue of character. Take, for example, the Trayvon Martin/George Zimmerman case. From the very beginning of the media's shining of the spotlight on the case, the main issue was about character – both Zimmerman's and Martin's. Strategically, the Martin family's legal team presented a literal picture of the "all American" school boy doing a normal childhood activity – going to the corner store to get candy and a drink.[50] Immediately, people all over the country – black, white, Latino, Asian – connected with the photos that were circulated of Trayvon Martin as a young child.[51] People, including President Obama (and myself) could envision this young boy as their own.[52] Conversely, the picture presented of George Zimmerman in the media was not very flattering at all. His photo presented him looking a little overweight and aloof (even mean). We were also told that he had been arrested before on a domestic violence charge and also for assaulting a police officer. Furthermore, we were told that he was white – and not just by media outlets, but, interestingly, by the police in the police report. When Zimmerman, through his representatives, finally started to speak for himself, much of those communications were efforts to rebuild his character. They painted a portrait of a man who not only was not a racist, but was a minority himself (as if to imply that minorities cannot hold and act upon biases against other minorities) who had fought alongside blacks in his community to combat racial injustice.

The media, therefore, provided distinct character profiles of both the victim and the alleged perpetrator. Of course, these profiles have changed over time with the further development of the case. But this was the initial picture of these two persons. And for many, this will always be their impression of them.

In his discussion of *Plessy v. Ferguson*, Professor Carbodo notes that the Supreme Court invited Homer Plessy to "litigate his racial identity" and then poses a question about the historical relevance of *Plessy* today: "Asked more pointedly, do people continue to litigate their race?" The answer is a resounding yes. The litigation of race is, perhaps, more multifaceted and can be subtle, but it certainly persists. The pretrial posturing in the Zimmerman/Martin case provides a modern example. On each side, the parties tried to mitigate the consequences of their race (or perceived race in the case of Zimmerman). Martin's parents and their advisors carefully crafted and molded his public image to evoke the type of sympathy (and empathy) that the more realistic picture – a complex, yet typical, teenage boy who sometimes got into trouble – would not because of Trayvon's blackness. Zimmerman, on the other hand, went to great lengths to identify as a minority, a person of color, who could not possibly be racist or racially biased against blacks. He eschewed the white credit that was initially afforded him because it benefitted his narrative much more in the court of public opinion – and racism deniers could point to the supposed absurdity that Zimmerman, a Hispanic man, could be racist. So he was white enough to get the initial benefit of the doubt from the police and colored enough to be the champion of those who want to silence discussions about racism. The chameleonic aspect of Zimmerman's race is not unlike that of Homer Plessy, who was an "octoroon." For Zimmerman, there has definitely been a property value in his "mistaken identity" as a white man who is actually Hispanic – the donations from his sympathizers are a perfect example.

There is value in having a racial-minority poster child for those who are a part of the "racism doesn't exist anymore" movement – simply ask any of those conservatives who are desperate to find their own ideological version of Barack Obama – someone who is a minority but also one with whom they can connect politically. In the Zimmerman trial, many were willing to demonstrate that value with their own money. And listening to the first juror who spoke out following the not-guilty verdict in the Zimmerman case, it seems that at least some of the jurors (nearly all of whom were white, and all of whom were women) connected with and sympathized with Zimmerman in much the same way as many of his white supporters in both the public and the media. Indeed, that first juror to speak out – Juror B37, in her interview with CNN's Anderson Cooper – repeatedly referred to Zimmerman as "George"[53] and clearly adopted his version of the facts, despite what many saw as a dearth of evidence to refute it and despite some evidence that contradicted it[54] (of course, Zimmerman did not have the burden of proving his innocence). Much of that juror's interview with Anderson Cooper was troubling because it revealed her seeming inability to connect with Trayvon, the victim, and Ms. Rachel Jeantel, Trayvon Martin's friend with whom he was having a cell phone conversation at the time of his encounter with Zimmerman.[55] Juror B37 referred to Ms. Jeantel and presumably Trayvon as "they" and talked about the way that "they" were living and expressed her sympathy for Ms. Jeantel, a young black woman, whom she thought was intimidated and out of place in the courtroom.[56] Juror B37 seems to have used Trayvon and Ms. Jeantel's race as evidence.

Consider how we make judgments about persons based on their appearances – their clothes, their accessories, their hair – and the way that they speak. All of these things have meaning; they evidence something to the observer (and they can be racialized). Similarly, and even more powerfully, race in and of itself has come to evidence something about a person's character in this country. Race conveys a narrative about a person based on the biases and experiences of the observer. Studies have shown that in self-defense cases, the actions of blacks are more likely to be perceived as aggressive as opposed to the same actions by whites.[57] Studies have also shown that the darker and more Afro-centric a murder defendant's features are, the more likely he is to receive the death penalty.[58] So even within the black race, the "blacker" the person is, the more his character evidences negativity.[59]

A few years ago, my husband and I were traveling from our current home in Alabama to the hometown in which we both grew up in Louisiana. We made a quick stop for gas at a station right off of the interstate in Clinton, Mississippi. After pumping the gas, my husband made his way into the store to purchase snacks and a drink (I stayed in the car with our young son). As I glanced through the window, I noticed my husband handing his driver's license to a police officer who had pulled up beside him on his way into the store. The two had a brief conversation and then my husband went inside the store. When he returned, I asked him what had happened and why he had been asked to show his driver's license to the officer. He simply replied, "Life of a black man," and changed the subject.

I reflected for much of the remaining trip on Interstate 20 to Louisiana on why the officer stopped him for no apparently good reason. My husband, a high school math teacher and basketball coach, often dresses in "sports casual" attire. That day he did have a sporty athletic look – much like many young urban males of all races. Perhaps this look, coupled with his race, gave rise to the officer's suspicion. My husband certainly thought this to be the case. Indeed, his simple, brief comment after the encounter suggested to me that he was resigned to the negative character implications that his "black maleness" conveys.

The same initial impressions that shape a layperson's views of a person's character – such as with the media coverage of the Zimmerman/Martin case – shape those of officials in the legal system, including the police, prosecutors, defense attorneys, judges, and jurors; hence, my husband's experience with the police. Generally, however, our rules of evidence purport to exclude the use of a person's character as evidence that the person acted in conformity with their character on a particular occasion. But there are so many exceptions to this general principle. And also, in practice, nearly everything about a trial is about character.

The criminal side of the judicial system is rooted in a fundamental principle: "[C]haracter is never an issue in a criminal prosecution unless the defendant chooses to make it one."[60] The seminal case that espouses this principle is *People v. Zackowitz*, authored by then Judge Cardozo. In that case, Judge Cardozo argued that prosecutors had painted an unfair picture of the defendant, who had been convicted of murder and sentenced to die. The defendant admitted to shooting a man who had hurled profanities at the defendant's wife. The prosecutors, according to Cardozo, had presented evidence of the numerous weapons from which the defendant selected the murder weapon, prominently laying those weapons before the jury. The obvious point was to show the defendant's violent nature – the nature he acted upon in killing the victim. He noted that the law is "not blind to the peril to the innocent if character is accepted as probative of crime."[61] There was no other purpose for which the prosecutor presented the guns (they were not used to commit the crime) other than "to generate an atmosphere of professional criminality." Thus, Judge Cardozo ordered that the defendant's conviction be reversed.

I have taught this case a number of times. Recently, after having the usual debate about whether there was a legitimate purpose, other than character, for presenting the evidence of the extra guns to the jury, a student approached me to discuss the case after class. He inquired about the race and nationality of the defendant, whose last name "Zackowitz," which suggested to the student that he might have been an immigrant. Perhaps he thought that would add another dimension to the character profile. It would also – in my student's view, perhaps – explain why Judge Cardozo went to the trouble of rehabilitating Mr. Zackowitz's character, even as he was reversing and remanding the case for a new trial. Judge Cardozo made a point of emphasizing that Zackowitz "was engaged in a decent calling, an optician regularly employed without criminal record, or criminal associates."[62]

The Zackowitz case laid the foundation for Rule 404 of the Federal Rules of Evidence, which basically provides that *generally*, evidence of a person's character is not admissible to show that the person acted in conformity with that character on a particular occasion.[63] The way that we normally demonstrate a person's character would be by the person's previous acts. Thus, the rule specifically says that a person's prior acts cannot be used to show that he has a propensity to act in a certain manner.[64]

As first-year law students quickly learn, the most important aspects of most rules are the exceptions to those rules. And the general ban on character-propensity evidence is wrought with exceptions. There are a host of "legitimate" reasons for which the law permits the use of a person's prior or other acts – often their other *bad* acts. For example, going back to the Trayvon Martin case, Mr. Zimmerman's defense team repeatedly argued that Martin was the first aggressor – that *he* started the altercation that ultimately resulted in his death. In the court of public opinion, they depicted Trayvon as a bad kid always looking for trouble. In the court of law, they were limited by the rules of evidence in how they were able to portray Trayvon, but ultimately they were able to use Trayvon's race as evidence.

In the media campaign, Zimmerman's defense team focused on Trayvon's academic records, which indicated that he had gotten into some trouble at school, which involved drug possession and suspensions. Ultimately, the court did not allow evidence of Trayvon's school suspensions.[65] The judge did, however, rule (correctly, in my view) that evidence of traces of marijuana in Trayvon's system admissible to explain why

Zimmerman thought that he was behaving strangely when he encountered the teen (Zimmerman's defense team ultimately did not focus on this evidence despite the favorable ruling).[66] And significantly, the defense did not present evidence of Trayvon Martin engaging in fights prior to his encounter with Zimmerman.[67]

To be sure, however, criminal defendants can present evidence of a victim's violent character under certain exceptions to the general ban on character evidence. Indeed, criminal defendants can use evidence of a homicide victim's violent character to help prove that the victim was the first aggressor, although their methods of proof may be limited depending on the circumstances.[68] The evidence rules seem straightforward enough, as did the judge's application of those rules at the Zimmerman trial. But race complicated the entire picture in the Zimmerman case (and in numerous cases unfolding around the country every day that receive no media attention). Nowhere in the Rules of Evidence is race mentioned or even acknowledged to be an issue when dealing with character evidence. Yet, it was the dominant issue in this case, especially with respect to the character evidence. If you disagree, just consider the tone of the media coverage in this case. Furthermore, go to any major news outlet's website and find any given archived article on this case; then read the viewer comments. Race *was* evidence in this case, as it is in so many others.

Furthermore, and disturbingly, the court in the Zimmerman case allowed race to be used as character evidence. The judge did limit specific bad character evidence about Travyon, such as his school records and some of his marijuana use. But remarkably and disturbingly, the court allowed the defense to elicit witness testimony regarding burglaries that occurred in the apartment complex where Zimmerman killed Trayvon and that were allegedly committed by young black males who had absolutely no connection to Trayvon – other than their race.[69] That's just plain old-fashioned racism – the ignorant notion that because some black people commit crimes, then we should suspect all of them.[70] As legal commentator Lisa Bloom succinctly put it, "To attribute the wrongs of two African-American men to all African-Americans is the definition of racism."[71] Anderson Cooper's interview of Juror B37 confirms that this evidence had an impact in the jury's deliberations. The defense saddled Trayvon with the burden of paying for the crimes of other black youth whom he did not even know. When judges apply our rules of evidence in a manner that allows this type of racial bias to permeate the proceedings, they inadvertently, for the most part at least, legitimize race as character evidence. This is exactly what the trial judge in the Zimmerman case did.

For the most part, race is a social construct, an amalgamation of our reactions to various experiences and social influences.[72] If most of our encounters with persons of another race have been negative, and if most of the images that we see of persons of another race are negative, then it seems quite natural that we will have negative stereotypes about all persons of that race. Even when a counterexample to the stereotype is presented, the negative images can persist,[73] and the counterexample might simply be considered the exception to the general rule.[74]

Professor Cynthia Lee's work has argued that stereotypes about race have a significant influence on views of what constitutes self-defense.[75] She demonstrates how various stereotypes regarding blacks, Asians, and Latinos have had very real consequences in self-defense cases and in other criminal cases where minorities have been victims.[76] Consider the following stereotypes of minorities, and one can see how those stereotypes, if held by alleged perpetrators, can affect whether or not certain actions are perceived as threats: "Black-as-criminal"; Asian-as-foreigner; Asian-as-Martial Artist; Latino-as-foreigner or "illegal"; Latino-as-criminal.[77]

The unfortunate truth for many minorities, particularly minority men, is that they are perceived in a negative light on a regular basis, and from as early on as preschool. As the mother of a little black boy, I have witnessed this firsthand. Moreover, having had numerous conversations with other mothers of black boys, what I have witnessed is not unique.

A few years ago, one of my friends – a black female partner at a global law firm – forwarded to me a copy of an e-mail that she sent to the headmaster of her son's exclusive private school in the heart of a major U.S. city. The e-mail was regarding the casting decisions made for the school's upcoming musical production of *The Bremen Town Musicians*. My friend was deeply disturbed upon learning that her son, a second-grader at the time and one of a handful of black children in the school, had been cast in the musical as the robber. Sure, given the production that the school chose, someone had to play the robber. The question is, why did they choose the little black boy? Moreover, as a school that purported to be committed to promoting diversity and cultural sensitivity, there was good reason to avoid casting the black child as the robber, as doing so would most certainly reinforce well-known negative stereotypes of blacks as criminals. My friend's advice to me – my little boy was only one or two years old at the time – was to get my "boxing gloves" out because I would constantly have to advocate for my child.

My friend's story raises the question about how teachers, principals, and other adults in the school system – public and private – perceive black children. Teachers, principals, and other adults in the school system come from the same society in which black criminality has been deeply engrained in the American psyche. Indeed, it has been well documented that black students are far more likely than white students to be suspended or expelled from school.

What does all of this have to do with the character evidence rules? Remember in the Zimmerman case, his attorneys fought to use Martin's school records, arguing that they were relevant to his self-defense claim. Indeed, one of the first questions that I and many others had as this case unfolded on the national scene was: Why was Martin suspended from school in the first place? Apparently, he had been suspended because "traces" of marijuana were found on some of his belongings in his backpack. Thus, he was suspended pursuant to a "zero tolerance" policy. My concern is that these policies have been used disproportionately to discipline black youth in the school system.[78] Indeed, the way that these policies and other school discipline policies have been implemented has helped to criminalize a generation of black youth in America.[79] The Martin case represents an all too-common trap that young black boys fall into, and as they stand now, our evidence rules are woefully inadequate to address the situation.

Indeed, Rule 403 would likely limit significantly the degree to which a prosecutor could attempt to explain the racial biases in the public school system that might have led to a school discipline record like Trayvon's. Rule 403, a catchall provision in the rules of evidence provides:

> The court may exclude relevant evidence if its probative value is substantially outweighed by a danger of one or more of the following: unfair prejudice, confusing the issues, misleading the jury, undue delay, wasting time, or needlessly presenting cumulative evidence.

This rule is significant because it gives trial judges a tremendous amount of discretion in determining whether to exclude evidence that may otherwise be relevant. Rule 403 is often interpreted to exclude evidence that would lead to a so-called mini-trial.

Perhaps no rule demonstrates the idea that race is evidence more than the prior conviction impeachment rule embodied in Federal Rule of Evidence 609. Rule 609 allows for the admissibility of a witness's prior convictions as impeachment evidence.[80] In other words, if someone takes the stand as a witness, even a criminal defendant testifying on his own behalf, his prior convictions can be used as evidence that he lacks credibility.[81] Rule 609 provides for the admissibility of all convictions that are punishable by imprisonment for more than one year or by the death penalty. It also provides for the admission of all convictions, regardless of the available punishment, for which the prosecution had to prove that the defendant made a dishonest or false statement.[82]

Anyone who regularly watches crime shows on television has probably seen Rule 609 in action. After a witness who is subject to impeachment via Rule 609 testifies, the opposing side's lawyer will approach the witness and ask if they are the same Jane Smith who was convicted of robbing a bank three years ago. The point is to discredit the witness and convince the jury (or judge if it is a bench trial) that her testimony ought to be discounted or altogether disregarded. If the judicial system has previously determined that someone is guilty of a felony, it has also simultaneously judged that person's character for *truthfulness* even if the crime for which the person was convicted had nothing to do with dishonesty or making a false statement. And of course, the same is true for crimes that actually involve dishonesty or false statement.

So what does all of this have to do with race? Almost every aspect of the rule has racial implications. The common law rule, which is the predecessor of Rule 609, came about after the post-Civil War liberation of the competency rules that had prevented blacks, criminal defendants, and convicted felons from testifying as witnesses in court.[83] The justice system considered persons in each of these categories as presumptive liars.[84] Although the old competency rules were ultimately abolished, the prior-conviction impeachment rule served as a reminder that certain people still could not be trusted to tell the truth on the stand – and given the large number of former slaves who were criminalized and imprisoned after the war, a lot of those people were black.[85] The rule was codified during the "tough on crime era" in the 1970s,[86] an era that marshaled in the "New Jim Crow."[87]

By virtue of data on arrests (particularly for drug crimes), formal charges (that are not reduced), and ultimate convictions, those most likely to have a felony in the United States today are African Americans and Latinos.[88] Thus, people of color are most likely to be adversely affected by the rule. But it goes deeper. The reasons for the disproportionate numbers of African Americans and Latinos having felony records include the disproportionate targeting of these groups by police, the "war on drugs," and other "wars" on crime. Moreover, studies have shown that even when whites engage in the same or similar behavior as blacks and Latinos, they are more likely to get lighter charges or not to be charged at all.[89] In fact, an empirical study by the *Miami Herald* of more than 700,000 cases revealed that whites were far more likely than blacks and Latinos to receive a "withhold of adjudication,"[90] which essentially allows defendants to complete diversion programs in exchange for the "withholding" of a felony conviction on their records.[91]

How can this type of bias occur on such a broad scale? Judicial bias, among other factors, contributes to the problem. Indeed, in a study regarding bias in the criminal justice system, one white judge even admitted that he viewed black youth differently from white youth, even when charged with similar crimes.[92]

I recall several years ago, when I was practicing civil litigation in Texas, going to a small courthouse in Huntsville for a hearing on a case. In that court, the judge presided over both civil and criminal cases. The partner with whom I was working on the case accompanied me. We had to sit through several hearings on the criminal docket before the judge got to our case. We observed the judge dispose of several criminal cases involving young white men for various offenses – assault, driving under the influence (DUI), robbery. They all resulted in the same outcome. The defendants were released with credit for the few days that they had served in jail and placed on probation. *None* of them were sentenced to prison. By the time that they came before the judge, they had all been released from jail on bond, so they were all dressed appropriately for court – in business casual attire or in suits. Then, entered the black defendants. They were shackled from head to toe it seemed, and they were all in prison jumpsuits. For what were nearly identical offenses as the white defendants, they were all given substantial jail terms of a year or more. The differential treatment of these defendants was quite striking. The law partner with whom I was working on my case – a highly successful black male partner who had graduated from an elite law school and was a stark contrast to the young black men who surely appeared destined to life behind bars – gave me a knowing glance after what we witnessed. I will never forget that scene.

Rule 609, however, takes none of the disparities in the criminal justice system into account. It simply stands in judgment – once a criminal, you are never to be trusted. Furthermore, it helps to keep young men like those whom we saw in Huntsville ensnared in the system. Once a person has a criminal record and is "in the system," he is on the radar screen of the police. When attempting to solve crimes, for example, police often look to the "usual suspects"; that is, those with criminal records. Police and prosecutors know very well that prior convictions can be used against defendants under Rule 609 and also under other rules such as Rule 404, discussed earlier, and under other rules that I will discuss later. A recent empirical study, published in the *Cornell Law Review*, revealed that evidence of criminal defendants' prior convictions had a substantial impact in cases that otherwise should have resulted in acquittals.[93] In cases with weak evidence of guilt, evidence of prior convictions was outcome determinative.[94] Thus, prosecutors are regularly using these prior convictions to obtain new convictions. Many defendants realize this, accept plea "deals" and avoid going to trial altogether.[95] Indeed, evidentiary rules that permit the admissibility of prior convictions are a large part of the reason that around 95 percent of criminal cases in this country are adjudicated through the plea bargaining process.[96]

Rules 413–415 of the Federal Rules of Evidence, and many state rules modeled after them, present a problem similar to the prior-conviction impeachment problem but in the context of sexual offenses. These rules were enacted in 1995 as a result of intense efforts to protect children and adults (mostly women) from sexual predators, who were thought to be the most likely criminals to recidivate.[97] Under these rules, which are true exceptions to the general ban against the character-propensity evidence rule embodied in Rule 404, a person's prior or "other" sexual offenses can be used against him or her in a trial involving a claim of sexual misconduct.[98] These rules are considered "true exceptions" to the character propensity rule because they allow the other offenses to be used as evidence that the person who committed a previous sexual offense is more likely because of his history to have committed the offense of which he is currently accused. Under Rule 404(b), in contrast, when other or prior acts are admissible as evidence, it is because they show something that is relevant to the case *other* than character and action in conformity with that character.

The prior sexual offense/molestation exceptions were quite controversial when they were enacted. There is a good deal of debate as to whether sex offenders are more likely to recidivate than others with criminal records, such as drug dealers, for example.[99] The exceptions were also controversial because everyone knew that the group that would most likely be disproportionately affected by the enactment of these laws were minority men. As Professor Katharine K. Baker argued,

> Police are more likely to be aware of the histories of men who have already encountered the criminal justice system – a class of men that is overwhelmingly poor and minority. The added police incentive to arrest and prosecute alleged prior offenders, coupled with the established juror belief that rapists are naturally recidivistic, will increase the chances of wrongfully convicting those men who are least likely to have access to high quality legal counsel and most likely to be victims of discrimination. *Poor, minority men with an alleged prior record will be much more likely to be falsely identified, improperly tried, and wrongfully convicted for stranger rapes that they did not commit.*[100]

Professor Baker's argument goes further, however. She aptly points out that the disproportionate enforcement of sex crimes against minority men, aided significantly by Rule 413, will perpetuate historical and modern-day stereotypes about rape and who commits rape.[101] History teaches that a common stereotype of the black male was the black-male-as-rapist stereotype;[102] in particular, the myth existed of the black brute desirous of ravaging white womanhood. These stereotypes were embodied in the slave codes and the black codes, as noted earlier. This stereotype persists today. It is obviously harmful to black males, who are the constant object of suspicion in American society. It is also, however, harmful to women whose perpetrators do not fit the stereotype:

> The law will continue to excuse men who, by virtue of class or race privilege, are much less likely to have experience with the criminal justice system and are therefore much less likely to be the targets of prosecution. Thus, the legal system will fail to reflect precisely what feminist scholarship has fought to establish: that rape is a crime across all classes, among all races, and by all sorts of men . . . Middle class

> white men – a significant percentage of whom admit to raping – will continue to go free.[103]

Accused rapists who do not already have records and are not "in the system" are seen as more difficult to prosecute without Rule 413-type evidence. Thus, the cycle repeats itself, and an entire class of rapists will go free. Professor Baker's theory, which is supported by empirical evidence,[104] is really a black tax/white credit theory. Moreover, it shows that race can be evidence in many rape and sexual assault cases. Surely, the rule writers were aware, as with Rule 609, of the disproportionate impact that such rules have on minorities (minority men, in particular).

### "I'm Not Like Them"

The previous discussion illustrates that race is evidence in society and in the courtrooms to which society turns to seek truth and justice through litigation. For racial minorities in particular, race is prima facie bad evidence historically and today, which means that there is a burden to disprove what people see when they look at you if you are a person of color.

And as reflected in the discussion on the black tax, one of the burdens of minorities in this country is that we often have to disprove stereotypes, which requires us to work "twice as hard" (or three, four, five, ten times as hard). An additional and overlapping strategy is for minorities to continuously strive to demonstrate that we are not like those minorities who actually do confirm negative stereotypes. In Professors Devon Carbado and Mitu Gulati's *Cornell Law Review* article, "Working Identity," they discuss "comforting strategies" that some minorities use to deal with negative stereotypes in the workplace. Some of those strategies are effectively attempts by certain outsiders (racial minorities, for example) to show insiders (whites) that they are not really like other outsiders, thus encouraging insiders to engage in "outsider exceptionalism."[105]

The comforting strategies might include avoiding eating certain types of foods that are stereotypically associated with a particular outsider group, such as spicy foods if the person is Asian[106] or fried chicken if the person is black. The strategies might also influence the name that a person chooses to use in the workplace (an Asian person might choose a more "American-sounding" name) and the persons with whom the minority chooses to associate at work (he might avoid other minorities of the same race).[107] As someone who has admittedly considered and even engaged in what are probably comforting strategies (like many people of color), I know firsthand that these strategies do indeed require a great deal of work and attention to detail and can be stressful. For example, there have been times when I have pondered whether to order fried chicken during a casual business lunch, and I have spent countless hours – like many black women – in hair salons getting my hair styled in a manner that would be more acceptable[108] (albeit completely unnatural) in a workplace dominated by a white majority. President Obama's overly effusive patriotic rhetoric in his own personal civil rights narrative, which Professor Brillaint points out is objectionable to some civil rights historians as conceding too much, is a comforting strategy to counter the stereotype of black Americans as anti-patriotic (Mrs. Obama and Obama's former pastor, Jeremiah Wright, come to mind as examples of blacks portrayed as anti-patriotic). Despite the tremendous effort, comforting strategies may not even work (Obama's detractors still see him as un-American), and moreover, such efforts to disprove negative stereotypes through comforting strategies used by the individual can have the perverse and damaging effect of reinforcing them for the outsider group.[109]

Professor Paul Butler, in his book *Let's Get Free*, discusses the strategies that he used as a black federal prosecutor trying cases against young black male defendants in Washington, DC.[110] In one of the most interesting passages in his book, Professor Butler provided an example of how he used his race and status when prosecuting a typical black criminal defendant:

> I loved it when the defendant took the stand. The judge would ask 'Does the government have any questions?'
>
> 'Yes, Your Honor!' I would leap up from the government's table, stand my full six feet three inches, and stare hard at the bad guy. On the street everybody might be scared of this dude (like they were scared of me, late at night, if I wasn't wearing my suit), but at this moment, I – on behalf of the United States of America – was running the show.
>
> I paced the entire well of the courtroom but avoided going anywhere near the defendant . . . I tried to convey to the jury through my movements as well as my words that the drug dealer on trial was a piece of garbage.

Professor Butler then provides a sample cross-examination (similar to what he would have conducted when he was prosecutor) of a black criminal defendant, whom he simply refers to as "Cretin."

ME (Butler): Where were you on the night of August 5?
CRETIN: Over to my baby mama's house.
ME: What is your wife's name?
CRETIN: Her name LaShonda, but she not my wife.
ME: I see. Then you left your baby mama's house and went to stand on the street corner, is that right?
CRETIN: I saw my boy and stopped to talk.
ME: What's your boy's name?
CRETIN: Lil' Boo. I meant that's what everybody calls him – I ain't know his real name.
ME: And when you and Mr. Boo saw the police, you threw your cocaine on the ground and ran away, didn't you?
CRETIN: Naw man.
ME: No further questions, your honor.

Professor Butler then provides more context for the cross-examination. When performing before a black jury that might be hesitant to send yet another young black male to prison, he had to show the stark differences between him and Cretin. As Cretin's speech became more inarticulate, Butler's "diction became more precise." In what is probably the most powerful passage in the book, Butler says:

> Here's what they don't teach you in law school: As you, the black prosecutor, button your jacket and head back to the government table, you look at the jurors and then you glance back over at the defendant. You can't actually say these words, but this is what you mean: *Ladies and gentlemen of the jury, I am an African America. You are African Americans. The defendant over there – that's a nigger. Lock him up.*[111]

Professor Butler notes that the office where he had worked, the U.S. Attorney's Office for the District of Columbia, had the highest percentage of black attorneys than any other U.S. Attorney's office in the country. At the same time, he notes that the DC office imprisoned black citizens at a higher rate than "than virtually any other office. .... [O]n a given day half of all the young black men in the city had a criminal case – they were either in prison, on probation or parole, or awaiting trial."[112] He suggests that the reason for the high percentage of black prosecutors in the DC U.S. Attorney's office was for those black attorneys to serve a "legitimization function": "[O]ne doesn't have to be a conspiracy theorist to think the correlation between the number of black prosecutors and black inmates is more than a coincidence."[113] In a lamenting tone, Professor Butler acknowledges that he had the highest conviction rate of anyone else in his section.

Professor Butler's approach as a prosecutor was to make use of race as character evidence – good and bad. Who he was – a highly educated, articulate, well-dressed black man – was good character evidence that he effectively presented on behalf of the government. Professor Butler's good character evidence was maximized and most effective against defendants such as Cretin, making blacks appear even worse before the jury than they already would because of negative stereotypes. Furthermore, the bad character evidence working against Cretin – his poor diction, accent, marital status, status as a criminal defendant, status as a *black* criminal defendant, among other likely factors such as his socioeconomic status – made Butler's good character evidence all the more effective.

But the problem with this strategy is actually revealed most poignantly in the first part of Butler's book, where he recounts that while in the midst of preparing for the biggest case of his career, he was actually arrested and charged in connection with an incident involving one of his neighbors.[114] Butler became the victim of the system. He was forced to go to trial, in one of the very same courtrooms where he had prosecuted Cretins, in the face of lying witnesses, including the neighbor – a woman named "Detroit" – and the police.[115] He was ultimately acquitted (helped no doubt, as he candidly concedes, because of his money, which allowed him to hire the best defense attorney in town, and his education and training, which enabled him to appeal to the jury).[116] But his story demonstrates that the "I'm not like them" strategy is ultimately harmful. Although not every minority who engages in this strategy will have it directly backfire in such a dramatic way, the "I'm not like them strategy" can be damaging to minority communities.

## Reverse 404(b): Flipping the Script?

A version of the "I'm not like them" strategy is embodied in a variant of Rule 404(b) that some criminal defendants, typically minority men, have used in relatively recent cases.[117] Recall that Rule 404(b) forbids the use of other acts, crimes, or wrongs as evidence of a person's character to show action in conformity with that person's character on a particular occasion. Some criminal defendants have successfully argued for the admission of evidence showing that someone else committed a crime similar to the crime that the defendant has been charged with and that the person who committed the other crime likely committed the one that is the subject of the present case. *United States v. Stevens* is a leading reverse 404(b) case.[118]

In *Stevens*, the victims were a white male and a white female – both were Air Force police officers.[119] The perpetrator was black. The male victim, McCormack, was robbed at gunpoint, and the female, whom the majority refers to as Smith to protect her identity, was sexually assaulted.[120] The assailant threatened to kill her companion if Smith did not comply with the perpetrators demands. The facts regarding the sexual assault were particularly vile and disturbing. After the robbery and assault, the victims immediately went to the military police station, where they chose the defendant's picture from a "Wanted Board." At Stevens's first trial, the jury could not reach a verdict, so there was a mistrial. At the second trial, Stevens was convicted and appealed, arguing several evidentiary errors. Among other errors, he argued that the trial court should have allowed the testimony of his expert regarding the "lack of correlation between confidence and accuracy in eyewitness identification," although the district court had permitted the defendant's expert to testify regarding the problems of unreliability with respect to cross-racial identification. Also, the defendant argued that he should be have been allowed to present the testimony of Tyrone Mitchell, a black male who had been robbed at gunpoint by another black male who, based on Mitchell's description, "resembled" the defendant. The court laid out the defendant's argument for admissibility, or the "syllogism" (as the court called it), as follows:

> In view of the many parallels between the two crimes, one person very likely committed both; and because Stevens was exonerated by Mitchell, a black man whose identification (or lack thereof) is

arguably more reliable than that of the two white victims, Stevens was not that person.

The appellate court agreed that Stevens should have been allowed to present the Mitchell testimony as well as other evidence regarding the Mitchell robbery.[121] In fact, the court noted that there were "significant" similarities between crimes involving Smith and McCormack and the one involving Mitchell. The crimes took place around the same place and time of day and were committed against military personnel by a black male whom the victims had similarly described (there was no sexual assault in the Mitchell robbery, but Mitchell did not have a female companion). The most "striking" parallel between the two crimes was that items that were taken during both robberies (which occurred at Fort Dix, New Jersey) turned up near Fort Meade, Maryland. In fact, the police investigating these crimes were convinced, at one point, that both were committed by the same person.[122]

The use of reverse 404(b) evidence, as Stevens and other minority men have demonstrated, presents another instance of race as evidence. As Professor Butler did when he was a prosecutor and as some minorities do when "working their identity," Stevens had to disprove the presumption of criminality by presenting evidence of criminality by another black male. And to be sure, this is precisely what Professor Butler and other minorities have done, albeit in different contexts. Professor Butler describes his and other black prosecutors' roles, intended by those who hire them, as legitimizing a racially unjust system that criminalizes blackness. They come into the criminal courtroom and stand in stark contrast to the stereotypical black criminal defendant. Even though (in Butler's cases) he was the prosecutor, he was really on trial, too – or more, accurately, his race was on trial. The nominal defendant, when he is black, carries the heavy presumption of guilt because of his color in our system. But as Butler brilliantly proves in his book, so does the black prosecutor (and any other black professional on any given day depending on whom we encounter). And when race is on trial, it takes strong evidence to combat its probative value. Butler's excellence and skill as a black prosecutor stood in stark contrast to the black Cretins whom he prosecuted. If you focus on Butler (his race) being on trial, then you can see that the Cretins were effectively reverse 404(b) evidence. The system has to exonerate some people to appear legitimate – hence the presence of black prosecutors in their "legitimization" role. When those prosecutors put on a display like the one that Butler described in his sample cross-examination, they are – for that moment – exonerated. But because color does not tend to rub off easily (for most of us), the reprieves are only temporary. We are constantly on trial because of our race – mostly outside of the courtroom, of course. And sometimes we use reverse 404(b) evidence – such as comforting strategies – as a way to cope and to survive.

And reverse 404(b) evidence certainly is powerful. Indeed, the appellate court in *Stevens* saw the power in the defendant's reverse 404(b) argument, calling it "striking." What is striking and troubling to me, however, is that Stevens was even charged in the first place, based on the facts as laid out in the appellate court's opinion. There seemed to be some serious problems with the identification of Stevens as the assailant.

According to the court, the identification was not made in the context of a "traditional investigative photographic array," but instead was "a collection of random sketches and photographs that had been assembled in order to facilitate chance identifications like the one that occurred here."[123] Also according to the court, one of the police officers assisting the victims had merely "offhandedly (and not unreasonably) suggested to the victims that they glance at the wanted board, not really expecting them to find their assailant." The defendant, however, argued that there were numerous problems with the identification, including that it was impermissibly suggestive and made it substantially more likely that he was misidentified as the assailant. He noted that there were eight posters on the wanted board and that only three, including that of his own, contained actual photographs, whereas the others contained composite sketches. The defendant's photographs were the only ones in color (the others were in black and white), and his photographs were twenty-five times the size of the other photographs. There were other problems with the prosecution of Stevens, including the lack of physical evidence.[124] I am left to wonder if the police and prosecutors even cared at all if Stevens was guilty of the charged crime. I cannot help but think that his race was on trial more so than he was. As experienced in the *Stevens* case, the 404(b) issue demonstrates the high level of evidentiary proof that minority men who have likely been misidentified might have to present if they hope to be acquitted. Do they all need a black "Cretin" to shift the burden of their presumed black criminality onto? Do they all need a Tyrone Mitchell, who was a black member of the military, to come in and point the finger at the black Cretin? My point is that even if a black defendant is acquitted in a case like *Stevens* because he had reverse 404(b) evidence pointing to another black person, race has still been tried and convicted even though the person who committed the crime is nowhere to be found. Given the strength of the reverse 404(b) evidence, Stevens should simply not have been arrested, charged, and tried, nor should any other criminal defendant where there is such strong evidence that someone else committed the crime.

## Reconsidering the American Civil Rights Story

As we reflect on this country's civil rights story, we should consider how character evidence has shaped past narratives and be mindful of how we use it to create future ones. Character evidence has been the centerpiece of the American civil rights story both inside the courtroom and also on the frontlines of the movement. Those leaders and strategists who have orchestrated some of the most celebrated legal cases and protest events have done so by telling masterful stories using the type of character evidence that makes a morally compelling case for equal treatment. There was tremendous value in utilizing "good character" evidence, as illustrated by the story of Rosa Parks, the upstanding light-skinned black woman chosen as one of the faces of the movement over Claudette Colvin, a darker skinned, cursing teenager who had, like Mrs. Parks, refused to give up her seat. The recent case regarding young Trayvon Martin is another example of the value, in terms of garnering attention and empathy from the American public, of crafting a narrative with good character evidence to counter the "bad character" evidence that has historically been used to justify the subordination of disfavored groups.

But what are the implications of the heavy reliance on character evidence as a justification for equality? As the Martin case has demonstrated, undue (and perhaps unwise) use of character evidence can backfire and actually be counterproductive in the vindication of rights. For the same reasons that the law governing trials *purports* to be skeptical regarding the utility of character evidence, so, too, should those creating strategies for the ongoing civil rights agenda. We should not engage in reverse 404(b) racial politics to advance the civil rights cause, particularly in the criminal justice arena. When civil rights leaders and attorneys highlight (or even manufacture) supposedly good character evidence in a discrimination victim whose cause they chose to champion, while ignoring (at least publicly) the causes of those who might confirm negative stereotypes, those leaders and attorneys are engaging in an implicit reverse 404(b) approach. They are actually using those stereotypes passively (and sometimes more expressly) to disprove the presumption of bad character in their chosen victim. But one racial minority's legitimacy should not be dependent on the illegitimacy of other persons of that race. To state it another way, we should not attempt to disprove illegitimacy in one person by confirming it in another. Doing so is ultimately counterproductive. Given the pervasiveness of the use of race as character evidence, however, I know that this proposal is easier said than done.

## Notes

1. http://www.law.ua.edu/programs/symposiums/civil-rights-in-the-american-story/
2. See, e.g., "Birmingham Celebrates 50 Years of Civil Rights History," *USA Today*, January 18, 2013. Retrieved from http://www.usatoday.com/story/travel/destinations/2013/01/18/birmingham-celebrates-50-years-of-civil-rights-history/1846549/. "Michigan Department of Civil Rights to Celebrate 50th Anniversary with Event in Holland." Retrieved from http://www.michigan.gov/mdcr/0,4613,7–138–302477–,00.html. "Southern Cities to Celebrate Civil Rights 50th Anniversary," *Scripps Howard Foundation Wire*, May 18, 2013. Retrieved from http://www.shfwire.com/southern-cities-celebrate-civil-rights-50th-anniversary. The following are just a sampling of the numerous websites commemorating the fiftieth anniversary of the civil rights movement across the country: http://birminghamal.org/events/50th-anniversary-of-the-civil-rights-movement-in-birmingham/ (Birmingham, AL); http://www.tougaloo.edu/anniv/ (providing information on Tougaloo College's events, Jackson, MS); http://www.clemson.edu/administration/diversityoffice/50-years/ (providing information on Clemson University's events, Clemson, SC); http://columbiasc63.com/index.html (Columbia, SC).
3. The Sentencing Project, May 18, 2013. Retrieved from http://www.sentencingproject.org/doc/publications/rd_crisisoftheyoung.pdf. Emphasis added.
4. The Federal Bureau of Justice Statistics, May 18, 2013. Retrieved from http://www.bjs.gov/content/pub/pdf/piusp01.pdf.
5. See Chris Weaver and Will Purcells, *The Prison Industrial Complex: A Modern Justification for African Enslavement?* 41 Howard Law Journal 349 (1998).
6. See Katy Hall, "CCA Letters Reveal Private Prison Industry's Tactics," *Huffington Post*, April 11, 2013. Retrieved from http://www.huffingtonpost.com/2013/04/11/cca-prison-industry_n_3061115.html.

7. http://racerelations.about.com/od/understandingrac1/a/Quotes-About-The-Myth-Of-Reverse-Racism_2.htm (accessed May 18, 2013) (quoting Bill Maher, who said during a television interview that "[i]n today's GOP there is only one correct answer to the discussion about racism. And that is: There is no racism in America anymore. Except reverse-racism against whites... Denying racism is the new racism. To not acknowledge those statistics, to think of that as a 'black problem' and not an American problem. To believe, as a majority of FOX viewers do, that reverse-racism is a bigger problem than racism, that's racist.")
8. Author unknown, "GOP Rep Wilson Yells Out," *Huffington Post*, September 9, 2009. Retrieved from http://www.huffingtonpost.com/2009/09/09/gop-rep-wilson-yells-out_n_281480.html (discussing Congressman Joe Wilson's angry outburst during President Obama's health care speech).
9. Joshua Green, "The Democratic Roots of the Birther Movement," May 30, 2012. Retrieved from http://www.businessweek.com/articles/2012-05-30/the-democratic-roots-of-the-birther-movement (noting that "[A]t its root, birtherism is the extreme manifestation of the belief that Obama is, by virtue of his race, name, and background, something other than fully American.")
10. See Campbell Robertson, "Alabama Gets Strict Immigration Law as Governor Relents," *New York Times*, May 18, 2012. Retrieved from http://www.nytimes.com/2012/05/19/us/alabama-gets-strict-immigration-law-as-governor-relents.html?_r=0 (noting that Alabama's immigration law is "considered the strictest and most sweeping in the country"); Lawrence Hurley, "Justices Refuse Alabama's Immigration Law Appeal," April 29, 2013. Retrieved from http://www.reuters.com/article/2013/04/29/us-usa-court-immigration-idUSBRE93S0GD20130429 (noting that the "Alabama law is considered one of the toughest state immigration statutes in the country").
11. See Ala. H.B. 56.
12. Fed.R.Evid. 401.
13. Montré D. Carodine, "The Mis-Characterization of the Negro: A Race Critique of the Prior Conviction Impeachment Rule," 84 *Indiana Law Journal* (2009), 521.
14. 33 Ky. (3 Dana) 382, 385 (1835).
15. Id. (emphasis added).
16. Id., 382.
17. Id., 385.
18. Id., 387.
19. *Hudgins v. Wrights*, 11 Va. (1 Hen. and M.) 134 (1806) ("Where *white* persons, or native *American Indians*, or their descendants in the maternal line, are claimed as slaves, the *onus probandi* lies on the claimant; but it is otherwise with respect to native *Africans* and their descendants, who have been and are now held as slaves"). Emphases in original.
20. Id.
21. Id., 141.
22. Carissa Byrne Hessick, "Race and Gender as Explicit Sentencing Factors," 14 *J. Gender Race and Justice* (2010), 127, 130.

23. Id.
24. Priscilla A. Ocen, "Punishing Pregnancy: Race, Incarceration, and the Shackling of Pregnant Prisoners," 100 *California Law Review* (2012), 1239, 1259.
25. Jason A. Gillmer, "Poor Whites, Benevolent Masters, and the Ideologies of Slavery: The Local Trial of a Slave Accused of Rape," 85 *North Carolina Law Review* (2007), 489, 514.
26. Paul Finkelman, "The Crime of Color," 67 *Tulane Law Review* (1993), 2063, 2101.
27. Karin S. Portlock, "Status on Trial: The Racial Ramifications of Admitting Prostitution Evidence Under State Rape Shield Legislation," 107 *Columbia Law Review* (2007), 1404, 1413.
28. See *Calhoun v. United States*, 113 S. Ct. 1136, 1137 (2013) (discussing *Holland v. State*, 247 Ala. 53 [1945] and *Taylor v. State*, 50 Tex. Crim. 560, 561 [1907]); Carodine, supra note 13, 548 (also discussing Taylor) and 570 (discussing "prosecutors' misuse of race as evidence" in modern cases).
29. Calhoun, 113 S. Ct. 1137–38.
30. William Carter, Jr., Race, Rights, and the Thirteenth Amendment: Defining the Badges and Incidents of Slavery, 40 U.C. Davis L. Rev. 1311, 1373 (2007).
31. Jody David Armour, *Negrophobia and Reasonable Racism: The Hidden Costs of Being Black in America*, New York and London: New York University Press, p. 13.
32. Id.
33. Carolyn C. Jones, "Mapping Tax Narratives," 73 *Tulane Law Review* (1998), 653, 658–659.
34. Erik Eckholm, "Study Documents 'Ghetto Tax' Being Paid by the Urban Poor," *New York Times*, July 19, 2006, at A14.
35. Id.
36. Id.
37. Dorothy Brown, "How Home Ownership Keeps Blacks Poorer than Whites," *Forbes*, December 10, 2012. Retrieved from http://www.forbes.com/sites/forbesleadershipforum/2012/12/10/how-home-ownership-keeps-blacks-poorer-than-whites/, last visited May 14, 2013.
38. Id.
39. See, e.g., Dorothy A. Brown, "Shades of the American Dream," 87 *Washington Law Review* (2010), 329, 332 (discussing tax subsidies for homeownership); Dorothy A. Brown, "Race and Class Matters in Tax Policy," 107 *Columbia Law Review* (2007), 790 (discussing earned-income tax credit); Dorothy A. Brown, "The Tax Treatment of Children: Separate But Unequal," 54 *Emory Law Journal* (2005) 755.
40. Jarrett Bell, "Bell: Geno Smith the Latest to Pay the Black Tax," *USA Today*, April 21, 2013. Retrieved from http://www.usatoday.com/story/sports/nfl/2013/04/21/bell-geno-smith-racial-bias/2101977/, last visited May 10, 2013.
41. Id.
42. Id.
43. Id.
44. Id.

45. Armour, supra note 31, 113–114.
46. Jones, supra note 33, 658.
47. Cheryl I. Harris, "Whiteness as Property," 106 *Harvard Law Review* (1993), 1709, 1726.
48. "Sandy Hook Victims," CNN, December 2012. Retrieved from http://www.cnn.com/interactive/2012/12/us/sandy-hook-victims/index.html?hpt=hp_c3, last visited May 14, 2013.
49. Robert McCoppin, "CHI Cops: City Ends 2012 with 506 Homicides – a 16 Percent Increase over 2011," *Chicago Tribune*, January 1, 2013. Retrieved from http://articles.chicagotribune.com/2013-01-01/news/chi-cops-city-ends-2012-with-506-homicides-a-16-percent-increase-over-2011-20130101_1_homicide-surge-homicide-toll-chicago-homicide-victims. Author Unknown, "Illinois Second-Largest City Ends 2012 Murder Free," NBC, Retrieved from http://www.nbcchicago.com/news/local/Illinois-Second-Largest-City-Ends-2012-Murder-Free-185416762.html.
50. Affidavit of Probable Cause – Second Degree Murder, April 11, 2012. Retrieved from http://i2.cdn.turner.com/cnn/2012/images/04/12/zimmerman.affidavit.pdf, last viewed May 14, 2013.
51. Petition by Tracy Martin and Sybrina Fulton. Retrieved from http://www.change.org/petitions/prosecute-the-killer-of-our-son-17-year-old-trayvon-martin, last visited May 14, 2013. Mary Wisniewski, "Rallies Held around Country for Trayvon Martin," March 25, 2012. Retrieved from http://www.reuters.com/article/2012/03/25/us-usa-florida-shooting-rallies-idUSBRE82O0OZ20120325, last visited May 14, 2013.
52. Krissah Thompson and Scott Wilson, "Obama on Trayvon Martin: 'If I Had a Son, He'd Look Like Trayvon,'" *Washington Post*, March 23, 2012. Retrieved from http://www.washingtonpost.com/politics/obama-if-i-had-a-son-hed-look-like-trayvon/2012/03/23/gIQApKPpVS_story.html, last visited May 14, 2013.
53. http://ac360.blogs.cnn.com/category/juror-b37/.
54. Id.
55. Id.
56. Id.
57. Cynthia Kwei Yung Lee, "Race and Self-Defense: Toward a Normative Conception of Reasonableness," 81 *Minnesota Law Review* (1996), 367, 400–401.
58. R. Richard Banks, Jennifer L. Eberhardt and Lee Ross, "Discrimination and Implicit Bias in a Racially Unequal Society," 94 *California Law Review* (2006), 1169, 1175–1176.
59. Id.
60. *People v. Zackowitz*, 254 N.Y. 192, 193–99 (1930).
61. Id.
62. Id.
63. Id.
64. Id.
65. http://www.flcourts18.org/PDF/Press_Releases/Order_on_States_Motions_in_Limine.pdf.

66. http://www.talkleft.com/story/2013/7/9/155955/6327/crimenews/Zimmerman-Trial-Marijuana-Evidence; http://www.talkleft.com/story/2013/7/10/172233/115/crimenews/George-Zimmerman-Trial-Defense-Rests.
67. http://www.talkleft.com/story/2013/7/10/172233/115/crimenews/George-Zimmerman-Trial-Defense-Rests.
68. Fed.R.Evid. 404; http://lawprofessors.typepad.com/evidenceprof/2013/05/section-90404of-the-florida-statutes-generally-precludes-parties-from-presenting-propensity-character-evidence-such-as-evid.html.
69. http://www.nytimes.com/2013/07/16/opinion/zimmerman-prosecutors-duck-the-race-issue.html?_r=0&adxnnl=1&adxnnlx=1382383415-/YfTgr1G1hHeu/T2hfpJjA
70. Id.
71. Id.
72. See Lee, supra note 57, 400–401.
73. Donna Coker, "Foreword: Addressing the Real World of Racial Injustice in the Criminal Justice System," 93 *Journal of Criminal Law and Criminology* (2003), 827, 868–869 (noting that "stories that contradict stereotypes may not change a person's belief in the general truth of the stereotype").
74. Id.
75. Id.
76. Id.
77. Id.
78. Michael Rocque and Raymond Paternoster, "Understanding the Antecedents of the School-to-Jail Link: The Relationship between Race and School Discipline," 101 *Journal of Criminal Law and Criminology* (2011), 633, 642 (noting that "studies continue to show that race is significantly associated with being disciplined").
79. Kristin Henning, "Criminalizing Normal Adolescent Behavior in Communities of Color: The Role of the Prosecutors in Juvenile Justice Reform," 98 *Cornell Law Review* (2013), 383, 411.
80. See Fed. R. Evid. 609.
81. Id.
82. Id.
83. Carodine, supra note 13, 538–550.
84. Id.
85. Id.
86. Id.
87. Michelle Alexander, *The New Jim Crow: Mass Incarceration in the Age of Colorblindness* (2010), p. 194.
88. *See* Carodine, supra note 13, 561; Allison Chappell and Scott R. Maggard, "Applying Blacks' Theory of Law to Crack and Cocaine Dispositions," 51 *Int'l Journal of Offender Therapy and Comparative Criminal*, 264; Mike Males and Dan Macallair, *The Color of Justice: An Analysis of Juvenile Court Transfers in California* (2000); Gerald David Jaynes and Robin Murphy Williams, A *Common Destiny: Blacks and American Society* (WASHINGTON, DC: National Academy Press, 1989), p. 481.

89. Traci Schlesinger, "The Cumulative Effects of Racial Disparities in Criminal Processing," 7 *Journal of Institutional Justice and International Studies*, 261, 262–263 (noting differential treatment between black, Latino, and white defendants whose cases have "similar legal characteristics").
90. Manny Garcia and Jason Grotto, "Odds Favor Whites for Plea Deals," *Miami Herald*, January 26, 2004, at 1A.
91. Id.
92. Carodine, supra note 13, 577 (discussing John Cheves, "Detention of Black Teens Up for Scrutiny," *Lexington Herald-Leader*, September 7, 1999 at A1).
93. Theodore Eisenberg and Valerie P. Hans, "Taking a Stand on Taking the Stand: The Effect of a Prior Criminal Record on the Decision to Testify and on Trial Outcomes," 94 *Cornell Law Review* (2009), 1353.
94. Id., 1386.
95. Deborah S. Emmelman, *Justice for the Poor: A Study of Criminal Defense Work* (Burlington, VT: Ashgate, 2003), p. 41.
96. "Felony Defendants in Large Urban Counties" (U.S. Department of Justice: Bureau of Justice Statistics, 2002), p. 28 (2006).
97. Basyle J. Tchividjian, "Predators and Propensity: The Proper Approach for Determining the Admissibility of Prior Bad Acts Evidence in Child Sexual Abuse Prosecutions," 39 *American Journal of Criminal Law* (2012), 327, 342.
98. See Fed. R. Evid. 413–415.
99. Michael S. Ellis, "The Politics Behind Federal Rules of Evidence 413, 414, and 415," 38 *Santa Clara Law Review* (1998), 961, 982.
100. 110 Harvard Law Review 563, 592 (1997). Emphasis added.
101. Id.
102. Id., 586.
103. Id., 593.
104. Id.
105. Devon Carbado and Mitu Gulati, "Working Identity," 85 *Cornell Law Review* (2000), 1259, 1303.
106. Id., 1302.
107. Id.
108. See Angela Onwuachi-Willig, "Another Hair Piece: Exploring New Strands of Analysis under Title VII," 98 *Georgia Law Journal* (2010), 1079; Paulette M. Caldwell, "A Hair Piece: Perspectives on the Intersection of Race and Gender," 1991 *Duke Law Jounal* (1991), 365.
109. Id. at 1305.
110. Paul Butler, *Let's Get Free, A Hip Hop Theory of Justice*, (New York: The New Press, 2009).
111. Id., 103–105.
112. Id.
113. Id.
114. Id., 3–17.
115. Id.

116. Id.
117. See *United States v. Williams*, 458 F.3d 312 (10th Cir. 2006); *United States v. Montelongo*, 420 F.3d 1169 (10th Cir. 2005); *United States v. Seals*, 419 F.3d 600 (7th Cir. 2005); *State v. Johnson*, 568 N.W.2d 426 (Minn. 1997).
118. 935 F.2d 1380.
119. Id., 1384.
120. Id., 1384–1385.
121. Id., 1400–1407.
122. Id., 1401.
123. Id., 1391.
124. Id., 1390.

# Commentary on Chapter 2
# Race Is Evidence of Parenting in America: Another Civil Rights Story

Tanya Asim Cooper*

## Introduction

Professor Carodine invites us to question whether we have really progressed in matters of race and equality as the "civil rights rhetoric" has "romanticized,"[1] and demonstrates that we have not. "[R]acial disparities in the criminal justice system today" belie that myth.[2] Race, she shows, is paramount for accused persons of color and is often used against them as negative character evidence, which the seemingly color-blind rules of evidence allow.

In "Race is Evidence," Professor Carodine shines a brilliant light on several themes in "the modern realities of race,"[3] and as illustrated in the four sections of this commentary, many resonate: empirical data verify disproportionate representation of people of color in American institutions; stereotypes of racial minorities persist and influence negative outcomes; systems' players have varying levels of power, which they sometimes abuse; and many strategies exist for today's various civil rights campaigns. To comment on "institutional racism, particularly in the law,"[4] I offer another counter-narrative to question the notion of progress in the American civil rights story, and the "reality . . . especially for people of color – that racial inequality, although not formally tolerated, is a persistent part of the American story."[5]

Race matters in American foster care.[6] According to Professor Dorothy E. Roberts, it "is basically an apartheid institution."[7] This is one of the

* I thank Montré D. Carodine, Paul M. Asim, Ronald Krotoszynski, Susan Donovan, and Talitha Bailey for their support and assistance, and Austin Sarat for including me in this important project.

great civil rights problems of our time: the disproportionate representation of Native American and African American children in foster care and the disparities they experience. Children from these races are removed from their families at rates greater than any other race and stay longer in foster care, where ironically they are at great risk of harm by the system itself.[8] Researcher Joseph J. Doyle found that "[t]hose placed in foster care are far more likely than other children to commit crimes, drop out of school, join welfare, experience substance abuse problems, or enter the homeless population."[9]

Under Professor Carodine's theory, being a parent of color is presumptively "bad character"[10] evidence because stereotypes of bad parents abound, especially for African American and Native American parents who are often demonized. Yet the facially neutral laws allow evidence of race to figure prominently in various system players' decisions of whether and when to remove a child from the home, where to place the child, whether and which services are provided to the child and parent, and whether to terminate the parent-child relationship forever.

On a systems level, Professor Carodine illustrates where racial inequalities manifest within the process and procedure of criminal justice, which is meted out by the system's different players, sometimes unjustly. Systems thinking generally offers a panoptic view of this phenomenon in any institution by considering three salient features: the system's players or stakeholders; the dynamics and interconnections between those persons, including participation and power; and the system's true purpose, based on its behavior – not its rhetoric.[11] This lens also reveals leverage points or critical junctures of key decision making where racial bias appears today, and more important, where change happens.

## I. Families of Color Are Disproportionately Represented in Foster Care and Stereotypes of Families of Color Underlie Decisions to Sever Families

Looking at how America's foster care system has treated certain races historically helps inform whether we have progressed. Native American children, for example, were removed from their families en masse in what was known as the "Boarding School Era" that lasted that for 100 years.[12] In an effort to Christianize and "civilize" these children, they were sent to boarding schools, where they were forced to cut their hair and not allowed to speak their own languages. They were not educated, but instead taught to work as maids or farm laborers. Many children died.

These abuses in part led Congress to enact the Indian Child Welfare Act, which provides Native American families with the highest legal standard and burden of proof.[13] Yet, as National Public Radio's multiyear investigation highlighted, in places with high Native American populations such as South Dakota, hundreds of children are still removed from their families each year and swept up into foster care.[14] Nationally, Native American children are represented in foster care at twice the rate they comprise the general population.

The foster care system's treatment of African American children is also storied. At first, the foster care system ignored them because it was a segregated institution.[15] However, once "services shifted from institutions to foster care and from private to public agencies[,]"[16] the system began to recognize African American children, and the foster care population soared.[17] This is still evident.

Professor Dorothy Roberts invites us to:

> Spend a day at dependency or juvenile court in most major cities and you will see unmistakable evidence of the stark racial disparity in child welfare. Most of the families in these urban courts are black. If you came with no preconceptions about the child welfare system's purpose, you would have to conclude that it is an institution designed primarily to monitor, regulate, and punish poor black families.[18]

To be sure, what this institution has become is a direct reflection of America's deep-seated belief that interfering with or severing African American families is no big deal. Since Harriet Beecher Stowe portrayed slave-era attitudes in *Uncle Tom's Cabin*, America, it seems, has acted consistently:

> You see, when I any ways can, I takes a leetle care about the onpleasant parts, like selling young uns and that, – get the gals out of the way – out of sight, out of mind, you know, – and when it's clean done, and can't be helped, they naturally gets used to it. 'Tan't, you know, as if it was white folks, that's brought up in the way of 'spectin' to keep their children and wives, and all that. Niggers, you know, that's fetched up properly, ha'n't no kind of 'spectations of no kind; so all these things comes easier.[19]

As Professor Roberts puts it, "[b]ecause parents involved with child protective services are so often portrayed as brutal monsters, the public usually ignores the trauma of taking their children."[20] Indeed, despite comprising only 15 percent of the general population, African American children are represented at twice that rate – more than 30 percent of all children in foster care.

One reason for this is what Professor Carodine calls the "mischaracterization of blacks" through multiple negative stereotypes.[21] Demonizing stereotypes in the foster care system of Native Americans and African Americans persist to create a presumption that these parents are simply unfit. Native Americans are often stereotyped as alcoholics or gamblers who are deemed unable to parent their children. African American parents, especially single mothers, are caricatured as "welfare queens" or drug addicts, so naturally they are not capable of taking care of their children.[22] All of these negative and inaccurate stereotypes underlie the decision-making process and treatment of families of color in American foster care.

Researchers and scholars study why these disparities exist, and there is considerable debate nationally about whether there are, in fact, genuine differences in maltreatment rates of African Americans and Native Americans such that their children are at greater risk of harm than whites. As part of my larger agenda to bring some of this system's injustices to light, in another article, I present the national debate on why these minority children are so highly represented in American foster care and whether that is justified or biased.[23]

## II. Color-Blind Laws Foster Institutional Discrimination Against Families of Color

As Professor Carodine points out, "the law generally does not tolerate, for the most part, *formal* racism and its mischaracterization of [racial minorities]."[24] Instead the "varieties of racism that characterize our times,"[25] according to Professors Richard Delgado and Jean Stefancic, are "more subtle, but just as deeply entrenched."[26] They note, moreover, that "racism is normal, not aberrant, in American society. Because racism is an ingrained feature of our landscape, it looks ordinary and natural to persons in the culture."[27] So, within our color-blind laws, many might not notice its disparate application, and the legal standards and presumptions in which racism today manifests.[28]

According to the Supreme Court, the foster care system's overarching "best interests of the child" legal standard is suspect.[29] Its lack of definitive guidance allows foster care professionals and even judges to substitute their own judgment on what is in a child's best interest and allows unintended biases to permeate decision making. For example, as Justice Brennan wrote in *Smith v. Organization of Foster Families for Equality and Reform*:

> Studies also suggest that social workers of middle-class backgrounds, perhaps unconsciously, incline to favor continued placement in foster care with a generally higher-status family rather than return the child to his natural family, thus reflecting a bias that treats the natural parents' poverty and lifestyle as prejudicial to the best interests of the child.[30] . . . [J]udges too may find it difficult, in utilizing vague standards like the "best interests of the child," to avoid decisions resting on subjective values.[31]

Indeed, the Supreme Court "more than once has adverted to the fact that the 'best interests of the child'" standard offers little guidance to judges, and may effectively encourage them to rely on their personal values.[32]

Along similar lines, Professor Linda Berger has noted, "[t]he best interests of the child standard has been criticized almost since adoption because its indeterminacy invites the use of cognitive shortcuts; these shortcuts include stereotypes and biases as well as the scripts and models left behind by metaphors and stories."[33] This vulnerability in the legal standard allows the racial bias and stereotypes that have plagued our nation for centuries to creep in insidiously.

## III. Power and Abuse of Power in Foster Care

To highlight racial disparities in power and their abuse, Professor Carodine shares the story of Professor Paul Butler and the race and class "strategies that he used when he was a black prosecutor prosecuting young black men in Washington, DC."[34] Professor Angela Davis has similarly highlighted the power of the American prosecutor, and how race heightens the power imbalance.[35] Professor Davis notes, "[t]hrough the exercise of prosecutorial discretion, prosecutors make decisions that not only often predetermine the outcome of criminal cases, but also contribute to the discriminatory treatment of African Americans as both criminal defendants and victims of crime."[36] Elsewhere, I have also commented on the power that prosecutors wield and abuse, even unwittingly, toward child victims and witnesses in the criminal justice system; racial differences in that context – and especially unconscious insensitivity – heighten the risk of secondary harm that prosecutors might inflict.[37]

In America's foster care system, families of color who are haled into court lack power and resources.[38] As Professor Annette R. Appell notes, they are not entitled to the same privacy as most Americans and are under greater scrutiny because they often receive public assistance.[39] Instead, decision-making power shifts between the professionals (caseworkers, judges, and lawyers, including civil prosecutors) in the system and as the research of Professors Sandra Azar and Philip Atib Goff revealed, "moment-by-moment appraisals . . . may be infused with biases, differing values, and stereotypical views, which can then alter child welfare and legal professionals' interactions with families, and ultimately culminate in faulty decision making."[40] "Conversely," they found, "members of ethnic and racial minorities within our society can have a similarly negatively colored schema regarding professionals and the institutions in which they exist. They may expect prejudicial treatment and may not see themselves as having power or control in transactions."[41]

## IV. Strategies for Changing Foster Care's Role in the American Civil Rights Story

Several potential strategies already exist to address civil rights violations today. Professors Carodine and Susan Sturm in this symposium offered several promising ideas. According to Professor Carodine, "we should consider how character evidence has shaped past narratives and be mindful of how we use it to create future ones."[42] Professor Sturm suggested the collective impact framework (stakeholders working together toward a common goal) as a modern-day civil rights strategy.[43]

Consider their strategies applied to the foster care system. Under a systems thinking lens, there are many places or leverage points where agency caseworkers, social workers, lawyers, and judges make subjective decisions about children and families, decisions themselves vulnerable to unintended bias and underlying stereotypes. Because there are so many different leverage points where those critical questions of removal, placement, and services arise, using litigation to test those subjective decisions and power imbalance for parents of color helps, but according to Professor Sturm, not as much as collective impact.[44] Collective impact is more effective because all stakeholders come together willingly and equally "to examine the domain in which sets of interlinked decisions are producing these disparate outcomes for families of color."[45] Then change happens. Professors Azar and Goff likewise highlight this research-based practice in the foster care system, often referred to as Family Group Conferencing.[46]

Bringing historically disenfranchised players to the table would represent a recognition that these families are not inherently inferior or less equipped to care for their own children, and perhaps end the cycle of "bad character" evidence that Professor Carodine highlights as a pitfall.[47] This shift would not necessarily eliminate the role of government in protecting children who are truly at risk. However, the power would then be distributed horizontally, as opposed to hierarchically. Families of color would no longer be passive, voiceless subjects of the state's paternalistic directives, but rather, active participants in the determination of their own destinies.

## Notes

1. Montré D. Carodine, Chapter 2 of this volume at 66.
2. Id. See also Michelle Alexander, *The New Jim Crow: Mass Incarceration in the Age of Colorblindness* (New York: The New Press, 2010).
3. Carodine, Chapter 2 of this volume at 67.
4. Id., 71.
5. Id., 64.
6. Dorothy E. Roberts, "Child Welfare and Civil Rights," 2003 *University of Illinois Law Review* (2003), 171, 174.
7. Id., 172.
8. Robert B. Hill, "An Analysis of Racial/Ethnic Disproportionality and Disparity at the National, State, and County Levels," Casey-CSSP Alliance for

Racial Equity in Child Welfare (2007), retrieved from http://www.aecf.org/~/media/Pubs/Topics/Child%20Welfare%20Permanence/Other/AnAnalysisofRacial EthnicDisproportionalityand/Bob%20Hill%20report%20natl%20state%20racial %20disparity%202007.pdf.; Roberts, "Child Welfare and Civil Rights" at 173; Sandra T. Azar and Philip Atiba Goff, "Can Science Help Solomon? Child Maltreatment Cases and the Potential for Racial and Ethnic Bias in Decision Making," 81 *St. John's Law Review* (2007).

9. See, e.g., Joseph J. Doyle, Jr., "Child Protection and Child Outcomes: Measuring the Effects of Foster Care." 97 *The American Economic Review* (2007), 1583.
10. Carodine, Chapter 2 of this volume, at 70.
11. Donella H. Meadows, *Thinking in Systems: A Primer* (White River Junction, VT: Chelsea Green, 2008).
12. Lewis Meriam, *The Problem of Indian Administration* (Baltimore, MD: Johns Hopkins Press, 1928); Marsha King, "Tribes Confront Painful Legacy of Indian Boarding Schools," *Seattle Times*, February 3, 2008.
13. The Indian Child Welfare Act of 1978, 92 Stat. 3069, 25 U.S.C. §1901 *et seq.*; *Mississippi Band of Choctaw Indians v. Holyfield*, 490 U.S. 30 (1989).
14. Laura Sullivan and Amy Walters, "Native Foster Care: Lost Children, Shattered Families," National Public Radio, October 25, 2011. http://www.npr.org/2011/10/25/141672992/native-foster-care-lost-children-shattered-families. Please note that since I submitted this commentary, the article cited in this endnote has been criticized by NPR's ombudsman but not on the point that hundreds of children are still removed from their families. Please compare Edward Schumacher-Matos, *S. Dakota Indian Foster Care 1: Investigative Storytelling Gone Awry*, National Public Radio (August 9, 2013), available at http://www.npr.org/blogs/ombudsman/2013/08/09/186943929/s-dakota-indian-foster-care-1-investigative-storytelling-gone-awry (last visited August 30, 2013) (responding as NPR's ombudsman to the criticism by South Dakota and finding after his own investigation, the reporting was deeply flawed and without hard proof of biases against Native Americans in South Dakota's foster care system) with Kinsey Wilson & Margaret Low Smith, *Editor's Note*, National Public Radio (August 9, 2013), available at http://www.npr.org/2013/08/09/210615253/editors-note (last visited August 26, 2013) ("NPR stands by the stories."). Ultimately, this reflects the ongoing debate of racial bias in American foster care.
15. Dorothy Roberts, *Shattered Bonds: The Color of Child Welfare* (New York: Basic Civitas Books, 2002).
16. Id., 7.
17. Id., 7–10. See also Leroy H. Pelton, For Reasons of Poverty: A Critical Analysis of the Public Child Welfare System in the United States (New York: Praeger, 1989).
18. Roberts, "Child Welfare and Civil Rights," 172.
19. Harriet Beecher Stowe, *Uncle Tom's Cabin; or, Life Among the Lowly* (Boston: John P. Jewett and Company, 1852).
20. Roberts, "Child Welfare and Civil Rights," 173.

21. Carodine, Chapter 2 of this volume, at 71.
22. Dorothy Roberts, "Shattered Bonds," 64–67.
23. Tanya Asim Cooper, "Racial Bias in American Foster Care: The National Debate," 97 *Marquette Law Review* (forthcoming 2014).
24. Carodine, Chapter 2 of this volume, at 71 (emphasis in original).
25. Richard Delgado and Jean Stefancic, eds., *Critical Race Theory: The Cutting Edge* (Philadelphia: Temple University Press, 2000), at xvi.
26. Id.
27. Id.
28. See generally, Azar and Goff, "Can Science Help Solomon?"
29. *Smith v. Organization of Foster Families*, 431 U.S. 816, 834 (1977) (noting within the legal standard the unconscious bias against parents' poverty and lifestyle); *Lassiter v. Department of Social Services*, 452 U.S. 18 (1981) (Justice Blackmun dissenting with whom Justices Marshall and Brennan joined) (noting that several courts have invalidated parental termination of parental rights statutes based on this vague standard).
30. *Smith v. Organization of Foster Families*, 431 U.S. 816, 834 (1977) (citations omitted).
31. Id., 835 n.36.
32. *Lassiter v. Department of Social Services*, 452 U.S. 18, 46 n.13 (1981) (Justice Blackmun dissenting with whom Justices Marshall and Brennan joined); *Quilloin v. Walcott*, 434 U.S. 246, 255 (1978) ("We have little doubt that the Due Process Clause would be offended '[if] a State were to attempt to force the breakup of a natural family, over the objections of the parents and their children, without some showing of unfitness and for the sole reason that to do so was thought to be in the children's best interest.'")(quoting *Smith v. Organization of Foster Families*, 431 U.S. 816, 862–863 [1977]).
33. Linda L. Berger, "How Embedded Knowledge Structures Affect Judicial Decision Making: A Rhetorical Analysis of Metaphor, Narrative, and Imagination in Child Custody Disputes," 18 *Southern California Interdisciplinary Law Journal* (2009), 298. Pointing to work by social psychologists, Berger laments how difficult it can be for lawyers to counter these influences and "persuade people to adopt a view that conflicts with what they [think they] already know." Id., 299.
34. Carodine, Chapter 2 of this volume, at 89 (citing Paul Butler, *Let's Get Free, A Hip Hop Theory of Justice* [New York: The New Press, 2009]).
35. Angela J. Davis, *Arbitrary Justice: The Power of the American Prosecutor* (New York: Oxford University Press, 2007); Angela J. Davis, "Prosecution and Race: The Power and Privilege of Discretion," 67 *Fordham Law Review* (1998), 18.
36. Id.
37. Tanya Asim Cooper, "Sacrificing the Child to Convict the Defendant: Secondary Traumatization of Child Witnesses By Prosecutors, Their Inherent Conflict of Interest, and the Need for Child Witness Counsel," 9 *Cardozo Public Law, Policy and Ethics Journal* (2011).

38. *Lassiter v. Department of Social Services*, 452 U.S. 18, 43 n.10 (Justice Blackmun dissenting with whom Justices Marshall and Brennan joined) ("the State and indigent parent are adversaries, and the inequality of power and resources is starkly evident").
39. Annette R. Appell, "Protecting Children or Punishing Mothers: Gender, Race, and Class in the Child Protection System," 48 *South Carolina Law Review* (1997), 584.
40. Azar and Goff, "Can Science Help Solomon?" 534.
41. Id., 549.
42. Carodine, Chapter 2 of this volume, at 95.
43. Susan Sturm, Reframing the Equality Agenda, Civil Rights in the American Story Symposium, University of Alabama School of Law, March 8, 2013. Retrieved from http://www.law.ua.edu/resources/podcasts/symposia/civilrights_session_3.mp3.
44. Id.
45. Id. (referencing Lani Guinier and Gerald Torres, *The Miner's Canary: Enlisting Race, Resisting Power, Transforming Democracy* [Cambridge, MA: Harvard University Press, 2002]).
46. Azar and Goff, "Can Science Help Solomon?" 562–563.
47. Carodine, Chapter 2 of this volume, at 95; Berger, "How Embedded Knowledge Structures Affect Judicial Decision Making," 301 (suggesting that "[o]nce advocates or policy makers are able to imagine alternatives, rhetorical analysis can be used to discover underlying conceptual frames and devise more accommodating ones").

# 3

## Blurring the Color-Blind Line

### Eroding the Dichotomy between Color-Blindness and Color-Consciousness in Civil Rights in the American Story

Mark Brilliant

Shortly before his untimely death in 1950, Charles Hamilton Houston declared, "The struggle for civil rights in America is won." By this he meant the dismantling of state-sanctioned segregation, which he understood merely as a beginning – a first step in the direction of a society, as he put it, that "guarantees justice and freedom for everyone." Thus, four years before the U.S. Supreme Court ruled in *Brown v. Board of Education*, Houston, the National Association for the Advancement of Colored People's (NAACP's) principal architect of the litigation strategy in *Brown*, was looking past *Brown*.[1] In fact, he was doing more than looking. He was also serving as a leading figure in the development of state fair employment practices laws. In this role, he advanced what legal historian Kenneth Mack describes as "a vision of New Deal-era regulation" for targeting "race discrimination by private actors in a wide swath of industry."[2]

What Houston envisioned for employment, his Los Angeles-based NAACP counterpart, Loren Miller, sought for housing. Miller developed the strategy and shouldered the bulk of the legal work against racially restrictive housing covenants that African-American migrants to Los Angeles during World War II encountered, making Los Angeles the nation's epicenter of this type of litigation. Miller's efforts earned him a place alongside Thurgood Marshall in the U.S. Supreme Court case – *Shelley v. Kraemer* – that struck down the constitutionality of judicial enforcement of racially restrictive housing covenants in 1948.[3] Following the decision, Miller cautioned against "overestimat[ing] [*Shelley*'s] immediate effect on residential segregation." Although "the last legal prop had been knocked from under the ghetto," numerous other impediments remained.[4] An editorial in *The Crisis* captured some of these obstacles when it described the upshot of *Shelley*. "It means that if Negroes have the money and can find sellers, and are willing to take their chances in a hostile atmosphere, they can now buy and move in."[5] These were enormous ifs. They represented part of what *The Crisis* described as "the Goliath in [the] path away from ghetto evils of overcrowding, exploitation, crime, disease, and death" that remained in the aftermath of the dismantling of court-enforced racially restrictive housing covenants. They represented, as well, the targets of subsequent Miller-led campaigns in the battle against housing discrimination, beginning in the early 1950s with what the NAACP West Coast Regional Office's Legal Redress Committee described as the "the first . . . legal challenge [in the country] to the pattern of private discrimination" in the real estate market.[6]

The mid-twentieth century words and deeds of leading NAACP figures such as Houston and Miller challenge a fundamental commonality in two otherwise ideologically disparate interpretations of the civil rights era – what historian Nancy MacLean has described as a "nearly hegemonic" view in the "existing literature . . . of a mid-sixties break between an earlier, allegedly narrow and formalist understanding of civil rights and a subsequent more robust conception that included economics and substantive equality."[7] On the one hand, they are hard to reconcile with those, often on the political right, who maintain that the end goal of the civil rights movement was color-blindness – formal legal equality embodied in the uprooting of legalized discrimination in a variety of venues such as schools, buses, neighborhoods, lunch counters, voting booths, and marriage. From this perspective, the turn to color-conscious policies, most typically associated with the rise of affirmative action in employment and higher education admissions in the mid- to late-1960s, marks both a rupture and betrayal of original intent. On the other hand, the positions of Houston and Miller on employment and housing are equally hard to reconcile with those, often on the political left, who view the Cold War as causing the NAACP to "abandon . . . economic issues" in favor of the pursuit of color-blindness through formal legal equality.[8] The Cold War, in other words, marks a break and a betrayal of original intent reflected in the more robust understanding of civil rights that flourished during the New Deal and World War II eras. Therefore, the turn to color-conscious policies in the mid- to late-1960s represents both a rupture and a return, albeit one to be celebrated rather than castigated.

This essay seeks to downplay the "mid-sixties break" to which MacLean refers and to erode the color-blind/color-conscious distinction that cuts through these two dominant and ideologically divergent views of civil rights in the American story. To this end, it will begin by drawing from the words of Barack Obama to sketch what is arguably the most popular rendering of the American story and situate civil rights within it. It will then delve into a critique of this particular rendering of civil rights in the American story advanced by the most recent trend in civil rights historiography. This scholarship has been driven, in part, by contemporary political concerns. It has sought to offer an antidote and corrective to the "New Right," which historian Jacquelyn Dowd Hall has excoriated for reducing the civil rights movement's "singular objective" to "color blindness," meaning "the elimination of racial classifications and the establishment of formal equality before the law."[9]

Ironically – and this is the argument I would like to develop – the attempt to make "civil rights harder," as Hall describes the ambitions of the recent civil rights historiography, can serve to reinforce the very thing it seeks to rebut.[10] That scholarship typically posits a sharp chronological and conceptual distinction between a robust New Deal and World War II civil rights movement that was focused on securing something more substantial than mere color-blindness and a tepid Cold War civil rights movement that aspired to accomplish little more than formal legal equality. From this perspective, then, the New Right's vision of the ultimate color-blind aim of the civil rights movement is at least half right.[11]

In fact, however, I believe it is all wrong and thus a mistake (historically and politically) to cede any ground to it. Instead, as I hope to demonstrate, elements of color-blindness and color-consciousness were *always* (Cold War included) intertwined within the aspirations and actions of mainstream civil rights activists, as well as within the operation of the antidiscrimination laws they advocated. In short, I will contest altogether, rather than concede in part, the color-blind to color-conscious phase/distinction (and other related ones). In the process, I will make the case for blurring the color-blind line that cuts through both popular and academic narratives of civil rights in the American story.

By blurring, I do not mean erasing. There are meaningful and useful conceptual distinctions to be drawn between dismantling legalized segregation and enacting antidiscrimination. Moreover, there are meaningful and useful conceptual distinctions to be drawn between less (initially) and more (subsequently) color-conscious approaches to antidiscrimination (e.g., a fair employment practices approach that focuses on recruitment versus one that focuses on goals and timetables in hiring). Yet, those distinctions – as I have alluded to with the opening examples of Houston and Miller, and hope to develop in the pages that follow – are better viewed as gradual shifts in emphasis rather than radical ruptures in ideology. They are the products of strategic and pragmatic thinking, with litigation and legislation choices rooted in a tactical sense of what was possible in particular moments and venues. As cases were won, as bills were passed, as lessons were learned, and as times changed, civil rights reformers expanded their reach into realms that they had previously perceived as beyond their practical grasp (but not their ideological vision).

"Patriotism," Samuel Johnson sneered in 1775, "is the last refuge of a scoundrel." By Johnson's definition, Republicans have been the "scoundrels" of American politics for much of the past sixty years. Whereas Democrats rallied the country around the flag in campaigns against the economic depression at home and fascism abroad during the 1930s and 1940s, Republicans seized the patriotism banner during the Cold War, leading the crusades to label as "Un-American" anyone but the most staunchly anticommunist.

Republican patriotism reached its apotheosis with Ronald Reagan. In his January 1989 "Farewell Address to the Nation," President Reagan identified the "resurgence of national pride" (or "new patriotism"), as he put it, as among his "proudest" achievements in office. At the core of this resurgent national pride resided what Reagan referred to as "an unambivalent appreciation of America." He continued, "[t]hose of us who are over thirty-five or so years of age grew up in a different America." Tellingly, Reagan's choice of periodization corresponded to 1954 – with the year of *Brown v. Board of Education* marking the end of when Americans' harbored an "unambivalent appreciation" for their country, at least until Reagan claimed to have revived it during his presidency.[12]

For Reagan, an "unambivalent appreciation of America" was synonymous with "informed patriotism." And if this was patriotism, many Democrats scoffed, then Samuel Johnson was right, and the Republicans could keep it. America's history, they reasoned, was simply too complex, too contradictory, too conflicted to allow for any kind of "unambivalent appreciation" of it. Only an actor turned President – along with the legions of fans who swooned at his sentimental schtick – could take seriously the notion that "informed patriotism" could be gleaned from pre-civil rights era movies and television that, as Reagan put it, "celebrated . . . the idea that America was special."[13] Such sentiments smacked of exceptionalism, at best, and jingoism, at worst.

That is why they sounded so strange coming from the mouth of a young, Democratic candidate for the U.S. Senate in 2004 – a black man who then aspired to become only the third black U.S. Senator since Reconstruction. Sounding strikingly Reagan-esque in his keynote address to the Democratic National Convention, Barack Obama spoke of the United States as a "magical" place; a country of "greatness" and "genius"; "a beacon of freedom and opportunity"; a "tolerant" and "generous" land brimming with "possibilities" where "you don't have to be rich to achieve your potential."[14] Obama's speech captivated the convention and catapulted him to national attention.[15] It marked the beginning of Obama's effort to reclaim the patriotism banner from the Republicans for the Democrats.

That endeavor included taking a page out of Reagan's playbook. To this end, Obama began his 2006 book, *The Audacity of Hope*, by paying tribute to Reagan for "offer[ing] Americans a sense of common purpose that liberals seemed no longer to muster." He then concluded his book, and effectively commenced his presidential campaign, with a line that might have made Reagan himself blush: "My heart," Obama gushed, "is filled with love for this country."[16]

Over the course of his presidential run, Obama would profess his love for country in myriad ways, including most profusely in a speech devoted to patriotism delivered in Independence, Missouri on June 30, 2008. In that speech, Obama referred to the United States as "the greatest country on earth" – "a force for good in the world" to which "other nations and other people have looked" upon as "the last, best hope on earth." Here, in a single sentence, Obama summoned no less than John Winthrop,

Abraham Lincoln, *and* Ronald Reagan. Elsewhere, Obama burnished his patriotic credentials by taking shots at a couple of favorite Republican punching bags, implicitly repudiating multiculturalism and identity politics and explicitly renouncing counterculturalism.[17]

With respect to multiculturalism and identity politics, Obama recoiled at the "confines of the categories that supposedly define us."[18] These categories, he suggested, had the unfortunate effect of accentuating the *pluribus* almost to the exclusion of the *unum* in *e pluribus unum*. Alluding to Teddy Roosevelt's early twentieth-century criticism of "hyphenated" Americans, Obama insisted, "There's not a black America and white America and Latino America and Asian America; there's the United States of America."[19]

With respect to counterculturalism, Obama blasted those 1960s radicals who went beyond "merely . . . criticizing . . . government policies" and "attack[ed] the symbols, and in extreme cases the very idea of America itself" through flag burning, country blaming and bashing, and, "most tragically," Vietnam veteran spurning, "something that remains a national shame to this day."[20] To drive home this point – and dagger – Obama's first inaugural address not only paid tribute to those who "fought and died" for "us" in Concord, Gettysburg, and Normandy, but also Khe Sanh, Vietnam.[21]

More than any other patriotic appeal, Obama tapped his "own American story" – the "son of a black man from Kenya and white woman from Kansas," raised in Hawaii "without . . . a father's steadying hand" to guide him, but rather the hands of his white World War II veteran grandfather and Rosie the Riveter grandmother. "In no other country on earth," Obama asserted in speech after speech, "is my story even possible."[22]

Wrapped into Obama's American story – indeed, quite literally spliced into Obama's genetic code – were some of America's most hoary stories: the immigrant flocking to America's shores (Obama's father), the pioneer lighting out to America's western territories (Obama's maternal grandparents), and the boundless opportunity each would find in America's teeming cities and wide-open frontiers. Obama was, in this sense, a living, breathing advertisement for the patriotic product he pitched. That Obama was also the Columbia- and Harvard-educated child of an interracial marriage that would have been banned in roughly half the states in the country when it took place in 1960 made his patriotic pitch all the more convincing and compelling. His life walked his campaign's patriotic talk, which perhaps goes some distance to explain the chants of "USA! USA!" that often accompanied his speeches.

Of course, Obama did not simply parrot Reagan on patriotism. Rather, he sought to *redefine* patriotism. In much the same way that he distinguished hope from blind optimism, he distinguished his brand of patriotism from blind allegiance. To appreciate Obama on patriotism, it is helpful to *contrast* him with Reagan, rather than *compare* him as I have done thus far. Reagan offered a *retrospective* or backward-looking patriotism. The "unambivalent appreciation of America" he pined away for existed in an idealized (and foregone) past when, as Reagan put it, "we absorbed, almost in the air, a love of country and an appreciation of its institutions."[23]

Obama, by contrast, offered a *prospective* or forward-looking patriotism. His campaign's two signature words – hope and change – alluded to an idealized (and as yet unrealized) more-perfect future. "The most American of ideas," he said in his Iowa Caucus victory speech, is "that in the face of impossible odds, people who love this country can change it."[24] Some version of this line became one of the most common refrains in Obama's speeches. It stood in marked contrast to conservative patriotism, which by definition sought to *conserve* something from the past, rather than *construct* something for the future.

To say that Obama's patriotism was prospective (rather than retrospective) and forward-looking (rather than backward-looking) is *not* to say that it was altogether unmoored from the past. On the contrary, Obama anchored the brand of patriotism he preached firmly in America's history. Some of his historical references were straight out of any old-fashioned text book: the "band of colonists" who rose "up against an empire";[25] "the creed" that the "founding fathers" among them inscribed into "the founding documents that declared the destiny of a nation" and which was subsequently "sung by immigrants as they struck out from distant shores and pioneers who pushed westward against an unforgiving wilderness"; the "president who chose the moon as our new frontier."[26] Other of Obama's historical references were more likely to be found in more recent multicultural textbooks: the slaves who "endured the lash of the whip" and joined abolitionists to "blaze a trail toward freedom"; the workers who "toiled in sweatshops," stood on "picket lines" and "organized" unions; the "women who reached for the ballot"; the students who sat at "lunch counters and brave[d] fire hoses" for "freedom's cause" and propelled the "king who took us to the mountaintop and pointed the way to the promised land."[27]

Taken together, Obama's historical references told an American story, a metanarrative with a moral: there is America in theory, there is America in practice, and over time, America in practice has grown closer to America in theory. By America in theory, Obama meant, as he put it, the "set of ideals that . . . stir our collective conscience" and "bind us together despite our differences."[28] These "ideals" that "light the world," included, above all, the Declaration of Independence's "simple premise" that "[w]e hold these truths to be self-evident that all men are created equal," which then found expression in the Constitution's "core . . . ideal of equal citizenship under the law."[29] By America in practice, Obama meant the flouting of the ideals that constituted America in theory – above all, "the original sin of slavery" that "stained the Constitution" and left a legacy of racism, which persists right down to the present. Although there has always been a gap between America in theory and America in practice, that gap – in Obama's rendering of America's story – has closed over time. As he put it, "[t]hrough protests and struggle, on the streets and in the courts, through a civil war and civil disobedience and always at great risk," the country's true patriots have helped "narrow [the] gap between the promise of our ideals and the reality of their time."[30]

The story of civil rights in the American story is simply a microcosm of Obama's American story. As Obama explained in his address to the NAACP on the occasion of its 100th anniversary in 2009, "[b]ecause of what they did" – "they" here referring to *both* leaders like DuBois and King who spearheaded civil rights litigation and legislation campaigns *and* ordinary "people" who boycotted or freedom rode on buses, sat-in at lunch counters, registered voters, and risked and endured violence and, sometimes, death – "we are a more perfect union."[31]

Not surprisingly, civil rights historians take exception to those who wax too whiggish about civil rights in the American story, those who forget the qualifying "more" from Obama's "more perfect union," those who view the election of the nation's first African-American president as evidence that the racial gap between America in theory and America in practice has disappeared and with it so, too, should go the policies that helped diminish it. This, for example, was the implicit message in Senator John McCain's 2008 presidential campaign concession speech, in which he spoke – in past tense – of the "old [racial] injustices that once stained our nation's reputation and denied some Americans the full blessings of American citizenship."[32] In such renderings, the civil rights movement's supposed "singular objective" of "color blindness," as historian Jacquelyn Dowd Hall has described the New Right's caricature of it, has been achieved.[33]

In part in response to this caricature of civil rights in the American story, a new, so-called long civil rights movement historiography has emerged in the past decade or so. This scholarship has expanded the temporal, geographical, and substantive boundaries associated with the "dominant" or "master" narrative of the civil rights movement it seeks to revise. Chronologically, the long civil rights movement historiography locates the civil rights movement's origins during the New Deal and its acceleration during World War II, rather than in the mid-1950s. Geographically, it highlights the breadth and depth of civil rights struggles in various northern locales occurring contemporaneous with, rather than subsequent to, those in the South. Substantively, it emphasizes how the movement's reform aspirations were broader than the attainment of formal legal racial equality through the dismantling of Jim Crow laws, at least until the Cold War descended and banished the movement's radical members and their more-robust agenda and gave rise to a tepid "racial liberalism."[34]

From this perspective, as the iron curtain fell abroad and the anticommunist chill set in at home, civil rights groups directed their attention to "legal challenges... to patterns of [de jure] segregation."[35] This legalistic focus on noneconomic civil rights issues was the hollow hallmark of "racial liberalism," which was the "most influential," if ineffectual, strand of civil rights activism throughout much of the civil rights era.[36] Racial liberals accentuated the "moral and psychological roots of racial inequality" – a diagnosis that pointed to changing "hearts and minds of misguided whites" as the prescription.[37] They represented a "biracial elite" who demanded little more than mere "formal equality," the dismantling of statutory segregation.[38] Wrongheaded in its diagnosis and feckless in its prescriptions, racial liberalism stands in contrast to "racial literacy," and racial liberals stand in contrast to civil rights structuralists who espoused an "economic understanding of racial inequality," recognizing that "jobs were necessary for freedom and unionism was a prerequisite to civil rights."[39] Racial liberalism, according to its long civil rights movement critics, was the faint echo of what had been a resounding call for "civil rights unionism" or "labor-infused civil rights."[40] Its rise signaled a demise, "the lost promise of civil rights."[41]

Antidiscrimination measures, most notably state fair employment practices laws that spread across the country (excluding the South) beginning with New York in 1945, marked this declension. They embodied what Thomas Sugrue, perhaps the leading long civil rights movement historian, calls "normative color blindness," which he defines as "a rejection of all color-based categories and a skepticism of any official recognition of racial difference." For proponents of normative color-blindness, "racial categorization, however well-intentioned, reinforces or reifies a problematic, essentialist understanding of race. The best way to ensure opportunities... is to stop talking about race."[42] Here, Sugrue implicitly posits a sharp line between color-blindness and color-consciousness, with state fair employment practices laws embodying the former.

In fact, that line was never clearly demarcated, and its blurriness challenges one of the most basic tenets of civil rights in the American story espoused by both conservative politicians and pundits and, ironically, some of their leading progressive, long civil rights movement historian critics. The color-blind/color-conscious distinction these otherwise ideological opposites find in the civil rights movement works much better as a heuristic than history, as I would now like to illustrate by drawing upon examples from California's civil rights history.

In December 1946, members of the Richmond, California branches of the NAACP and Progressive Citizens of America (PCA) met with representatives from Lucky Stores, Inc., an Oakland-based supermarket chain. At the time, Lucky did not employ a single African-American in its stores, including the five it operated in Richmond. In their meeting, the Richmond NAACP and PCA representatives, according to PCA leader John Hughes, "asked Lucky to consider the hiring of Negro clerks in proportion to Negro trade." Lucky refused. Instead, Lucky agreed to "experiment" with the hiring of a single black clerk in a handful of their Richmond stores "before giving consideration to the hiring of more Negro clerks." Dissatisfied with this "token-hiring," Richmond NAACP and PCA representatives demanded another meeting with Lucky officials. Once again, they asked Lucky to increase African-American hiring until African-American employment was "roughly equal" to African-American patronage. Once again, Lucky refused.[43]

In response, a small group of Richmond NAACP and PCA members picketed a single Lucky store. To stop the picket, Lucky sought an injunction in Contra Costa County Superior Court, which was granted in June 1947. Hughes and Louis Richardson of the Richmond NAACP, however, disregarded the court order, and once again staged a picket with signs that read, "Lucky's Won't Hire Negro Clerks in Proportion to Negro Trade, Don't Patronize." Their efforts earned them a contempt of court citation, for which their punishment was to be two days in jail and a $20 fine each. Lawyers for Hughes and Richardson appealed, and what began as the case of *Lucky Stores vs. Progressive Citizens of America* turned into *Hughes v. Superior Court*.[44]

As it made its way up to the California and U.S. Supreme Courts over the course of the next several years, *Hughes* posed a difficult dilemma for regional and national NAACP leaders. On the one hand, they steadfastly supported state and national efforts to enact fair employment practices laws. Richmond made a particularly compelling case for such measures. As the city hemorrhaged Kaiser shipyard's World War II jobs, a worried Walter White wrote in July 1945, "[s]ome of the city officials, among whom I understand the Mayor is most active, are advocating sending newcomers 'back where they came from,' especially Negroes."[45] On the other hand, regional and national NAACP leaders, including Thurgood Marshall and Robert Carter, rejected the means – that is, hiring in proportion to patronage – through which the Richmond branch of the NAACP and PCA sought to achieve the ends of "greater opportunity" for African-American employment.[46]

Whatever dilemma *Hughes* may have posed to the NAACP, it presented no such problem for the California and U.S. Supreme Courts. On November 1, 1948, the California Supreme Court upheld the injunction that the Contra Costa County Superior Court had issued against the picketing of Hughes and Richardson. The picketers' demand for hiring in proportion to patronage, the court majority held, was illegal. It called for "arbitrary discrimination upon the basis of race and color alone, rather than a choice based solely upon individual qualification for the work." If the picketers' prevailed, they would set a dangerous precedent, in that "other races, white, yellow, brown, and red, would have equal rights to demand discriminatory hiring on a racial basis." Because the picketers' demand was illegal, so, too, was their picket.[47] A year and a half later, a unanimous U.S. Supreme Court offered similar reasoning to reach a similar decision.[48]

Nearly three decades later, Thurgood Marshall confronted the legality of another "quota system," this time as a member of the U.S. Supreme Court. At issue in the *University of California Regents v. Bakke* was a University of California, Davis medical school admission program that reserved sixteen (out of 100) slots for "Blacks," "Chicanos," "Asians," and "American Indians."[49] Marshall was one of four justices to join sections of Justice Lewis Powell, Jr.'s opinion, thereby cobbling together a one-vote majority on behalf of a particular, "diversity" defense of affirmative action in university admissions. At the same time, he filed a separate opinion in which he blasted the limited reach of Powell's reasoning. Focusing exclusively on African-Americans, Marshall described their history as "different in kind, not just degree, from that of other ethnic groups." Normatively, that history warranted the "consideration of race in making decisions about who will hold the positions of influence, affluence, and prestige in America." Legally, there was nothing unconstitutional about such color-conscious considerations. The exceptionally invidious history of antiblack racism in the United States merited "greater protection under the Fourteenth Amendment to remedy the effects of past discrimination."[50] Race-conscious policies in the past (of one kind) required race-conscious policies in the present (of another kind) in order to realize a color-blind future.

For some scholars (and other commentators), Marshall's journey from *Hughes* to *Bakke* – from eschewing racial quotas in the one case to embracing them in the other case – represents an act of apostasy, a renunciation of a commitment to color-blindness as the ideal and goal of civil rights.[51] For other scholars (and other commentators), Marshall's journey from *Hughes* to *Bakke* represents an act of epiphany. Propelled by the proselytizing of the people in the pews (or, more accurately, the rank-and-file participants in the black freedom movement), Marshall finally saw the light and realized that "freedom [was] not enough," as historian Nancy MacLean puts it; that "formal" equality – the dismantling of statutory segregation and the passage of antidiscrimination legislation – was distinct from, and no substitute for, "substantive" equality.[52]

Despite their different normative stances, scholars from both of these camps espouse similar historical perspectives. For them, Marshall's path from *Hughes* to *Bakke* is a microcosm of a broader transformation – a qualitative shift – within the civil rights movement encapsulated in a series of related dichotomies: from color-blind to color-conscious, from equality of opportunity to equality of results, from antidiscrimination to affirmative action, from formal equality to substantive equality, from individual rights to group rights, from disparate treatment to disparate impact, and from racial liberalism to racial literacy.[53]

Such starkly drawn distinctions, I believe, work much better as abstract conceptual devices than as accurate empirical descriptors. Even though Marshall, for example, may have rejected color-conscious "quotas" in *Hughes* – "oppos[ing] a proportional or quota system in hiring" and insisting that "persons must be given job opportunities in accordance with ability rather than in accordance with race or color" – he did not reject the color-conscious notion of inferring racial discrimination from racial underrepresentation, noting how black unemployment in Richmond was "greatly disproportionate to unemployment among whites."[54] Similarly, although Marshall may have embraced color-conscious "quotas" in *Bakke* – thereby endorsing the University of California, Davis medical school admission's program – he did so in the name of color-blindness, that is, as a necessary step toward becoming a "fully integrated society, one in which the color of a person's skin will not determine the opportunities a ailable to him."[55]

In both of these instances, even though separated by three decades, elements of color-blindness and color-consciousness were intertwined and thus hard to reconcile with a view that posits – for better or worse – a fundamental rupture in the civil rights movement between color-blind (or formal equality) and color-conscious (or substantive equality) phases. As the legal historian Kenneth Mack has written, this "distinction" – between "formal equality (removing explicit barriers to participation) and substantive equality (actual African-American participation in the nation's institutions)" – "isn't so neat."[56]

Just as color-blindness and color-consciousness were intertwined within the aspirations and actions of mainstream civil rights activists like Thurgood Marshall, so, too, were they intertwined within the operation of the antidiscrimination laws they advocated beginning in the

1940s. Consider the case of the California Fair Employment Practice Act.

In his dissenting opinion in *Hughes* in 1948, California Supreme Court Justice Roger Traynor noted the absence of a state fair employment practices law. Without such a law, Traynor argued, there existed no prohibition against businesses such as Lucky to discriminate in "favor or against Negroes." Lucky, therefore, could very well, if it so chose, adopt a "policy of proportionate hiring" in favor of black job applicants in order to offset "the fact that everywhere [black job seekers] turn for jobs they are likely to encounter the barrier of discrimination." Although a state fair employment practices law that "prohibited consideration of the race of applicants for jobs . . . might" render "the demand for proportional hiring" illegal, "[n]either the Legislature nor the people have adopted such a statute."[57]

In fact, California lawmakers and voters repeatedly rejected state fair-employment practice proposals throughout the 1940s and into the 1950s, a reflection of how the Cold War hobbled the push for civil rights in the Golden State beyond the dismantling of legalized segregation, which had occurred in rather short order in the second half of the 1940s.[58] As leaders in the California Federation of Civic Unity observed in 1948, "[u]nfortunately, it is becoming increasingly difficult to undertake any kind of activity in the area of civil rights of racial and/or religious minorities without being forced to face the charge of Communism."[59] This observation would be borne out, for example, by the eleven years that would have to pass before California began venturing down the antidiscrimination legislation roads that commenced where anti-legalized segregation litigation roads had concluded in the late 1940s. Desegregation, in other words, might have been a Cold War imperative, girding many states and the federal government into action against legalized segregation.[60] By contrast, antidiscrimination litigation and legislation on behalf of fair employment practices, initially, and fair housing, subsequently, faced stiff and insurmountable Cold War head winds for many years. Opponents of such measures often cast them as encroachments on the sacred right of private property and thus of a piece with a "communistic plan" to sow "discord in democratic communities," as foes of a fair employment practices ballot proposition in California in 1946 charged.[61]

In the face of such resistance, however, California racial liberals did more to narrow the composition of their membership – distancing themselves from communists – than they did to narrow the domestic civil rights content of their aspirations.[62] For example, from the time it opened its doors in 1944, the NAACP's West Coast Regional Office (NAACP-WC), led initially by Noah Griffin, made securing a state fair employment practices law its top legislative priority. Such a measure, Griffin maintained, represented a response to the NAACP-WC's "paramount concern" – namely, the threat of massive postwar job losses.[63]

Securing a fair employment practices law remained the NAACP-WC's top state legislative priority, which finally came to fruition in 1959 when California became the fifteenth state to enact such a measure.[64] The California Fair Employment Practice Act forbid "discrimination or abridgment on account of race, religious creed, color, national origin, or ancestry" in employment. For enforcement, it established a Fair Employment Practice Commission (FEPC) composed of five gubernatorial appointees, each of whom had a small staff to investigate and resolve employment discrimination cases. If the FEPC then found unlawful discrimination, it could, among other things, order the employer to "take such affirmative action, including (but not limited to) hiring, reinstatement or upgrading of employees, with or without back pay." Refusal to abide by the FEPC's ruling constituted a misdemeanor, punishable by up to six months in jail and a $500 fine.[65]

Historian Nancy MacLean implicitly links state fair employment practices laws to "legal freedom, formal equality," as opposed to "genuine inclusion," which, she says, would not arrive until the second half of the 1960s when "ordinary workers [African-Americans, at first]" spurred the creation of "an innovative and effective national policy: affirmative action."[66] Similarly, historical sociologist Anthony Chen distinguishes between fair employment practices and affirmative action – tracing the "remarkable journey" from the one to the other – with the latter emerging in the late 1960s as a result of a "color conscious turn" reflected in affirmative action's use of "'goals and timetables' for increasing the representation of selected groups over time."[67] MacLean and Chen echo Sugrue, who draws a sharp line between color-blindness and color-consciousness, with state fair employment practices laws embodying the former.

In fact, members of the California FEPC espoused a more nuanced view from almost the moment the law went into effect. They recognized what veteran California civil rights activist and California FEPC executive director, Edward Howden, described in 1961 as a "classic dilemma" between the "case for color-blind policy" and the "problem of achieving integration" in the workplace.[68] The law's provisions – and the California FEPC's administration of them – reflected that tension. On the one hand, they forbid inquiries into race (as well as religion and place of birth) when it came to hiring. On the other hand, those "forbidden inquiries" did not apply "once . . . employer[s] . . . decided to hire . . . applicant[s] and so informed [them]." Only by such a "liberalized" view of the state's fair employment practice law, as the FEPC described its interpretation of when race could or could not be taken into account in employment, would "survey[s] of ethnic pattern[s]" in work places be permissible.[69] And only with the data revealed by such surveys – a "solid basis of relevant facts" – could "equal opportunity for Negro Americans, Mexican Americans, and other minorities" be achieved, as the California FEPC explained in a 1963 "Statement on Surveys and Statistics as to Racial and Ethnic Composition of Work Force or Union Membership."[70] Thus, rather than hewing to the color-blind side of a sharply drawn line between color-blindness and color-consciousness, the California FEPC blended the two and thereby blurred the boundary between them. It sought to reconcile the "classic dilemma" between the "case for color-blind policy" and the "problem of achieving integration," as Howden described it, by employing color-conscious means to achieve color-blind ends.[71]

Attorney General Stanley Mosk endorsed this approach. "A pattern of systematic exclusion may be overcome by a policy of deliberate inclusion," Mosk wrote in an April 1964 explication of the state fair employment practice law. Supreme Court Justice John Marshall Harlan's oft-quoted line in his dissent in *Plessy v. Ferguson* that "the Constitution is color blind," according to Mosk, "was never intended to blind the law to inequities which arise out of color distinctions or to cripple the democracy in its efforts to eliminate such inequities." This did not mean that "quotas" were legal, wrote Mosk, citing and affirming *Hughes*, but it did mean that the pursuit of "reasonable racial balance" was.[72] Mosk's view reflected that of Governor Pat Brown, who exhorted the state FEPC in 1962 to "engage industry and labor" through recruitment reviews, employment surveys, and "everything else needed to accelerate employment integration throughout California."[73] Fair employment practices, in other words, entailed opportunity as well as outcomes, and outcomes required more than a narrow interpretation of the law that limited compliance to investigation of individual complaints on a case-by-case basis. There was a "broad consensus" among FEPCs across the country, Howden told Congress in 1963, that such an approach was "haphazard, piecemeal, and wholly inadequate."[74]

To avoid that, the California FEPC not only promoted racial and ethnic surveys of workforces and unions, but also launched "affirmative actions" in places where "a seriously deficient situation in terms of percentage and distribution of minority employees is discovered."[75] The first "formally designated affirmative action" took place in 1963. However, according to the California FEPC, kindred efforts in "positive compliance" had been occurring since the law went into effect. Although more time consuming and costly to conduct than investigations into individual complaints, affirmative actions offered the promise of "more comprehensive effect in terms of broadened job opportunities."[76]

This promise – as yet unfulfilled because investigations into individual complaints about workplace discrimination (nearly 90 percent of which were brought by African-Americans) constituted the bulk of the FEPC's work in its formative years[77] – prompted multiple members of the FEPC, including Howden and C. L. Dellums, a veteran labor and NAACP leader in California, to comment in late 1963 that there were "powers in the [fair-employment practices] law that hadn't been fully harnessed."[78] To harness at least some of those powers, the California FEPC more than doubled the number of affirmative actions it launched between July 1964 and July 1966, from seventeen to forty-one. It also called for an amendment to the California Fair Employment Practices Act to require "ethnic pattern reports" from all employers and unions covered by the law, rather than simply from those against whom the FEPC had initiated an investigation.[79]

The California FEPC's and state attorney general's position on affirmative actions reflected similar positions being staked out at the time by leading civil rights groups. (The "top down," in other words, proceeded in lockstep with the bottom up, as opposed to one following the other as historians of affirmative action have debated.[80]) In October 1963, the Urban League's Whitney Young called for a "Domestic Marshall Plan" for African Americans. Although eschewing a "quota system," Young's proposal required the collection of statistical data in employment in order to reach beyond "'tokenism'" and ensure that "*qualified* Negroes [were placed] in all categories of employment at all levels of responsibility."[81]

Concurrently, the San Francisco-based western regional office of the Congress of Racial Equality (CORE), established in May 1962, was pressuring selected employers throughout California, such as Lucky [Grocery] Stores, for a "statistical breakdown of all employees by job category and race (White, Negro, Spanish-American, and all other minorities)," as well as an "account of progress" reflected in the those statistics.[82] Lucky acceded to this demand, unlike it had done when faced with the picketing for proportional hiring in the late 1940s that led to the *Hughes* case. In November 1963, it (as well as Safeway) agreed to provide CORE with "progress reports on the hiring, training and advancement of non-whites." CORE hailed this as a "major employment breakthrough."[83] Over the next couple of years, CORE would negotiate 260 other similar employment agreements, resulting in hundreds of jobs.[84]

These included Bank of America, the state's largest employer in an industry that CORE described in early 1964 as "completely closed . . . to Negroes and non-whites."[85] Initially, the bank consented only to "cooperative effort [with CORE] to find qualified applicants" and resisted "demands for masses of statistical data," which it deemed in violation of the California Fair Employment Practice Act.[86] Such data, CORE retorted, was essential to buttress the case for "preferential hiring," which was essential to achieving the "equal [employment] opportunity" of the state fair employment practice law.[87] The California FEPC sided (for the most part) with CORE, brokering an arrangement whereby Bank of America agreed to provide the FEPC with the statistical data that CORE wanted. This "example of the FEPC's affirmative action program," its chair asserted in June 1964, "was a major step in furthering the cause of equal employment opportunity."[88] It would yield a nearly 40 percent increase in African-American employment in its first three months.[89] It would also buttress the California FEPC's well-established view that the kind of "affirmative actions" the law permitted held the greatest hope for prying open "whole plants, firms, and industries," as a 1965 *Stanford Law Review* article characterized it, based on interviews of California FEPC commissioners and staff, among others.[90]

One year later, however, that hope would be derailed. In November 1966, Ronald Reagan became governor of California, defeating Pat Brown, who had signed the California Fair Employment Practice Act into law in 1959. Although Reagan did not oppose the law on the campaign trail (as he did the state's fair housing law), his first year in office witnessed a substantial shift in the FEPC's administration of the law away from affirmative actions. After increasing under Brown, the number of FEPC-initiated affirmative actions plummeted from forty-one to nine from July 1, 1966–June 30, 1967.[91] The following year, the California legislature passed a law that defined affirmative action in the narrowest possible terms – as "educational activity for the purpose of securing greater employment opportunities for the members of such groups on a voluntary basis" – and the number of FEPC-initiated affirmative actions fell to a mere two, even as the number of individual cases that opened steadily grew.[92]

If his FEPC's actions are any indication, Reagan did not need anything like the subsequent arrival of the Philadelphia Plan's "goals and timetables" for minority hiring nor the University of California, Davis Medical School's racially tiered admissions program to find fault with affirmative action. He could find it instead in the affirmative actions undertaken by the California FEPC under Brown. These different approaches to enforcing the same fair employment practice law – Reagan's more narrow, Brown's more expansive – underscore how "the formal and the substantive interpretations of antidiscrimination law, the restrictive and the capacious" have long been intertwined, as historian Nancy MacLean puts it, rather than mutually exclusive and chronologically sequential.[93] In the process, they provide additional proof of just how blurry the color-blind line was in civil rights history and therefore ought to be presented in civil rights historiography and memory. To fail to appreciate this blurriness is to cede unwarranted historical ground to the more contemporary politically conservative equation of civil rights with color-blindness. It is to concede the existence of a color-blind phase in the civil rights movement rather than contesting altogether the color-blind/color-conscious dichotomy by blurring the boundary between it across the civil rights era, as this essay has sought to do.

## Notes

1. Houston quoted in Patricia Sullivan, *Lift Every Voice: The NAACP and the Making of the Civil Rights Movement* (New York: The New Press, 2009), p. 383.
2. Kenneth W. Mack, "Bringing the Law Back into the History of the Civil Rights Movement," 27 *Law and History Review*, no. 3 (2009), 662.
3. *Shelley v. Kraemer* 334 U.S. at 1 (1948).
4. Loren Miller, "A Right Secured," *Nation* (May 29, 1948), 599.

5. "No Support for Covenants," *The Crisis* (June 1948), 169.
6. NAACP West Region Annual Report 1954, National Association for the Advancement of Colored People, West Coast Regional Office, Region I, Records, The Bancroft Library, University of California, Berkeley (hereafter NAACP-WC). For more on Miller's housing covenant litigation in California during the 1940s, see Mark Brilliant, *The Color of America Has Changed: How Racial Diversity Shaped Civil Rights Reform in California, 1941–1978* (New York: Oxford University Press, 2010), chapter 4.
7. Nancy MacLean, "Response to Ken Mack – and New Questions for the History of African American Legal Liberalism in the Age of Obama," 27 *Law and History Review*, no. 3 (2009), 672.
8. Jacquelyn Dowd Hall, "The Long Civil Rights Movement and the Political Uses of the Past," 91 *Journal of American History*, no. 4 (2005), 1250.
9. Hall, 1237.
10. Hall, 1235.
11. For a similar point, see Mack, 666.
12. Ronald Reagan, "Farewell Address to the Nation," January 11, 1989.
13. Reagan, "Farewell Address."
14. Barack Obama, "Keynote Address to the Democratic National Convention," July 27, 2004.
15. Barack Obama, *The Audacity of Hope* (New York: Three Rivers Press, 2006), p. 354.
16. Obama, *The Audacity of Hope*, 32, 362.
17. Barack Obama, "The America We Love," June 30, 2008.
18. Barack Obama, "South Carolina Primary Speech," January 26, 2008.
19. Obama, "Keynote Address."
20. Obama, "The America We Love."
21. Barack Obama, "First Inaugural Address," January 20, 2009.
22. Barack Obama, "A More Perfect Union," March 18, 2008.
23. Reagan, "Farewell Address."
24. Barack Obama, "Iowa Caucus Speech," January 3, 2008.
25. Obama, "Iowa Caucus Speech."
26. Barack Obama, "New Hampshire Primary Speech," January 8, 2008.
27. Obama, "First Inaugural Address," "New Hampshire Primary Speech," "Iowa Caucus Speech."
28. Obama, *Audacity of Hope*, 8.
29. Obama, "First Inaugural Address," "A More Perfect Union."
30. Obama, "A More Perfect Union."
31. Barack Obama, "Remarks by the President to the NAACP Centennial Convention," July 17, 2009. Although he acknowledges the "many barriers" that persist, Obama, as historian Nico Slate writes, "is perhaps the most successful promoter of the view that the civil rights movement should be seen, in Hall's words, 'as a natural progression of American values.'" Nico Slate, "Glorious Burdens: Teaching

Obama's History and the Long Civil Rights Movement," 44 *History Teacher*, no. 4 (2001), 596.

32. John McCain, "Concession Speech," November 4, 2008.
33. Hall, 1237.
34. Hall, 1249.
35. William H. Chafe, "Race in America: The Ultimate Test of Liberalism," in William H. Chafe, ed., *The Achievement of American Liberalism: The New Deal and Its Legacies* (New York: Columbia University Press, 2002), 166.
36. Thomas J. Sugrue, *Sweet Land of Liberty: The Forgotten Struggle for Civil Rights in the North* (New York: Random House, 2008), 355, 34.
37. Sugrue, *Sweet Land of Liberty*, xxvi.
38. Lani Guinier, "From Racial Liberalism to Racial Literacy: *Brown v. Board of Education* and the Interest-Divergence Dilemma," 91 *Journal of American History*, no. 1 (2004), 93–95.
39. Guinier, 92; Sugrue, 34.
40. Hall, 1245–1246; Robert Rodgers Korstad, *Civil Rights Unionism: Tobacco Workers and the Struggle for Democracy in the Mid-Twentieth Century South* (Chapel Hill: University of North Carolina Press, 2003).
41. Risa Goluboff, *The Lost Promise of Civil Rights* (Cambridge: Harvard University Press, 2007).
42. Thomas J. Sugrue, *Not Even Past: Barack Obama and the Burden of Race* (Princeton, NJ: Princeton University Press, 2010), 114–115.
43. John E. Hughes, "To Defend the Legal Right to Picket in Protest of Anti-Negro Discrimination in Employment: Memorandum Concerning the Fight for 'Fair Employment' vs. the Monopoly Chain Store Lucky Stores Inc.," 1947, Carton 89, Folder 14, NAACP-WC.
44. Hughes, "To Defend the Legal Right to Picket in Protest of Anti-Negro Discrimination in Employment."
45. Walter White to Noah Griffin, July 16, 1945, Carton 89, Folder 13, NAACP-WC.
46. "Brief of the National Association for Advancement of Colored People as *Amicus Curiae*," October 1949, in *The Hughes Case*, The Bancroft Library, University of California, Berkeley. Amicus briefs filed by the CIO and ACLU took similar views. They supported the right of the Richmond NAACP and PCA activists to picket for employment opportunity, but spurned their demand for hiring in proportion to patronage. "Brief for the Congress of Industrial Organizations as *Amicus Curiae* and Brief for the American Civil Liberties Union, *Amicus Curiae*," October 1949, in *The Hughes Case*, The Bancroft Library, University of California, Berkeley.
47. *Hughes v. Superior Court*, 32 Cal. 2d 850 (1948). For Justice Felix Frankfurter, who wrote the Court's opinion, the "broad question" posed by the case was, "Does the Fourteenth Amendment of the Constitution bar a State from use of the injunction to prohibit picketing of a place of business solely in order to secure compliance with a demand that its employees be in proportion to the racial origin of its then customers?" The answer was no. Nothing in the Fourteenth Amendment,

nor, for that matter, the First Amendment, precluded the Contra Costa County Superior Court from acting as it did, given the "mischief furthered" by the "evil of picketing to bring about proportional hiring." To rule otherwise would open a Pandora's Box of "community tensions and conflicts." Echoing the California Supreme Court's concerns, Frankfurter wrote, "[t]o deny to California the right to ban picketing in the circumstances of this case would mean that there could be no prohibition of the pressure of picketing to secure proportional employment on ancestral grounds of Hungarians in Cleveland, of Poles in Buffalo, of Germans in Milwaukee, of Portuguese in New Bedford, of Mexicans in San Antonio, of the numerous minority groups in New York, and so on through the whole gamut of racial and religious concentrations in various cities."

48. *Hughes v. Superior Court*, 339 U.S. at 460 (1950).
49. *Regents of the University of California v. Bakke*, 438 U.S. at 265 (1978).
50. *Regents of the University of California v. Bakke*, 438 U.S. at 265 (1978).
51. See, for example, Hugh Davis Graham, *The Civil Rights Era: Origins and Development of National Policy, 1960–1972* (New York: Oxford University Press, 1990); Andrew Kull, *The Color-Blind Constitution* (Cambridge: Harvard University Press, 1992); Paul D. Moreno, *From Direct Action to Affirmative Action: Fair Employment Law and Policy in America, 1933–1972* (Baton Rouge: Louisiana State University Press, 1997); Hugh Davis Graham, *Collision Course: The Strange Convergence of Affirmative Action and Immigration Policy in America* (New York: Oxford University Press, 2002).
52. See, for example, Thomas J. Sugrue, "Affirmative Action from Below: Civil Rights, the Building Trades, and the Politics of Equality in the Urban North," 91 *Journal of American History*, no. 1 (2004), 145–173; Nancy MacLean, *Freedom Is Not Enough: The Opening of the American Workplace* (New York: Russell Sage Foundation, 2006); Thomas J. Sugrue, *Sweet Land of Liberty: The Forgotten Struggle for Civil Rights in the North* (New York: Random House, 2008); Anthony S. Chen, *The Fifth Freedom: Jobs, Politics, and Civil Rights in the United States, 1941–1972* (Princeton, NJ: Princeton University Press, 2009).
53. On the "two phases of the Civil Rights Era," see Graham (1990). On the distinction between formal equality and substantive equality and the progression from the former to the latter, see MacLean (2006, 2009), as well as Kenneth Mack's discussion of this aspect of MacLean's work inMack (2009). On the distinction between racial liberalism and racial literacy and the progression from the former to the latter, see Guinier.
54. "Brief of the National Association for Advancement of Colored People as *Amicus Curiae*," October 1949, in *The Hughes Case*, The Bancroft Library, University of California, Berkeley. Amicus briefs filed by the Congress of Industrial Organizations and American Civil Liberties Union took similar views. They supported the right of the Richmond NAACP and PCA activists to picket for employment opportunity, but spurned their demand for hiring in proportion to patronage. "Brief

for the Congress of Industrial Organizations as *Amicus Curiae* and Brief for the American Civil Liberties Union, *Amicus Curiae*," October 1949, in *The Hughes Case*, The Bancroft Library, University of California, Berkeley.

55. *Regents of the University of California v. Bakke*, 438 U.S. at 265, 400, 401 (1978).
56. Mack, 663.
57. *Hughes v. Superior Court*, 32 Cal. 2d 850, 868–869 (1948).
58. For more on the dismantling of legalized segregation in California in the second half of the 1940s, see Brilliant, chapters 2–4.
59. Josephine Duveneck and Ruth Kingman, "Brief Statement Covering Problems Facing California Federation for Civic Unity," February 26, 1948, Carton 3, Folder Board of Directors Meetings, California Federation for Civic Unity Records (hereafter CFCU), The Bancroft Library, University of California, Berkeley.
60. Mary Dudziak, *Cold War Civil Rights: Race and the Image of American Democracy*. (Princeton, NJ: Princeton University Press, 2000).
61. "Proposition 11: Fair Employment Practices Act," 1946. Retrieved from http://librarysource.uchastings.edu/ballot_pdf/1946g.pdf. For more on this point with respect to fair employment practices legislation, see, for example, MacLean, 30; Chen, 128–129; Daniel Martinez HoSang, *Racial Propositions: Ballot Initiatives and the Making of Postwar California* (Berkeley: University of California Press, 2010), chapter 2. For more on this point with respect to fair housing legislation, see Brilliant, 193–194; HoSang, chapter 3.
62. Shana Beth Bernstein, *Bridges of Reform: Interracial Civil Rights Activism in Twentieth-Century Los Angeles* (New York: Oxford University Press, 2011), introduction, chapters 4–5. See also Manfred Berg, "Black Civil Rights and Liberal Anticommunism: The NAACP in the Early Cold War," 94 *Journal of American History*, no. 1 (2007), 75–96. Berg views the NAACP's anticommunism as a pragmatic, political calculus of what was required "to keep the cause of black civil rights on the agenda" (77). That agenda, at least in California, remained consistent before and after the NAACP adopted its anticommunist policy in 1947, focusing from the 1940s into the 1960s on fair employment practices and fair housing. To the extent that the Cold War had a chilling effect, according to Sophia Lee, it was in the area of the "transnational fight against colonialism and for human rights," not over "workplace rights" that remained hotly contested. Sophia Z. Lee, "Hotspots in a Cold War: The NAACP's Postwar Workplace Constitutionalism, 1948–1964," 26 *Law and History Review*, no. 2 (2008).
63. Noah Griffin to Walter White, et al., September 8, 1944, Part 17, Reel 15, Frame 491, Microfilm of the NAACP.
64. *FEPC First Annual Report, September 18, 1959 – December 31, 1960* (Sacramento: State Printing Office, 1961), 7–8.
65. Chapter 121, 1959 Statutes of California.
66. MacLean (2006), 5, 76.
67. Chen, 7, 17.

68. Minutes of Special Executive Session of the California Fair Employment Practices Commission, May 25, 1961, Box 1, Fair Employment and Housing Commission, San Francisco.
69. *FEPC Reports: 1961 and 1962* (Sacramento, CA: State Printing Office, 1963).
70. California Fair Employment Practices Commission, *Statement on Surveys and Statistics as to Racial and Ethnic Composition of Work Force or Union Membership* (San Francisco, CA: Fair Employment Practices Commission, November 1963). See also California Fair Employment Practices Commission, *Promoting Job Opportunities: A Guide to Employers* (Sacramento, CA: Fair Employment Practices Commission, 1963).
71. According to Nelson Lichtenstein, other state FEPC's took a similar view and in so doing "began to put into place many of the legal strategies and administrative techniques that proponents of 'affirmative action'" would espouse. See Nelson Lichtenstein, *State of the Union: A Century of American Labor* (Princeton, NJ: Princeton University Press, 2009), 86–87.
72. Office of the Attorney General of the State of California, *Opinion Nos. 63–148 (43 Ops. Cal. Atty. Gen. 200, April 30, 1964)*. Mosk's position on the limits of color-conscious also echoed – and corroborated – the FEPC's from the year before: "Nothing in this statement is to be construed as sanctioning any quota or preferential hiring by reason of race, religion, or ancestry." California Fair Employment Practices Commission, *Statement on Surveys and Statistics as to Racial and Ethnic Composition of Work Force or Union Membership* (San Francisco: California Fair Employment Practices Commission, November 1963).
73. Brown quoted in John Anson Ford to Pat Brown, November 16, 1962, Reel 1, Frames 25–28, CORE Western Regional Office Microfilm.
74. Howden, quoted in Richard B. Couser, "The California FEPC: Stepchild of the State Agencies," *Stanford Law Review* 18, no. 2 (1965), 203, f.n. 119.
75. Couser, 195; *FEPC Report: January 1, 1963–June 30, 1964* (Sacramento, CA: State Printing Office, 1965).
76. *FEPC Report: January 1, 1963–June 30, 1964* (Sacramento, CA: State Printing Office, 1965).
77. *FEPC Reports: 1961 and 1962* (Sacramento, CA: State Printing Office, 1963).
78. Minutes of Special Executive Session of the California Fair Employment Practices Commission, June 10, 1963, Box 1, Fair Employment and Housing Commission, San Francisco. On Dellums, see C. L. Dellums, "International President of the Brotherhood of Sleeping Car Porters and Civil Rights Leader," Oral History Interview, Conducted 1973 by Joyce A. Henderson, The Bancroft Library University of California/Berkeley, for the Earl Warren Oral History Project.
79. *FEPC Report: July 1, 1964–June 30, 1965* (Sacramento, CA: State Printing Office, 1966); *FEPC Report: July 1, 1965–June 30, 1966* (Sacramento, CA: State Printing Office, 1967).
80. The historiography tends to fall into two camps about the forces driving the rise of affirmative action. One camp – led by Hugh Davis Graham and John David

Skrentny, among others – presents an inside-out (or top-down) interpretation, attributing the rise of affirmative action to administrators charged with implementing the provisions of fair employment practice laws. Another camp – led by Nancy MacLean and Thomas Sugrue – offers an outside-in (or bottom-up) interpretation, attributing the rise of affirmative action to the efforts of grassroots activists.

81. Whitney M. Young, Jr., "Domestic Marshall Plan," *New York Times*, October 6, 1963 (emphasis in original). John David Skrentny describes Young as "truly a man before his time" for his early advocacy of the kind of "race-targeted ideas" he called for in his "Domestic Marshall Plan." John David Skrentny, *The Ironies of Affirmative Action: Politics, Culture, and Justice in America* (Chicago: University of Chicago Press, 1996), 32.
82. Chet Duncan to Bryan Stokes, September 6, 1963, Reel 39, Frame 1239, Papers of the Congress of Racial Equality, Microfilm (18901).
83. "San Francisco Congress of Racial Equality Newsletter," November 1963, Reel 39, Frames 1264–5, Papers of the Congress of Racial Equality, Microfilm (18901).
84. Larry Raphael Salomon, "The Movement for Jobs in Civil Rights-Era San Francisco, 1963–64," M.A. Thesis, San Francisco State University, 1994.
85. "Employment Report," circa January 1964, Reel 25, Frame 258, Papers of the Congress of Racial Equality Addendum, Microfilm (20887).
86. Frank Young to William Bradley, April 10, 1964, Reel 3, Frames 773, CORE Western Regional Office, Microfilm.
87. Press Release, May 1964, Reel 3, Frames 814, CORE Western Regional Office, Microfilm.
88. Carmen Warschaw, "Comment on Agreement with Bank of America," June 1, 1964, Reel 3, Frames 247, CORE Western Regional Office, Microfilm.
89. Couser, 195, f.n. 69.
90. Couser, 201. See also, California Fair Employment Practices Commission, *Affirmative Actions in Employment: A Special FEPC Report* (San Francisco: Fair Employment Practices Commission), which stresses the "importance of moving increasingly through broad-gauged affirmative actions."
91. *FEPC Report: July 1, 1966–June 30, 1967* (Sacramento, CA: State Printing Office, 1968).
92. *FEPC Report: July 1, 1967–June 30, 1968* (Sacramento, CA: State Printing Office, 1969).
93. MacLean (2009), 675.

# Commentary on Chapter 3
# What Line?

Fredrick E. Vars

In his chapter, "Blurring the Color (Blind) Line," Mark Brilliant claims to "contest altogether" the idea of "a sharp chronological and conceptual distinction between a robust New Deal and World War II civil rights movement that was focused on securing something more substantial than mere color-blindness and a tepid Cold War civil rights movement that aspired to accomplish little more than formal legal equality."[1]

His evidence, however, is largely limited to the second half of this allegedly false dichotomy. To be sure, Brilliant convincingly shows that color consciousness (primarily affirmative action) and color-blindness were both present in the civil rights struggle between 1946 and 1978. But his evidence does not rule out a more muscular earlier movement. Indeed, in the question-and-answer session that followed the presentation of his chapter, Brilliant conceded that the pre-Cold War civil rights movement included a more radical "right to work" agenda premised on the Thirteenth Amendment. Brilliant's discussion of the "long" civil rights movement is consistent with that concession. If the right to work agenda was quickly shelved as too "Communist" around the start of the Cold War (or for some other reason), then there is more support for the challenged story than Brilliant's chapter admits.

Brilliant also omits the last decade of the Cold War. This omission is potentially significant to his argument: perhaps the claim that there was an abrupt shift from color consciousness to color-blindness is right, but it happened around the time *Regents of the University of California v. Bakke*[2] was decided (1978), not at the inception of the Cold War. In Part I of this response, I will fill this gap by discussing a seminal U.S. Supreme

Court opinion that was decided the same year the Berlin Wall fell, *City of Richmond v. J. A. Croson Co.*[3] I conclude that color consciousness and color-blindness appear to have remain commingled through the end of the Cold War. This half of Brilliant's thesis stands.

Taking as a starting point language from *Croson*, Part II will reexamine Brilliant's comparison of the rhetoric of Obama and Reagan. Brilliant identifies important commonalities and differences. One such difference in particular (nostalgia versus hope) deserves even more emphasis and, indeed, renders the similarities rather superficial. In this vein, Obama draws more on Clinton than on Reagan. Part III extends Brilliant's thesis forward in time and broadens it beyond race by analyzing the most significant post-Cold War federal civil rights enactment, the Americans with Disabilities Act of 1990. One could argue that the end of the Cold War coincided with a more muscular, substantial requirement for "reasonable accommodation." But what this requirement ultimately reveals is how equality can demand different things for different people. Brilliant successfully blurs the line between formal and substantive equality, but perhaps that is because, in some contexts at least, there is no such line.

## City of Richmond v. J. A. Croson Co.

Brilliant's history of the civil rights movement in California ends with the U.S. Supreme Court's 1978 decision in *Regents of the University of California v. Bakke*.[4] Five years later, the City of Richmond adopted a color-conscious set-aside program for certain government contracts.[5] Six years after that, a legal challenge to that program prevailed in the U.S. Supreme Court case of *City of Richmond v. J. A. Croson Co.*[6] By that time, "dozens" of other municipalities had adopted similar, color-conscious programs.[7]

The case is a landmark because it represented the first time the Court applied strict scrutiny to a remedial racial classification. In his dissent, Justice Marshall, along with Justices Blackmun and Brennan and most of the civil rights community, decried this development on at least three grounds: considering race may be needed to remedy past discrimination, such consideration need not stigmatize, and strict scrutiny is "fatal in fact."[8] I have elsewhere argued that *Croson* need not be fatal in fact.[9]

Color consciousness was very much alive in the civil rights movement, even though the Court was highly skeptical.

Indeed, color consciousness and color-blindness were intertwined. Justice Marshall reiterated Justice Blackmun's statement in *Bakke* that "[i]n order to get beyond racism, we must first take account of race. There is no other way."[10]

## The Reference Point in Rhetoric

In a separate dissent in *Croson*, Justice Blackmun, joined by Justice Brennan, struck a chord much like Obama and Reagan:

> "So the Court today regresses. I am confident, however, that, given time, it one day again will do its best to fulfill the great promises of the Constitution's Preamble and of the guarantees embodied in the Bill of Rights – a fulfillment that would make this Nation very special."[11]

Indeed, this statement could be said to combine Reagan's backward-looking patriotism with Obama's forward-looking version. The Court did its best in the past (specifically, during the Warren Court) and will again do its best in the future, even though today it moves backward.

But notice how much turns on the reference point. Indeed, nearly everything does. Brilliant recognizes this point and aptly describes the contrast between Obama and Reagan. The similarities between Obama's rhetoric and Reagan's are nonetheless striking, but Obama was certainly not the first Democratic candidate for President to borrow from the Reagan playbook.

In his 1996 speech accepting the Democratic nomination for President, William Clinton hit equally patriotic, Reagan-esque notes even though his major thrust was fixing the damage done by Reagan and Bush, Sr.: "The Cold War is over. Soviet communism has collapsed and our values – freedom, democracy, individual rights, free enterprise – they have triumphed all around the world."[12] Clinton recited the last line of the Pledge of Allegiance: "One nation, under God, indivisible, with liberty and justice for all."[13] "When we pull together, America will pull ahead. Throughout the whole history of this country, we have seen, time and time and time again, that when we are united we are unstoppable."[14]

Nor was Obama's twist toward forward-looking patriotism original. At the same convention speech, Clinton foreshadowed Obama's trans-partisan message:

> We offer our people a new choice based on old values. We offer opportunity. We demand responsibility. We will build an American community again. The choice we offer is not conservative or liberal. In many ways, it is not even Republican or Democratic. It is different. It is new. And it will work. It will work because it is rooted in the vision and the values of the American people.[15]

Hopeful patriotism was Clinton's theme well before Obama's. Clinton concluded his speech: "My fellow Americans, I end tonight where it all began for me – I still believe in a place called Hope. God bless you, and God Bless America."[16]

Both Obama and Clinton appear to have used Reagan's rhetoric as a reference point. And no doubt Reagan drew on countless politicians before him in extolling America's unique virtues. However, Obama's forward-looking version of patriotism much more closely resembles Clinton than Reagan.

## The Americans with Disabilities Act of 1990

If there was no abrupt shift toward color-blindness at the start of the Cold War or in the 1960s, then perhaps there should have been no abrupt shift back toward more muscular, substantive civil rights discourse after the fall of Communism. If color consciousness and color-blindness were intertwined, perhaps equal rights and special treatment were blended together in attacks on nonracial discrimination. The Americans with Disabilities Act (ADA) of 1990, passed just one year after the Berlin Wall came down, provides a unique lens through which one can assess these two extensions of Brilliant's thesis. Here are my conclusions: (1) Although the timing may be coincidental, the ADA does represent probably the most muscular federal civil rights legislation in history, and (2) the ADA embodies both formal and substantive equality and suggests that this distinction may not even be meaningful.

The ADA prohibits employment discrimination "on the basis of disability,"[17] just as Title VII bans racial discrimination.[18] But the ADA goes substantially further; it prohibits

> not making reasonable accommodations to the known physical or mental limitations of an otherwise qualified individual with a disability who is an applicant or employee, unless such covered entity can demonstrate that the accommodation would impose an undue hardship on the operation of the business of such covered entity.[19]

In other words, employers must modify their workplaces or procedures to accommodate the disabilities of applicants and employees.[20] The only exception is for "undue hardship." Hardship less than that must be borne.

On first blush, the 1990 passage of the ADA, with its bold "reasonable accommodation" requirement, just one year after the end of the Cold War, would seem to contradict Brilliant's thesis that the Cold War did not suppress more muscular civil rights discourse. But perhaps the timing is a coincidence. The fall of Communism could quite easily have been interpreted as further support for limiting the role of central government, not for expanding it through measures like the ADA.

The only mention of the Cold War I have located in the legislative history of the ADA does not resolve the question. Representative Hoyer of Maryland argued in favor of the ADA and against an amendment limiting remedies for violations thereof:

> This bill [the ADA] is about all men and women being created equal, endowed not by the State, not by Congress, as some of our Communist friends tried to sell the world and are now failing in doing so, but by their creator, with certain unalienable rights. If those rights are transgressed, then their remedies ought to parallel the remedies of a black citizen or a female citizen or an ethnic minority citizen or any other citizen in America who was not treated consistently with the principles that has made this Nation the object of envy throughout the world, because we have pledged and our law stands ensconced in the world as standing for the proposition that every individual will be granted equal rights and equal remedies.[21]

On the Cold War, the statement is inscrutable. Hoyer rails against statism in favor of the ADA, which includes a large state mandate. On the specific amendment at issue, however, this statement makes the clearest sense.

The amendment would have allowed for more limited remedies for ADA violations. Thus, the "equal remedies" point is valid.

The "equal rights" point is more complicated. Framed narrowly, the ADA gives the disabled a right to "reasonable accommodation," which others do not have. This is not equal. But, of course, others do not have such a right because they do not need it. The right at issue must be framed more broadly to see the point; for example, as the right to work. A person in a wheelchair may need a ramp to enjoy this right in the same way as someone with functioning legs.[22] Affirmative action arguably serves exactly the same function as the ramp. As Lyndon B. Johnson said: "You do not take a man who for years has been hobbled by chains, liberate him, bring him to the starting line of a race, saying, 'you are free to compete with all the others,' and still justly believe you have been completely fair."[23]

A commitment to equality – before, during, and after the Cold War – always and necessarily includes recognition and accommodation of group differences. Brilliant is quite right to correct historians who have implied otherwise.

## Notes

1. Mark Brilliant, "Blurring the Color (Blind) Line," Chapter 3 of this volume at 6, 115.
2. *Regents of the University of California v. Bakke*, 438 U.S. 265 (1978).
3. *City of Richmond v. J. A. Croson Co.*, 488 U.S. 469 (1989).
4. *Regents of the University of California v. Bakke*, 438 U.S. 265 (1978).
5. Croson, 488 U.S. 477.
6. Id., 469.
7. Id., 555.
8. Id., 552 (Justice Marshall, dissenting).
9. Ian Ayres and Fredrick E. Vars, "When Does Private Discrimination Justify Public Affirmative Action?" 98 *Columbia Law Review* (1998), 1577.
10. Croson, 488 U.S. 550.
11. Id., 562 (Justice Blackmun, dissenting).
12. William J. Clinton, "Address Accepting the Presidential Nomination at the Democratic National Convention in New York," July 16, 1992. Online by Gerhard Peters and John T. Woolley, The American Presidency Project. Retrieved from http://www.presidency.ucsb.edu/ws/?pid=25958.
13. Id.
14. Id.
15. Id.
16. Id.

17. 42 U.S.C. §12112(a).
18. 42 U.S.C.A. §2000e-2.
19. 42 U.S.C. §(b)(5)(A).
20. 42 U.S.C. §12111(9).
21. 136 Cong. Rec. H2599–01, *H2622.
22. Michael Ashley Stein, "Same Struggle, Different Difference: ADA Accommodations as Antidiscrimination," 153 *University of Pennsylvania Law Review* (2004), 579.
23. Lyndon B. Johnson, Commencement Address at Howard University on June 4, 1965. Retrieved from http://www.pbs.org/wgbh/amex/eyesontheprize/sources/ps_bakke.html (last visited May 8, 2013).

4

# Reframing the Civil Rights Narrative

## From Compliance to Collective Impact

Susan Sturm

### Introduction: Why Reframe the Civil Rights Narrative?

These are complicated and challenging times for those involved in the project of reducing inequality. By some measures, there has been considerable progress. Unlike fifty years ago, there is now a broad public consensus that deliberate discrimination is wrong, unacceptable, and illegal. Women and people of color hold some of the highest positions of public leadership, including the president of the United States and four out of nine Supreme Court justices. Women and people of color also head major private and non-profit institutions. People of color, women, and people with disabilities have made it into the middle class, and have opportunities to pursue a wide range of occupations, including many that used to be limited to nondisabled white men. Girls currently outpace boys at all levels of academic performance.

Nevertheless, we live in a world of increasing inequality, one in which a widening income, wealth, and opportunity gap intersects with age-old inequalities along racial, gender, ethnic, disability, immigrant, and age lines.[1] This growing inequality is entrenched in social and political arrangements – an "architecture" and "geography" that structures interactions, opportunities, and outcomes.[2] Race, gender, and class continue to shape people's positions, experiences, status, and mobility within many organizational settings. Occupational, educational, and social segregation and stratification are still pervasive and the gap between rich and poor has widened. The glass ceiling remains intact in many sectors of the economy. Disproportionate numbers of people of color and people from poor communities receive education in substandard schools, live in substandard housing with inadequate access to transportation, work in low-quality jobs for inadequate pay or are unemployed, and have inadequate health care. Many reports show that women of color and their communities have been hardest hit by the recession. Evidence shows that our society is more unequal now than it was three decades ago, and that this inequality profoundly affects the quality of life for people at both the top and the bottom of the spectrum.[3]

This contradictory equality landscape complicates the future of the civil rights project. The public discourse about the meaning of and proper approach to addressing race and gender disparities has become polarized and contentious. Different stakeholders seem to focus on different elements of the equality topography. Some claim that we are in a post-racial era, at the same time that studies document widening racial and gender disparities in access to key resources, institutions, and opportunities. People disagree about the language used for, the priority given and the meaning assigned to race, gender, and other categories of identity. These disagreements have become highly charged, with the courts' increasing insistence on color-blindness fueling the battle for hearts and minds. Concerns about inequality are now expressed in terms such as diversity and inclusion, with deep disagreements about the relationship of those terms to the kinds of inequality that matter. In the midst of an economic downturn, when scarcity forces hard choices, that battle has taken on particular urgency.

These disagreements about the language and meaning of discrimination coincide with the recognition that structural inequality is a multidimensional and embedded problem. At the micro-level, interactions among individuals influence whether and how people connect to resources, information, and forms of support that matter. Social psychologists have shown that people who take race or gender into account often do so not because they mean to, but because the stratified world around them produces cognitive frames that make identity categories matter to their decisions and interactions.[4] They have also shown that contexts can prime stereotypes that pose threats to individuals in high-stakes situations.[5] Economists, sociologists, organizational theorists, and network researchers have shown that micro-level interactions accumulate over time and space;[6] they are embedded in norms, social arrangements, and networks that produce and reinforce inequality for individuals, groups, organizations, and communities.[7]

Political scientists and historians have shown how these inequalities are embedded in policies – institutional and governmental arrangements that lock in barriers to access and participation for women and communities of color.[8]

Reducing embedded inequality requires operating both deeply within particular contexts (to get at the micro-level and cumulative interactions) and broadly across contexts (to enable the reworking of the environmental conditions and incentives that shape internal practices).[9] It thus requires addressing institutional climate, culture, and practices, as well as networks that shape the flow of information and mobility. These dynamics occur at the level of individual or group interaction, but are reinforced – and potentially transformed – through institutional policies, practices, and interventions, which are in turn encouraged by macro-level policies and incentives.[10] This challenge requires a framework that invites, bridges, and sustains the different goals and interventions needed to change systems.

These complications are compounded by the increasing unavailability or thinness of the paradigmatic civil rights tools as a means for addressing twenty-first-century inequality. The structural understanding of inequality – shared by a growing group of progressive scholars, advocates, and policy makers – is at odds with the prevailing conception of inequality animating the federal courts' interpretation of the civil rights legislation and the constitution.[11] The courts have embraced intentional discrimination, formal equality, and color-blindness as the hallmarks of judicially recognized inequality.[12]

Moreover, regulatory strategies relying on courts for enforcement have proven to be a blunt instrument for addressing the complex, structural, and systemic underpinnings of social inequality. This multifaceted form of inequality bears an uneasy fit with the most familiar methodologies of the civil rights era. The prototypical civil rights strategies – comprehensive civil rights legislation, impact litigation campaigns exemplified by *Brown v. Board of Education*, and large-scale protest movements – are both less available and more limited in their capacity to mobilize complex, long-term and collaborative change necessary to address embedded structural inequality.

Political gridlock and judicial conservatism make progressive legislative action seem remote and progressive change through the courts unlikely, at least for now. Technology has also dramatically altered the landscape and venues for mass mobilization.

A framing challenge also accompanies this search for effective approaches to persistent inequality. Frameworks play a critical role in organizing and prioritizing action and specifying the arenas and settings on which their application is focused. Frameworks "organize diagnostic and prescriptive inquiry" and help identify the elements (and the relationships among those elements) that are needed for institutional analysis.[13] Changing complex and interrelated systems requires frameworks that enable actors and analysts to meet the challenge of identifying the appropriate "chunk" or levels of analysis and action most relevant to addressing specified challenges.[14]

For many groups that are the focus of the civil rights project, the concepts of discrimination, diversity, and inequality do not adequately communicate their deepest and most urgent concerns and aspirations. Their concerns are grounded in the institutions and arenas that affect their quality of life – education, housing, health, transportation, criminal justice. Within these key institutions, group status continues to affect people's experience. People outside the "circle of concern" experience more limited trajectories and possibilities for engagement, mobility, and success. So, the equality agenda is deeply connected to broader concerns about the failure of our institutions to provide contexts enabling people to flourish.

Many of those who are committed to the civil rights agenda are searching for the tools and knowledge needed to get from here to there. How can we move forward to address inequality in the face of this complexity and controversy? Much of the civil rights scholarship and practice has been focused on critiquing the color-blindness framework for its misfit with the dynamics producing and sustaining inequality, and calling for expansion of that framework to include a structural inequality analysis. One response in progressive legal scholarship and policy has been to explore whether and how to expand the legal frame so that it covers the structural dynamics producing group-based inequality. This strategy entails shifting the focus from conscious intent to include the range of unconscious mechanisms leading people to decide and act based on race and gender, including implicit bias, stereotype threat, and in-group favoritism.[15] A second move calls for an expansion or shift in focus from individual to group-based discrimination and exclusion, and for some, shifting compliance responsibility from the judiciary to the regulatory arena. Richard Ford, for example, proposes that we limit individual entitlements based on specific evidence of discriminatory intent, and instead rely on comprehensive administrative regulation to address the problems of systemic inequality and bias.[16] A third shift involves broadening the frame beyond the question of mindset to take account of barriers and opportunity networks, and expanding the public venues and strategies that are the focus of inquiry and attention.[17] Recent work has identified practices in the regulatory arena as an unrecognized yet promising approach for promoting the civil rights agenda, and for expanding beyond an antidiscrimination frame to one focused on reducing racial disparities and promoting equity through audits and "equality directives."[18]

The preeminent scholarly, legal, and policy responses frame the equality agenda primarily under the civil rights banner of antidiscrimination, equity, and disparities reduction. Many responses remain focused on identifying disparate treatment, biased decision-making criteria, racial and gender disparities in access to opportunities, and barriers and practices that cause racial, gender, and other group-based disparities, along with developing remedies to eliminate those practices, reduce these disparities, and remove those barriers. They frequently locate equality work within a compliance mode, with regulatory agencies and courts at the center of equality policy and advocacy. A compliance orientation focuses on legally enforceable equality norms and requirements and marshalling adherence to those requirements. It is sometimes reflected in the way law and lawyers operate in the context of organizing efforts to advance equality.

These compliance-oriented civil rights initiatives still play a significant role in making visible and actionable the continued significance of race and gender in shaping people's life opportunities.[19] They have opened up positions and organizations previously closed to women and people of color, eliminated formal and intentional barriers to participation, and contributed to broad acceptance of formal equality and nondiscrimination as a consensus public value. Interventions aimed at reducing disparities, biases, and discrimination have produced tools and strategies to identify structural barriers to participation and to dis-entrench people and organizations that are maintaining a closed system of opportunity. They also can create important opportunities for mobilizing communities and advocates to change public policy.

The conventional civil rights narrative is, however, incomplete both as a comprehensive portrayal of activity advancing equality in the post-Brown era and, perhaps more importantly, as a framework guiding campaigns to transform the conditions that produce persistent inequality.[20] These accounts tend to place legal actors, norms, and institutions at the center of the narrative, and to focus on outcomes tied to litigation, legislation, or administrative enforcement. Change initiatives in nonlegal venues tend to be overlooked, along with their relationship to law and lawyers. Yet, a considerable amount of activity aimed at addressing structural inequality, including racial inequality, takes place outside judicial and regulatory venues, and frames racial, gender, and other civil rights issues as part of broader projects such as mass incarceration, school reform, and economic revitalization. Many organizations and activists involved in work carrying out the civil rights agenda do not define their work solely or primarily in terms of civil rights, but have squarely on their agendas the goal of reducing structural inequality and advancing the goal of full social, economic, and political citizenship (including for those without U.S. citizenship).

In addition to its descriptive incompleteness, a compliance-based civil rights framework is limiting as a "theory of change" for guiding efforts to improve the quality of lives of those who are the focus of the civil rights project. A theory of change makes explicit the intended relationship between strategies and desired outcomes – how a group committed to a particular outcome understands how to move from here to there.[21] A framework defined solely in terms of civil rights offers too thin a strand of analysis and intervention to reach the much thicker and more intertwined set of dynamics and activities perpetuating inequality. Equality analysis alone does not reach many of the concerns and hopes of those experiencing these conditions. Concerns about widening inequality implicate more than whether individuals or groups are being treated fairly or whether bias – either conscious or unconscious – is influencing outcomes. Often, this aspect of inequality is the tip of the iceberg because those being treated unfairly based on their identity are experiencing conditions that do not enable them to succeed or prosper in the settings that matter to their well-being. The civil rights framework alone does not invite the full range of questions or involve the necessary set of actors who must come together if we are to address these systemic dimensions of inequality or to mobilize the long-term systems change needed to address them.

This chapter identifies four features of the conventional civil rights framework that limit its efficacy as an overarching theory of change:

First, it under-specifies the problem and the interlocking dynamics producing structural inequality;

Second, it overrelies on identifying root causes as the methodology for developing goals and solutions;

Third, it does not take sufficient account of the dynamics enabling or preventing institutional and social change needed to remedy structural inequality; and

Fourth, it fails to provoke the elaboration of outcomes and institutional arrangements advancing the values and conditions we want to create.

This analysis builds on the premise that institutions are a crucial and neglected focus of analysis and intervention.[22] Institutions are "the prescriptions that humans use to organize all forms of repetitive and structured interactions."[23] They organize individuals' decisions and actions. They are both lasting and permeable. They mediate how norms and policies are translated into practice, and in turn, how practices shape our understanding and revision of norms. They are the sites in which individuals "face choices regarding the actions and strategies they take, leading to consequences for themselves and for others."[24] As John Powell has noted, "the more complex society becomes, the more our relationships and opportunities will be mediated through institutional arrangements. This is not just true in relationship to non-whites but for all groups in society."[25]

To reduce structural inequality, the frameworks guiding change efforts must take account of the institutions and settings that shape the way individuals interact and how policies are put into practice. Progress requires reframing problems and goals so that they advance the outcomes we want to achieve and the visions we want to pursue. The frames shaping these projects must also be ones that can mobilize the shared commitments and relationships needed to change systems. In other words, the civil rights agenda must be situated within a theory of change that can address complex, adaptive problems requiring systems change.

Collaborations and campaigns have recently emerged that continue to make race, gender and other identity categories crucial aspects of inquiry and concern, but that frame identity issues within the context of a broader, affirmatively articulated set of goals. A framework articulated in the language of "collective impact" and linked to goals of "full participation" has begun to orient a growing number of change initiatives among community and organizational leaders, advocates, policy makers, funders, and other change agents.[26] Race and gender have been incorporated as elements in broader strategies framed around a transformational agenda that not only addresses race, gender, and other categories of difference explicitly, but also situates these identity-based concerns within a broader substantive aim, such as transforming schools or increasing health outcomes. Compliance – including organizing to induce change – operates as a part, but not the overarching frame for this activity. Moreover, the dynamics entrenching inequality coexist with new sites and possibilities for mobilization and change, offered by technology and the proliferation of "third spaces" for collaboration and experimentation.[27] These forms of activism aimed at reducing structural inequality are not visible through a compliance lens. These projects include lawyers and even litigation as a tool, but not necessarily as an overarching frame.

This chapter first analyzes the limits of the civil rights/compliance framework as an overarching change theory for transforming institutions and systems, and then sketches out the features of a full participation framework grounded in a collective-impact approach to reducing structural inequality. Full participation is a framework that nests antidiscrimination within an affirmative vision connected to a theory of action, and a methodology aimed at systems change. It resonates with a wide range of emerging scholarship and activism aimed at advancing equality under conditions of complexity, changing demographics, decentered governance, privatization, and technological change. The framework draws on insights from extensive and ongoing field research, conducted by the Center for Institutional and Social Change at Columbia Law School, on the strategies and frameworks used in innovative initiatives taking a systemic approach to advancing equality. It integrates this practice-based knowledge with insights from cutting-edge, multidisciplinary scholarship on the multilevel dynamics affecting levels of engagement and participation by different groups. Most of this field research has been in the area of education and public employment, and thus, most of the illustrations of the ideas presented here will be in those areas. However, the research suggests that these ideas have broader applicability. The chapter identifies the features and potential of this framework, and considers its implications for public policy, law, and advocacy.

## The Incompleteness of the Conventional Civil Rights Framework for Designing and Enabling Institutional Change

As discussed previously, the framework used to address inequality shapes the public-policy agenda, the questions that are asked, the people who are at the table, and the way we think about problems and goals. A compliance-based civil rights frame for tackling structural inequality, although an important part of a larger inquiry, does not adequately construct the problem and solution space needed to enable structural inequality to be meaningfully addressed.

### A. Under-Specification of Problems, Causes, and Solutions

The civil rights lens focuses inquiry and intervention on differences in treatment or outcomes experienced by members of underrepresented, marginalized, or targeted groups, and how to reduce those disparities. So, for example, the focus in K-12 education has been on reducing segregation; in employment, it has been on reducing the operation of bias in employment decisions and the use of criteria that disproportionately exclude protected class members.

A change strategy framed under the umbrella of reducing racial and gender inequality through promoting compliance with legal or regulatory rights, although necessary, does not adequately focus inquiry on the range of practices combining to produce structural inequality, the relationship of those dynamics to overarching institutional practices that are problematic in other ways, the information needed to understand why those practices persist, or the mechanisms that will enable it to be changed. This observation follows from the way structural inequality operates. Racial and gender inequality is embedded in practices, processes, and policies that shape behavior and experience more generally. Although some of these dynamics are specific to particular identity groups (such as women or people of color), many are also linked to broader patterns of behavior, identities, and institutional arrangements. Inquiries framed in terms of race or gender may not uncover the broader dynamics that are now accounting for persistent inequality. Marginalized groups may disproportionately experience institutionally rooted patterns that can only be detected by examining general patterns of mobility and engagement. These institutional dynamics may be as – or more – important to the kinds of changes likely to reduce structural inequality affecting marginalized groups.

In addition, civil rights analysis, advocacy, and policy tend to focus on a single social category – race, gender, disability, age, or sexual orientation – as a focus of inquiry and intervention. Yet, as intersectionality analysis has shown,[28] people fall in many different categories of experience, and initiatives focused on one aspect of inequality distorts and sometimes polarizes change efforts. Changes at the organizational level must account for the experiences of many different groups, and that often requires a focus that extends beyond the impact on a particular marginalized group, even as that group's experience is instructive for more general patterns.

In addition, eliminating problematic or biased conditions revealed through structural inequality analysis may leave in place policies, practices, and arrangements that prevent genuine equality. This observation also follows from the embedded and interconnected nature of structural inequality. These dynamics are embedded in more general systems, relationships, and norms. Thus, addressing this complexity requires a more iterative process of inquiry that takes into account context, function, structure, and process.[29] A focus on the conditions producing exclusion or marginalization of particular groups, albeit important, may produce targeted interventions aimed specifically at reducing an identified bias, but fail to address other norms or processes sustaining inequality. For example, substantive ground rules often reflect the priorities and values put in place at a time when women and people of color were not part of the conversation. These ground rules involve important issues of value and merit, such as the value of time, the relative importance of different fields of work, and the attributes or qualities that signal success. These substantive ground rules are frequently taken for granted and not the subject of public deliberation; they also emerge from the accumulation of decisions made at an early time, and structures that reflect those accumulated decisions. They frequently have embedded within them assumptions that devalue work that women and people of color are more likely to do. Changing underlying systems, practices, and norms may be crucial to long-term change, but seen as tangential to the immediate issues facing these groups. Changing these ground rules depends on the participation of both institutional and community leaders who have broader responsibility for the governance of their domains, and who treat advancing full participation as one of a much larger set of values and concerns.[30]

Consider, for example, the challenge of increasing faculty and student diversity and engagement within academic departments comprised of predominantly white and male faculties and students.[31] Many race and gender initiatives have examined differences in access and success for women and people of color, and have worked toward removing the barriers that block pathways into and through higher education for these groups. This approach might include interventions designed to develop effective responses to sexual harassment, reduce the operation of bias in decision-making processes, or increase the mentorship, resources, and tools available to these group members.[32] However, these interventions often have limited systemic effect because the prevailing governance system and reward structure undercuts their importance to crucial actors when they determine how to allocate their time, influence, and attention. Strategies targeting only the mechanisms of group-based bias and exclusion do not necessarily invite inquiry about the larger values and governance structure. These "second generation" dynamics are difficult to see at the level of the individual interaction, and often go undetected and unremedied unless general patterns of participation and mobility are examined.

Both the importance and limits of the civil rights frame are illustrated by the controversy over the New Haven, Connecticut fire department's decision not to use a paper and pencil test because of its disparate impact on black and Latino firefighters, at issue in *Ricci v. DeStefano*.[33] A group of white fire fighters contested whether the city could lawfully disregard a promotion test that disproportionately excluded blacks and Latinos. The response of the advocacy community, in defense of the City's decision, focused attention on the history of deliberate discrimination in fire departments, and on whether the test and other aspects of the selection process still stack the deck in favor of white candidates.[34] However, the fire department's decision to scrap the test, even if it had been upheld, did not address the dynamics that make it difficult for Latinos and blacks to succeed in the fire department, nor did it address the interactions between the fire department and the diverse communities to which it is responsible. Indeed, the dispute over the validity of the test deflected consideration of the politicization of the fire department, or the disconnect between the selection criteria and the capacities required to meet the department's public mission as first responder.[35] The bias-reduction framework alone was insufficient to bring the community together around those deeper issues that had to be addressed for people of color to be able to participate in and be served by the fire department.[36] Unless these issues of minimizing bias and realizing institutional mission are addressed together – and the equality agenda is framed in terms of a priori institutional requirements – changes in the assessment process are likely to have only modest impact on the integration and mobility of firefighters from underrepresented groups.

These examples illustrate that racial and gender inequality often operates in conjunction with a broader set of problems and dynamics that must be linked with concerns about inequality in order to address that inequality. Selection, advancement, and governance practices can be problematic and unfair in ways that may be experienced more acutely by people of color and women, but that have far broader reach. Yet, framing issues or problems in terms of racial or gender disparities alone sometimes discourages the inquiry needed to identify the interconnections among these issues and dynamics. Some people who do not initially identify with issues of racial or gender equality may share an interest in changing the conditions perpetuating inequality, but will not become engaged with a project that defines its overarching goals in terms of racial or gender justice. The normative agenda that could mobilize effective change may be broader than the problem diagnosed in terms of racial or gender inequality. This dynamic frequently appears in research by the Center for Institutional and Social Change on higher education initiatives aimed at increasing access and engagement. When those initiatives were defined solely in terms of reducing racial or gender bias, they were more easily marginalized or limited in their scope and sustainability. When, however, those initiatives were reframed in terms of improving opportunities for success and thriving, including for women and people of color, they generated more willingness to consider and take action when inquiry revealed differential access or opportunities for under-served groups.

## B. Over-Reliance on Causes to Determine Goals and Solutions

The previous section sketched out the value of the structural inequality frame in focusing analysis on the dynamics that operate to produce racial and gender disparities. However, understanding the racialized or gendered origins and underlying causes of complex problems does not sufficiently answer the question of what to do to change those interlocking conditions and causes. Causal analysis also does not necessarily dictate the solution space or the scope of the normative agenda informing the definition of the action arena. To say it differently, understanding why problematic conditions exist does not tell you what should be done to change them. Versions of this insight are commonplace in psychology, public health, complexity theory, and even public law remedies. The remedy does not proceed logically or factually from the violation. And diagnosis does not dictate treatment.[37]

Structural inequality analysis of the U.S. education system, for example, has shown that tracking is a significant determinant of educational inequality for underrepresented minority students.[38] But this finding is only a starting point for figuring out how to address this problem. This is true for a variety of reasons. The dynamics producing complex problems most likely took place at a different time period and involved different actors than those in a position to change current and future practices. The values and dynamics sustaining the status quo may be different than those producing the problem. Moreover, the question of what works to produce full participation is not the same as the question of what caused that inequality in the first place. Knowing why an institution failed does not necessarily tell you about the dynamics, constituencies, opportunities, and practices that would enable movement toward greater equality.

For this reason, information about the scope and causes of racial or gender disparities is not sufficient to inform efforts to transform those conditions. Change agents require information about the operative mechanisms and leverage points that could produce change, as well as the assumptions and cultural practices that influence what people value and how they interact. The potential of the structural equality project to advance broader institutional goals, efforts, and interests – and the opportunities for related efforts, in turn, to advance full participation – is typically not systematically thought through upfront or realized in its design and execution.

## C. Under-Specification of a Theory of Sustainable Institutional and Social Change

Legal scholars, policy makers, and activists often focus their attention on the harm they seek to address and the wrongs they seek to right. They do not necessarily specify a remedial strategy or theory of change, and have a tendency to under-specify how change will be achieved, and over-rely on enforcement of legal norms. This lack of focus on getting from here to there undercuts the efficacy of civil rights efforts.

First, conventional civil rights analysis does not squarely pose the question, "What do I do now? And where, specifically, do I start?" Structural inequality analysis does not provide the tools to "chunk" systemic change into manageable, prioritized goals and locations.[39] Institutional change requires defining appropriate solution spaces, or action arenas, that are simultaneously delimited enough to enable meaningful action and to allow accountability for responsible actors, and at the same time, broad enough to engage the systems, actors, and levels needed to shift routines, practices, and incentives.[40] Without sufficient analytical tools, a focus on complex or subtle causes of inequality can communicate the idea that you have to change the whole system at once, which can overwhelm actors with a sense of impossibility or encourage them to abdicate responsibility. Or, it can justify an intervention that will produce an immediate victory without a realistic prospect for lasting change.[41]

Second, systemic change is difficult to sustain unless it can somehow be connected to core values, logics, and stakeholder interests within the institution.[42] It is important to be able to frame projects in terms that will bring the necessary and affected stakeholders to the table. Sometimes that can be done effectively under the rubric of a race or gender inequality frame. But under some circumstances, proceeding exclusively under the banner of race, gender, or other categories of inequality will limit who comes to the table or sees themselves as interested. An identity-delimited frame can create challenges in addressing the situations of other identity group members who are affected by the institutional dynamics, thereby limiting participation of crucial allies with overlapping concerns. Naming the overarching problem solely in the language of race or gender inequality sometimes makes it difficult to mobilize those who share interests in changing structures, but lack primary identification with the particular group named.

Finally, achieving sustainable institutional change ultimately requires a meaningful shift in individuals' mindsets and behaviors, at multiple levels and in multiple locations over time. Change occurs by building on convergences of commitment and energy to make positive change – enabling, connecting across, and building out from successful innovation – as well as destabilizing and delegitimizing resistance and backlash. These efforts must also be linked to engaging the large group in the middle. The project of advancing structural equality requires a framework that reaches these different yet related behavioral dynamics.

The source, position, and orientation of accountability mechanisms matter greatly to the dynamics of and possibilities for producing institutional change. Typically, civil rights analysis presumes a compliance frame for intervention.[43] This may be in part because of structural inequality's roots in unjust, state-sanctioned discrimination. A compliance frame defines the unit of analysis in terms of a case or regulatory violation. It focuses on judicial and regulatory agencies as the source of norms and enforcement. Its problem and goal definitions proceed under the rubric of judicial and administrative agency requirements, which focus on eliminating discrimination and reducing bias. The primary participants in the compliance-action arena tend to be agency personnel, internal regulatory actors, lawyers, judges, forensic experts, parties, and organizational actors who are directly responsible for compliance. The strategies and tools for promoting change are focused on tracking, addressing, and deterring problematic behavior, and they are generally defined in reference to the legal arena. They include regulatory reporting, monitoring and auditing, processing complaints, identifying abuses, providing compliance-related training, engaging in mediation or settlement, and deploying litigation-related tools such as discovery, experts, hearings, and remedy. The leverage points for mobilizing attention and action revolve around compliance-oriented activities, such as complaints, reports, investigations, mediations, settlements, audits, and litigation events.

Courts and compliance agencies – and their counterparts within organizations – are crucial destabilizers of stuck systems that are violating baseline norms.[44] But the compliance frame has limited capacity to encompass the heterogeneity of values, beliefs, and behaviors within the context of an institutional population and stakeholder set. To advance structural equality, it is necessary to engage a wider range of norms, actors, mechanisms, and leverage points.

Effective change at the institutional level also requires taking account of how different accountability systems interact within a particular setting. Compliance-oriented interventions can either reinforce or undercut the legitimacy and effectiveness of proactive initiatives aimed at addressing structural inequality. A single-minded focus on compliance-based approaches discourages the work of situating interventions targeting different types of behavior within a broader systems analysis. To do so effectively within a given context, it is necessary to integrate the analytical frame of structural inequality with the theory, disciplines, and site-specific realities of organizational and cultural change.

## D. The Missing Articulation of Affirmative Values and Institutional Aspirations

The previous section discussed the limitations of the structural inequality frame in identifying where and how to begin an effort to advance full participation. Of equal concern is its limitation in answering the questions, "What future state are we aiming to achieve, and how will we know we are making progress toward it?" A civil rights frame will generate significant insight into the locations at which the dynamics of inequality are produced and sustained, but it stops short of defining the specific outcomes, goals, and shifts required at key locations to advance the equality agenda. Moreover, it does not ask more fundamental questions like, "What do we want this institution (or specific institutional component) to be? What do we want it to be like? In what specific ways can we imagine it working differently and generating different outcomes?" From a problem-solving perspective, this move to define an affirmative vision is more integrative, intuitive, and imaginative than analytical; it complements the work of structural inequality analysis by prompting and engaging a different set of questions, processes, and mindsets.

In academic literature and policy papers, the majority of the energy is focused on problem identification and diagnosis. The paucity of attention devoted to specifying possible and desired future states – let alone how to move toward them in the realities of a complex system – limits the effectiveness and practicality of the analytical frame. Without an overarching framework that requires you to specify the normative vision in an integrated way, it is harder not only to see the big picture, but also to identify the component parts and how they fit together to drive the whole.[45] And without a specified future state and its attendant benefits and outcomes defined as an aim, it becomes more difficult to hold leaders accountable for achieving progress toward the broader goal; it lets them off the hook and concedes the conventional wisdom that the system is too large and too distant, so all we can do is spot and fight fires.

Because the systems producing structural inequality are so large and complex, actionable change requires that the equality agenda identify its operative institutional settings and define its aspirations in concrete terms situated in specific settings. The positive frame and affirmative values must be located in order to be meaningful, and they must delegitimize the acceptability of inaction in order to be effective. While structural inequality analysis produces significant and compelling findings identifying disparities, problems and root causes, the goal of advancing structural equality often remains an abstract ideal, difficult and daunting to approach. The tendency is to focus attention on remediating discrete problems and instances. This response may seem more imminently "addressable" on its surface but it avoids the imperative of identifying the leverage points for changing the system that produces – and will continue to produce – similar results in multiple locations. The project of advancing structural equality, therefore, requires a framework that forces accountability and specificity with regard to domain, goals, and desired outcomes. It calls for a compelling positive frame, supported by reasons to believe it is realistic and achievable.

Because structural inequalities by their nature are embedded, interconnected, and difficult to undo, the "street credibility" of an affirmative vision is vital to its chances of success. The equality agenda must, therefore, take into account the highly pragmatic consideration of individuals' intellectual and emotional connections to the effort, including its probability of sustainable progress, and its impact on them personally. Specifically, a project framed to be about inequality or injustice will typically galvanize the individuals who already embrace the structural inequality premise, but it risks alienating or simply failing to enlist the significant population of individuals who do not identify with its language or the phenomena it describes. In order to make real progress toward institutional change – let alone to sustain it – leaders at multiple levels will need to articulate a compelling vision and set of aspirations that will stand up against competing priorities, reinforce mission-critical goals, and elicit broad participation from key stakeholders. Analysis and dissemination of the stories of "positive deviants," organic to the institution and grounded in its lived experience, might play a critical role.[46] Just as the analysis of structural inequality works from micro- to macro-dynamics and impacts, the affirmative vision must draw credibility and insight from context-specific examples of new ways of thinking and behaving, as well as a unifying aspiration for the whole.

Therefore, a workable framework for addressing structural inequality must resonate with the pragmatic realities of the individuals and agents who are engaged in advancing the equality agenda. Even at a basic semantic level, even though structural inequality functions effectively as an analytical frame for scholars, it falls short as an overarching framework for institutional leaders and stakeholders whose vision, passion, and participation will be instrumental to its remediation. The project of advancing structural equality calls for an approach that prompts a broader set of questions – and points to a broader range of solutions – regarding the specific goals, mechanisms, agents, and motivations that will catalyze and sustain meaningful progress toward this aspiration within any given institutional ecosystem.

At the same time, it would be a mistake to step away from the civil rights project or from an explicit focus on race, gender, and other categories associated with durable inequality. Again to quote John Powell,

> To the extent we are concerned with racial justice, for a number of reasons, virtually all [universal programs] fail to promote this outcome. Ira Katznelson looked at some of the most popular universal programs coming out of the New Deal and World War II and concluded that these programs by and large benefited whites disproportionately. While the programs may have still benefited non-whites, they often exacerbated the disparities between whites and non-whites. In many instances, universalism will not work to address the needs of marginalized racial and ethnic groups.[47]

Race and gender continue to structure interactions and opportunities for participation and voice, and patterns of exclusion may well place groups outside the "circle of concern" and inhibit the capacity and opportunity of marginalized groups to participate or shape the agenda. Interventions focused on categories of difference that continue to shape people's experience are a necessary part of a larger strategy of collective impact, and the civil rights frame offers a powerful mechanism for mobilizing affected communities.

For this reason, the call for universal strategies that reject legal strategies or that do not explicitly take account of race, gender, and other categories of identity is also problematic. It is necessary to make a both/and move – one that frames the goals more broadly than compliance efforts to reduce inequality, but keeps inequality analysis and compliance strategies as a crucial tool to advance the work when appropriate. A framework of full participation has the potential to link these strategies, and has indeed been embraced either explicitly or in practice by collaboratives that include – but are not structured by – civil rights lawyers. The next section offers a direction for this crucial project of reframing the civil rights agenda, one that links the normative goal to an explicit theory of change. This full participation/collective-impact framework situates civil rights analysis within a broader umbrella of creating settings that build the capacity of relevant stakeholders to participate, succeed and thrive. It suggests the need to build into the design of the work the process of specifying the meaning of full participation within a particular context.

## Full Participation and Collective Impact as Frameworks for Addressing Structural Inequality

Broadening the lens from civil rights compliance to full participation and collective impact brings into view a broader, more systemic and holistic approach to scholarship, activism, policy development, and lawyering. Full participation advances goals that are central to the equality agenda and keeps equality concerns squarely on the table, but also enables us to move beyond the logjam and to solve the problems that now vex the equality/inequality discourse. Viewed through the lens of full participation, compliance with government regulation operates within a much broader institutional environment. Government involvement in elaborating public norms extends beyond the compliance arena. Regulatory compliance activities are not necessarily the location of decisions or conduct relating to the realization of public values. Yet, government is a crucial player in shaping the architecture within which institutions operate and providing the backstop.

Consider the following example to compare and contrast a full participation approach with a conventional civil rights framework. At a meeting of the Rutgers University's Board of Governors in 2007, the Board Chair – Dr. William Howard, a minister and respected community leader – posed the following question to the university's leadership: Why are so few students from Rutgers' host cities of Camden, Newark, or New Brunswick graduating from Rutgers? Dr. Howard acknowledged that, by the prevailing definitions of diversity, Rutgers is quite diverse: "11% of our students are African-American, 12% are Latino, 28% are Asian, 19% are Jewish. We are a very diverse institution, with students from 150 countries." But he went on to observe that "this diversity comes mostly from suburban and international minorities and not from the inner-cities in New Jersey or anywhere else." He urged the university to do what it takes to change this state of affairs, because doing so was necessary to fulfill the democratic and public mission of the university.

The leadership began its response by explaining why students from these communities do not compete successfully for a place at Rutgers. Many of them come from school districts that, generally speaking, do not prepare students for college. Camden, Newark, and New Brunswick are all "Abbott District High Schools" – thirty-one low-wealth urban school districts that were found by the courts to fall short of providing students with an adequate education, as required by the state constitution. Rutgers has not generally recruited students from those schools. A significant proportion of students from these communities do not graduate from high school. Most of their students do not have the academic credentials or test scores needed to get in to Rutgers. For the small proportion that do apply and are accepted to Rutgers, many cannot afford to come, particularly those who are undocumented, and thus not even eligible for financial aid. Those students who do come to Rutgers from these low-performing schools are disproportionately likely to struggle to succeed, thrive, and graduate. Many of them will not have the networks, preparation, scaffolding, and support needed for them to overcome the barriers and challenges they face.

Suppose the problem posed by Rutgers' board chair was processed through the lens of compliance/civil rights. Viewed through that lens, the search might be for discriminatory actions, evidence of bias, violation of statutory or regulatory standard, and corresponding legal claims that could be pursued alone or as part of mobilization strategy. Attention is also likely to focus on how current diversity-oriented strategies are affected by the Supreme Court's decision in *Fisher v. University of Texas*. Lawyers are likely to be central to this conversation, and to play a significant role in dictating the questions posed and strategies pursued.

The implications of framing the issue in terms of traditional rights discourse are profound. It would likely affect who sets the agenda, what arena becomes the focal point for discourse, how the issue or problem is framed, which strategies or mechanisms emerge, who participates in the mobilization process and what role they play, and whether the strategies match the presenting problems. This frame will likely fall short of meeting the aspirations underlying Chairman Howard's challenge to the leadership, or addressing the structural underpinnings that limit access and success for the largely nonwhite urban communities currently missing as a stakeholder of Rutgers. By conventional approaches to affirmative action, Rutgers has done all it can, taking advantage of the creativity of a creative lawyer and enrollment management staff insistent upon finding ways to diversify their student body. By conventional definitions of diversity, Rutgers is doing quite well. Indeed, its Newark campus is frequently at the top of the list of the most diverse in the country. It is taking all lawful and available steps to attract and admit students of color who meet the merit standards and add diversity to its community. By conventional definitions of discrimination, Rutgers is also in compliance. It does not discriminate or engage in biased decision making. On the contrary, Rutgers takes affirmative steps to include students of color. Poor students of color coming from urban schools are being treated equally. They just do not have the networks, resources or, in many instances, academic records required to attend Rutgers. And the problems with PreK–12 education, accounting for their lack of access to a college-going culture, lie beyond the scope of higher education's legal and regulatory responsibility. Given the high level of legally approved diversity, the absence of a constitutional right to higher education and the limited evidence of actionable bias, the conversation might not have gone any further.

But at Rutgers, like in a number of communities, a group of leaders came together from a variety of locations to mobilize a long-term project aimed at advancing full participation in higher education in New Jersey. This group of change agents viewed this admittedly lawful and, by prevailing definitions, nondiscriminatory and diverse situation to fall short of an affirmative set of commitments and values shared by a wide-ranging group of educational, government, business, and community leaders. So, a group with the power to influence Rutgers' policies and practices, which included members of the community, reframed the question. They asked: Why is it that people from the community to which Rutgers as a public university is accountable are not able to enter, thrive in, and graduate from Rutgers University? What can we do to change this situation, and to create higher education institutions that enable community members with potential from all backgrounds to enter, succeed, and thrive?

Lawyers participated in significant ways in facilitating this initiative, including as vice president and general counsel, members of the board, and collaborators in institutional design. But formal law did not dictate the change strategy. By framing equality in terms of an affirmative, collective-impact agenda, two crucial shifts occurred. First, the focus shifted to an affirmative goal: How can Rutgers University admit, support, and graduate students from its urban communities (many of whom are people of color from low-income families attending struggling schools) while remaining consistent with its overall mission of pursuing academic excellence and public leadership? Second, the unit of analysis expanded from individual students to the settings that influence their capacity to succeed. A group of stakeholders began to ask what it would take for Rutgers to participate in creating or transforming the settings that these students inhabit along the pathway into and through college so that students from urban schools could enter, do well, and graduate.

This reframing of the goal gave rise to a major, long-term, collaborative initiative called Rutgers Future Scholars. This initiative, now in its seventh year, has adopted a long-term goal of empowering, admitting, and graduating poor students from Rutgers' host cities, and in the process, building the capacity of the feeder schools to prepare and enable students to access post-secondary education. It invites – indeed, demands – a systems analysis of the dynamics that enable or prevent students from succeeding. It also catalyzes a process of addressing inequality by building social-capital networks, leveraging resources, and transforming systems that engage a broad range of participants over a long period of time, including community members, corporations with an interest in New Jersey, government leaders, foundations, school principals, teachers, faculty, lawyers, Rutgers students, artists, and parents. It has forced thinking and collaboration across conventional regulatory boundaries because the dynamics affecting students' academic success include their housing, nutrition, resources, health, access to cultural institutions, and relationships with the criminal justice system. This approach does not preclude the role of litigation, for example, in the school finance cases in New Jersey,[48] but the driving force for change comes from a newly constructed arena of mobilization focused on an affirmative vision.

Rutgers Future Scholars' strategy offers one illustration of a shift to an affirmative framework for addressing inequality, one focused on transforming settings to enable people from all different backgrounds – including those currently marginalized from opportunity – to enter, succeed, and thrive.[49] A similar move is apparent in other arenas. For example, the New York Reentry Education Network – a coalition of community-based organizations, government agencies, and higher education institutions that has emerged in New York City – focuses on making education central to reentry policy and practice, and building the networks, policy changes, and relationships necessary to move in this direction.[50] Restaurant Opportunities Council (ROC) has undertaken the affirmative goal of improving conditions for restaurant workers by making the restaurant industry a safe, healthy, and inclusive workplace for all workers, including those who are now in "the back of the house." The City of Cincinnati has adopted a "cradle to career" initiative under the name of Strive Together, which has undertaken the goal "Every Child, Every Step of the Way, Cradle to Career."[51] These strategies are also embodied in, and sometimes embedded in, a set of public policies, such as the Second Chance Act, the Promise Neighborhoods Initiative, and the Social Innovation Fund.

Importantly, inequality analysis remains an important part of these initiatives. For example, Rutgers Future Scholars includes a focus on racial and class dynamics in the classroom and community that have to be addressed as part of the process of removing barriers to students. Similarly, race powerfully interacts with criminal backgrounds in ways that prevent formerly incarcerated students of color from successfully navigating the transitions and milestones needed to succeed in college. ROC includes discrimination as part of its analysis of the dynamics producing "low road" conditions in the restaurant industry:

> There is a stark division between the treatment and experiences of the workers we see, or those with front of the house positions, who tend to fare somewhat better in terms of wages, hours, benefits, and working conditions, and those we do not, who work in the back of the house, where there is a greater likelihood that they will be subject to poor wages and working conditions. Additionally, factors such as gender, race, ethnicity, national origin, and immigration status have a significant impact on the nature and quality of the experiences of restaurant workers.[52]

This inquiry suggests that inequality goals can be most effectively and robustly advanced when they are situated within a broader framework aimed at advancing full participation in particular settings. This aim focuses on creating conditions such that people of all races, genders, incomes, religions, sexual orientations, and backgrounds can realize their capabilities as they understand them and participate fully in the life of the institutions that matter to their well-being.[53] "Full participation" has a positive valence; it engages participants in articulating an affirmative vision of full participation in their community and of building the capacity for individuals and groups to achieve those goals. This emphasis on realization of capabilities as the measure of participation resonates with Amartya Sen's idea of just institutions and equality as capabilities.

At an individual and experiential level, full participation describes a sense of belonging, mobility, engagement, access to networks and resources, and a sense of personal efficacy and capacity to influence the environment. Not only do individuals have institutional access, as measured by their representation as members of the institution – they are also enabled to contribute their capabilities and energy to animate the institution.

Although full participation articulates goals in affirmative terms, its pursuit provokes an inquiry about who is – and is not – included in the prevailing definitions and practices of full participation. It also includes an articulation of the processes involved in moving toward the desired outcome. What actions and decisions account for different patterns among different groups? Achieving full participation requires a critical assessment of the barriers and obstacles facing groups at the various institutional locations that shape inclusion and advancement. It also informs the targeting of initiatives to focus attention on groups and communities that are not flourishing within existing institutional arrangements.[54]

This affirmative framing of the problem and goal shows up in the branding of innovative initiatives that have successfully mobilized diverse coalitions to provide educational access and success for communities characterized by disinvestment: Promise Zones, Strive Together, the Kalamazoo Promise, Rutgers Future Scholars, College Initiative. Each of these initiatives has embraced an affirmative vision providing a sense of possibility and commitment. These projects grew out of a commitment to tackle dramatic and entrenched educational inequality. However, the goals were framed in terms of achieving high-quality education for every child; they nested inequality analysis within that affirmative vision, as a way to diagnose problems and catalyze the urgency of advancing that affirmative vision. The Strive Together program's motto is illustrative. Strive Together defines its goal as "bringing people together to improve results for every child, every step of the way, from cradle to career, in Cincinnati, Newport and Covington." Similarly, the mission of College Initiative, a reentry education program and network that supports access and success for formerly incarcerated students, is "to create pathways from criminal justice involvement to college and beyond and to establish and support communities invested in their own success."

These affirmative agendas typically emerged from a systematic analysis identifying profound barriers and disparities in access to social capital, resources and outcomes, showing that existing institutions were disproportionately failing people in low-income communities of color. An architectural approach invites consideration of these initiatives in relation to the systems within which they operate, the structures that shape their actions, the design that creates the structures, and the spaces within which they work. The systems approach exposes the interactions across different levels of the system (e.g., department, discipline, role, stakeholder, issue area), and how they affect the experience of full participation. Many of the features that affect whether and how full participation is achieved result from values, priorities, and patterns that cut across discrete programs, departments, and initiatives. So, for example, students' experiences of full participation and engagement are influenced by how and with whom they interact on the faculty, and these interactions are in turn shaped by the values affecting faculty members' choices and priorities. The value system of an institution, discipline, or field profoundly shapes how faculty members spend their time and how they are rewarded for those choices. These dynamics result from choices that are susceptible to change if they are made visible across these different contexts.

These programs use disparity analysis to focus urgent attention on the problem, target particular communities for sustained support, and assess outcomes. Yet, their overarching goals have not been specified solely in terms of eliminating those disparities. Each of these programs specifies a set of conditions and outcomes relating to the quality of support, levels of engagement, and success of outcomes for people in the relevant communities.

The norm of full participation provides a way to move beyond the concrete problems that produce inequality and about which people can agree, without having to reach agreement at the outset on the language or definition of inequality. Full participation also more accurately specifies the conditions necessary for people to thrive in an unequal world. Its emphasis is on people's lived experience in particular settings, and thus invites taking account of the complex dynamics that give rise to that experience. It includes the values of fair treatment and nondiscrimination, but takes account of the fact that eliminating bias, although necessary, will not itself suffice to produce conditions that will enable people from different groups and backgrounds to thrive in a society that continues to structure opportunity and resources unequally.

In this way, the goal of full participation enables a "both/and" move. It frames problems in a way that brings together groups of people who may disagree on the meaning of equality, some of whom would not come together around issues of race, gender, or other forms of inequality. Yet, full participation keeps issues of group-based inequality as a focus of explicit attention. Full participation does not embrace the value or practice of color-blindness. Race, gender, and other categories of difference are explicitly addressed as part of the analysis of who is not (yet) a full participant in the relevant context.

Where needed to address blatant discrimination and harassment, ROC supports workers seeking redress through litigation. Similarly, Strive Together has undertaken an initiative focused on increasing high school graduation and college access and success for black males. In the words of Eric Thomas, a task force member and director of the district's Office of Innovation, "every indicator you can come up with, whether it's the incarceration rate or the college-going rate, young men are on the negative side. This is a situation where unless we do something special with this subgroup, we won't succeed as a whole."[55]

Although racial, gender, or other types of group-based inequality may be the presenting condition (or the miner's canary), the project and vision is articulated in affirmative terms focused on creating a context in which every participant can succeed and thrive. The overarching goal is connected to issues of core concern among interlocking groups. This approach shifts the unit of analysis – from individual to relationships and contexts, with the nature of the relationship determined. The specified goals are pragmatic, but visionary, with success measured in terms of demonstrable movement toward a long-term goal rather than necessarily reaching ultimate success. For example, Strive Together has articulated the goal of creating a school system in which every child can succeed and progress to the next level from cradle to career. This articulation focuses on continuing advancement toward this affirmative vision, rather than on producing a final outcome of generative access.

This strategy thus entails a framing of the problem and goal that considers issues of bias and disparity within the context of a broader frame of making demonstrable progress toward an end state that reduces group-level inequality and advances core institutional values. To mobilize the systems change necessary to address structural inequality, it is necessary to frame the goal in affirmative terms, connected to a question of urgent concern among those who are affected by a common problem or change. The features of a system that lock in patterns of inequality are hard wired, and that hard wiring has to be revised in ways that take account of concerns beyond those visible through the lens of structural inequality. In addition, it is often difficult to identify where group status is operating to structure differential experiences if the focus is narrowly on how predefined groups (i.e., women, people of color, disabled people) experience exclusion. This broader framing is also important because it focuses attention on identifying what it would take to make change, not only on what it is that needs to be changed. It also allows for an articulation of goals that can mobilize the range of stakeholders who must participate to enable systems change, and puts on the table the incentives and values that underlie patterns of group-based marginalization. Systems change implicating core values and concerns must be made in order for group-based disparities to be addressed.

At the same time, the realization of broadly framed affirmative goals of enabling everyone to succeed and thrive depends on ongoing attention to structural inequality. What actions and decisions account for different patterns among different groups? This disparity/inequality question has to be asked as part of the full-participation question for full participation to be achieved. This is so for a variety of reasons. Because our society is so stratified, efforts to advance full participation without addressing inequality will replicate existing inequality. Moreover, if you do not pay explicit attention to issues of race, gender, disability, and so forth, they will continually be pushed off the table even when they are dramatically affecting whether people can succeed and thrive. Research demonstrates the limits of race-neutral interventions in enabling communities of color to participate fully in addressing racial disparities. The patterns preventing groups from fully participating are entrenched, cumulative, and difficult to see if you do not look for them. Institutional mindfulness about patterns of participation is necessary to enable full participation to be achieved. Achieving full participation requires a critical assessment of the barriers and obstacles facing groups at the various institutional locations that shape inclusion and advancement. It also informs the targeting of initiatives to focus attention on groups and communities that are not flourishing within existing institutional arrangements.

### *The Components of a Full-Participation Strategy*

What does it look like when equality initiatives explore questions concerning the impact and design of public policy, advocacy, and government intervention from the perspective of facilitating multilevel systems change that build settings where people from all different backgrounds, races, genders, and identities can succeed and thrive? This framework takes a focus of developing the capacity and incentives for institutions to advance public values, to facilitate movement from intractability to innovation. It places institutional change, motivated from multiple locations, at the center of the inquiry, design, and intervention process.

## ❖ Unit of Analysis: The Institutional Change Domain or "Action Arena"

Under this approach, the arena for analysis and intervention is not determined by legal or regulatory categories or fixed over time, but defined and revised through an analysis of the problem and the aspiration in relation to the actors who are located, and play a significant role within that arena. It focuses the change inquiry on change projects or initiatives. The locus of activity shifts from cases or regulatory actors to fields of practice. Action arenas provide a focus for inquiry and action, and are defined by a shared, ongoing project involving a set of "repeat players" who interact over time in relation to a common problem or goal, and who operate across the multiple levels that affect the choices and practices within that domain: the operational, collective action, constitutional, and meta-constitutional levels. These arenas often operate across formal organizational boundaries. The determination of the action arena includes consideration of (1) the identified organizations, programs, and people operating at different levels and shaping the context for decision making; (2) the actors in a position to set or change the rules of the game that shape the choices available to those whose decisions influence students' trajectories; and (3) the choice points for pivotal decisions shaping the contexts affecting relevant behaviors.

Action arenas might be defined geographically, in terms of an industry, or participants in a common enterprise. Institutional and cross-institutional levels are key, and action arenas cut across traditional boundaries to include the individual, collective, and institutional actors affected by and responsible for conditions in that arena. It focuses on networks and practice domains sharing common problems and concerns.

So, for example, at Syracuse University, inclusive urban education became an action arena involving the school superintendent, targeted schools, Syracuse University, local foundations, a major national foundation, a national evaluation organization, a set of community-based organizations, and parent advocacy organizations. This group connects to a national arena of districts experimenting with strategies for school turnaround. The Restaurant Opportunity Council has targeted the restaurant industry in New York City as the initial action arena for work related to improving conditions and practices affecting workers and customers.

It also has confederations of similar initiatives to address the industry nationally.

## ❖ Normative Frame: An Affirmative, Collectively Articulated Goal Defined in the Context of a Change Project

The normative frame is defined in relation to the problem it seeks to address and the affirmative vision of the kind of institutions it strives to create, with discrimination and bias included as a crucial, but not framing, component of that larger vision. Reducing inequality is part of the broader project, but does not define the ultimate outcome, which is an affirmative one of creating settings enabling the realization of affirmative goals, such as full participation (described in this chapter). The goal is not necessarily limited to – or framed in terms of – reducing inequality or bias, although these goals are a necessary part of the larger project. This articulation of the goals and vision links material conditions of education and employment to broader individual and institutional goals. It connects addressing discrimination with the need to rethink larger institutional missions and practices. It situates challenges to discrimination and disparities within a broader set of imperatives, such as building effective schools that serve the communities.

The requirement to articulate and move toward an affirmative vision creates a different dynamic. It forces thinking through both what an inclusive and participatory institution looks like, who is not currently succeeding or thriving within the setting, who is left out of the "circle of concern," what are the barriers to achieving the desired setting, and the strategies and roles for making it happen. This normative articulation pushes for development of an affirmative institutional-transformation strategy, tailored to the context of the project.

## ❖ Strategic Development of Primary Roles

The roles and participants emerge under this framework from a strategic analysis of the action arena, and the location of actors in a position to promote or impede movement toward the articulated vision. It cuts across formal and informal roles, as well as organizational and legal boundaries. It takes account of the multiple positions occupied by actors in a position of influence in relation to the articulated goals.

Participation is defined not by formal position, but instead by one's stake in and responsibility for change. The agenda has to be framed in a way that enables necessary and diverse stakeholders to understand the urgency of the goal or problem, and to care about the solution. Change often occurs by energizing both insiders and outsiders – people who might experience race and gender as a defining feature of their experience within the setting and those who do not initially gravitate to problems organized around identity, but who care about the broader affirmative goal, such as enabling students to thrive. This kind of change requires not only the involvement of both the people who "get it" and experience it, but also those whose participation is necessary to change practices. Stakeholders must be able to see why this project matters, and why it matters to them. This process requires bottom-up and top-down leadership and participation, as well as the capacity to address resistance and push back. So, how the problem is defined matters a lot for the ability to mobilize the groups of people inside and outside the institution to participate in a long-term change project.

Collective-impact projects thus devote considerable attention and energy to identifying and involving appropriate stakeholders, who could include multilevel leadership inside and outside organizations, institutional intermediaries (including foundations and public/government agencies), community-based organizational leaders and activists, compliance officials within organizations, lawyers, government regulators, and the courts.

## ❖ Government Role: Governance, Capacity Building, Accountability

In this framework, compliance remains part of the picture, but is not necessarily the starting point or the organizing principle defining the role of government actors participating in the change project. The approach engages the full range of practices, resources, and roles that can be played by government in contexts where responsibility for addressing inequality has been acknowledged. This range of practices and roles includes: funding and shaping the practices of grantees, capacity building, pooling knowledge, convening, accrediting, licensing, and compliance.

Government actors sharing the change-oriented goals of the project bring the range of tools into that work, with compliance as one of those tools, but not necessarily the one framing the overarching enterprise. This approach takes explicit account of the impact of government policy and action dynamically and institutionally: Government's role is considered not only in terms of desired policies and outcomes, but also with an eye toward developing the architecture for ongoing institutional transformation. How does government involvement advance these objectives, and do we want it to shape design making, role creation, and accountability at the institutional and network levels? What impact does and can government and other quasi-public actors have on crucial aspects affecting whether institutions are "influenceable"?

Government's role is considered not only in terms of desired policies and outcomes, but also with an eye toward developing the architecture for ongoing institutional transformation. It asks how interventions and initiatives shape the internal design of organizations, the way issues and problems are framed, the opportunities and incentives for learning, innovation, the leverage points for mobilization, accountability and change, and the relationship between compliance and other approaches for addressing structural inequality.

## Implications for Policy, Advocacy, and Law

Racial justice work since *Brown* thus is framed in language that includes, but is not necessarily limited to, civil rights. What would it look like to design and assess public policy, advocacy, and government intervention from the perspective of a collective-impact strategy focused on facilitating settings that enable all relevant stakeholders to fully participate, succeed, and thrive? This framework encourages a more architectural approach that enables a wide range of stakeholders, including regulatory actors, to engage in a multilevel systems analysis. Public policy and law would be designed to encourage multi-stakeholder projects and experiments to advance shared goals. Whatever the entry point, those engaged in structural inequality projects would ask how their work connects to a broader set of actors who need to be linked to each other around a common goal to achieve systems change.

This might encourage a shift of the unit of regulatory intervention from a single regulator to constructed arenas of mobilization around crosscutting projects. This could be achieved by constructing a broad, but thin, set of norms, thereby establishing a minimum conduct floor, and a much thicker and project-driven set of collaborations across regulatory and social fields. It would also broaden and shift the center of gravity for normative elaboration and realization. Funding, licensing, assessing, budget cutting, convening around public values – all of these are increasingly significant sites for normative elaboration.

This approach might also encourage greater attention to the question of which actors are in a position to influence behavior of the field in a desired direction. What are the available normative frames to different regulatory and public actors? How embedded is the particular regulator entity in the interactions shaping core practices? What networks can they leverage? How much access, credibility, and influence do they have with people in key decision-making positions? What resources can they mobilize to build capacity and influence behavior? Change agents would have the strategic capacity to pay careful attention to the development of social spaces for innovation and experimentation, boundary-spanning intermediaries, mechanisms prompting participatory reflection and accountability, and the cultivation of leadership in multiple locations that need to activate change.

Finally, this framework would encourage the linkage of compliance-oriented approaches – which have been the focus of most of the scholarly and advocacy activities in the equality arena – to other important arenas of activity. It might also encourage greater attentiveness to how change takes place in the way cases are selected, priorities established, and remedies designed.

## Notes

1. Richard Wilkinson and Kate Pickett, *The Spirit Level: Why Greater Equality Makes Societies Stronger*. New York: Bloomsburg Press, 2009.
2. O. Johnson, "Disparity Rules," 107 *Columbia Law Review* (2007), 374; Patrick Sharkey, *Stuck in Place: Urban Neighborhoods and the End of Progress toward Racial Equality*. Chicago: The University of Chicago Press, 2013; S. Sturm, "The Architecture of Inclusion: Advancing Workplace Equity in Higher Education," 29 *Harvard Journal of Law and Gender* (2006), 247.
3. S. Treuhaft and D. Madland, "Prosperity 2050: Is Equity the Superior Growth Model?" (2011), available at http://www.policylink.org/site/apps/nlnet/content2.aspx?c=lkIXLbMNJrE&b=5136581&ct=9359713; Picket and Wilkinson, *The Spirit Level*.

4. S. L. Gaertner and J. F. Dovidio, "Understanding and Addressing Contemporary Racism: From Aversive Racism to the Common Ingroup Identity Model," 61 *Journal of Social Issues* (2005), 615, 625; For summaries of the psychological literature, see T. Green, "Discrimination in Workplace Dynamics: Toward Structural Account of Disparate Treatment Theory," 38 *Harvard Civil Rights-Civil Liberties Law Review* (2003), 91; 854–857; L. H. Krieger, "The Content of Our Categories: A Cognitive Bias Approach to Discrimination and Equal Employment Opportunity," 47 *Stanford Law Review* (1995), 1161, 1186–1188; R. Lenhardt, "Understanding the Mark: Race, Stigma, and Equality in Context," 79 *New York University Law Review* (2004), 803, 879–896.
5. C. M. Steele, *Whistling Vivaldi* (New York: W.W. Norton, 2010).
6. Deirdre A. Royster, *Race and the Invisible Hand: How White Networks Exclude Black Men from Blue Collar Jobs*. Berkeley: University of California Press (2003); V. Valian, *Why So Slow: The Advancement of Women*. Cambridge: Massachusetts Institute of Technology Press, 1999.
7. G. C. Loury, "Discrimination in the Post-Civil Rights Era: Beyond Market Interactions," *Journal of Economic Perspectives* (Spring 1998), 117, 118–119; Deidre A. Royster, *Race and the Invisible Hand: How White Networks Exclude Black Men from Blue Collar Jobs*. Berkeley: University of California Press, 2003.
8. M. Brilliant, "Blurring the Color-Blind Line," Chapter 3 of this volume; I. Katznelson, *When Affirmative Action Was White*. New York: W.W Norton, 2005.
9. S. Sturm, "The Architecture of Inclusion." Note 2.
10. For a general theory of multilevel institutional analysis in advancing systems change, see *Understanding Institutional Diversity*. Princeton: Princeton University Press, 2005.
11. R. Siegel, "Discrimination in the Eyes of the Law: How Color Blindness Discourse Disrupts and Rationalizes Social Stratification," 88 *California Law Review* (2000), 77.
12. See *Adarand Construction, Incorporated v. Pena*, 515 U.S. at 200 (1995).
13. The Frameworks Perspective: Strategic Frame Analysis, available at http://www.frameworksinstitute.org/perspective.html (this is an on line report).
14. E. Ostrom, *Understanding Institutional Diversity*. Princeton: Princeton University Press, 2005, p. 28.
15. Green, "A Structural Approach"; L. J. Krieger, "The Content of Our Categories: A Cognitive Bias Approach to Discrimination and Equal Employment Opportunity," 47 *Stanford Law Review* (1995), 1161, 1213; J. Kang and M. Banaji, "Fair Measures: A Behavioral Realist Revision of Affirmative Action," 94 *California Law Review* (2006), 1063, 1072. In the criminal context, see D. M. Kahan et al., "Whose Eyes Are You Going to Believe: *Scott v. Harris* and the Perils of Cognitive Illiberalism," 122 *Harvard Law Review* (2009), 838.
16. R. Ford, "Civil Rights and the Myth of Moral Progress," Chapter 5 of this volume.
17. Richard Ford's contribution to this volume calls for a move from individual to group action arenas.

18. O. Johnson, "Beyond the Attorney General: Equality Directives in American Law," 87 *New York University Law Review* (2012), 102.
19. John Powell, "Poverty and Race through Belongingness Lens," Policy Matters. Retrieved from http://www.issuelab.org/resource/policymatters_poverty_and_race_through_a_belongingness_lens.
20. Michael McCann, *Rights at Work: Pay Equity Reform and the Politics of Legal Mobilization*. Chicago: University of Chicago Press, 1994; Michael Paris, *Framing Equal Opportunity: Law and the Politics of School Finance Reform* New York: Bloomsbury Press, 2009.
21. "Organizational Research Services, Theory of Change: A Practical Tool for Action, Results, and Learning," The Annie Case Foundation (2004). Retrieved from http://www.google.com/url?sa=t&rct=j&q=&esrc=s&source=web&cd=1&ved=0CCsQFjAA&url=http%3A%2F%2Fwww.aecf.org%2Fupload%2Fpublicationfiles%2Fcc2977k440.pdf&ei=f5RmUqPeG5CvkAers4HIBA&usg=AFQjCNHTTj4ldTzMOHMyb_Ow4KrU63qGTg&bvm=bv.55123115,d.eWo.
22. Sturm, "Architecture of Inclusion," p. 249.
23. For a general theory of multilevel institutional analysis in advancing systems change, see *Understanding Institutional Diversity*. Princeton: Princeton University Press, 2005. Elinor Ostrom, *Understanding Institutional Diversity* (2005).
24. Id.
25. John Powell, "Post Racialism or Targeted Universalism?" 86 *Denver University Law Review* (2009), 1.
26. The goal of full participation has been adopted as an organizing framework for several national networks, including Imagining America and the Creating Connections Consortium. The concept of "collective impact," first articulated by John Kanner and Mark Kania, has become the centerpiece of a growing set of public-private collaborations. See J. Kanner and M. Kania, "Collective Impact," *Stanford Social Innovation Review* (Winter 2011), 36.
27. Sharkey, supra; Sturm, supra; X. de Souza Briggs, Introduction, in *The Geography of Opporunity*. Washington, DC: Brookings Institution Press (2005).
28. K. Crenshaw, "Demarginalizing the Intersection of Race and Sex: A Black Feminist Critique of Antidiscrimination Doctrine, Feminist Theory and Antiracist Politics," *University of Chicago Legal Forum* (1989), 139.
29. Jamshid Gharajedaghi, *System Thinking: Managing Chaos and Complexity*, 2nd ed. Amsterdam: Elsevier, Inc 2006, p. 112.
30. See S. Sturm, "Negotiating Workplace Equality: A Systemic Approach," *Negotiation and Conflict Management Research*, 2 (2009), 92; Mark Suchman and Lauren Edelman, "Legal Rational Myths: The New Institutionalism and the Law and Society Tradition," 21 *Law and Social Inquiry* (1996), 903, 905.
31. See Eckel, P., Hill, B., and Green, M. (1998). *On change: En route to transformation*. Occasional paper no. 1. Washington, D.C.: American Council on Education. Sturm, supra note; Daryl Smith, *Diversity's Promise for Higher Education: Making it Work*. Baltimore: Johns Hopkins University Press (2009).

32. See, e.g., Keivan Stassun, Susan Sturm, K. Holley-Bockelman, A. Burger, D. Ernst & D. Webb, The Fisk-Vanderbilt Master's-to-Ph.D. Bridge Program: Recognizing, enlisting, and cultivating unrealized or unrecognized potential in underrepresented minority students, 79 *American Journal of Physics* (2011), 374; Damon Williams, *Strategic Diversity Leadership: Activating Change and Transformation in Higher Education*. Sterling: Stylus Publishing, Inc. (2013); S. Sturm, E. Freudenberger, J. Howard & E. Juaregio, "Linking Mobilization to Institutional Power: The Faculty-Led Diversity Initiative at Columbia" in *Reconstructing The Academy: Faculty Take the Lead*, Newark: Rutgers University Press (2008).
33. 129 S. Ct. 2658 (2009).
34. "Candidates without $500 for the study materials or a relative or friend from whom they might borrow the books were put at a disadvantage. Moreover, it was the firefighters union, which sided with the white firefighters in the Supreme Court, that negotiated the contractual mandate giving disproportionate weight to the multiple-choice test. Those negotiations occurred two decades ago when the leadership of the department was virtually all white." Lani Guinier and Susan Sturm, "Trial by Firefighters," *New York Times*, July 11, 2009.
35. "America at Risk, America Burning Recommissioned" (2002). Retrieved from http://www.usfa.dhs.gov/downloads/pdf/publications/fa-223-508.pdf.
36. L. Guinier and S. Sturm, "Trial by Firefighters," *New York Times*, July 11, 2009.
37. I am grateful to Liz Emens for this analogy.
38. Anthony Carnavale and Jeff Strohl, *Separate and Unequal: How Higher Education Reinforces the Intergenerational Reproduction of White Racial Privilege*. Georgetown Public Policy Institute (2013), available at cew.georgetown.edu/separateandunequal/; Jeannie Oakes and Marisa Saunders, Multiple Pathways: Promising to Prepare All High School Students for College, Career, and Civic Participation," in Beyond Tracking: Multiple Pathways to College, Career and Civic Participation (J. Oakes and M. Saunders, ed). Cambridge: Harvard Education Press (2008).
39. Ostrom, supra note, at 34.
40. Ostrom, supra note.
41. A good example is the proposal to respond to cognitive bias by hanging portraits of women and people of color. C. Sunstein and C. Jolls, "The Law of Implict Bias," *California Law Review*. 94 (2004), 969, 983–84.
42. Thornton and Ocasio, "Institutional Logics," in R. Greenwood, C. Oliver, R. Suddaby, and K. Sahlin-Andersson, eds., *The Sage Handbook of Organizational Institutionalism*. London: Sage Publications LTD 2008, pp. 99–129.
43. See, e.g., S. Bagenstos, "The Structural Turn and the Limits of Antidiscrimination Law," *California Law Review* 94 (2006), 1; Green, supra; Krieger, "The Content of Our Categories."
44. C. Sabel and W. Simon, "Destabilization Rights: How Public Law Litigation Succeeds," *Harvard Law Review* 117 (2004), 1015; S. Sturm, Second Generation

Employment Discrimination: A Structural Approach," *Columbia Law Review* 101 (2001), 458.

45. The collective-impact analysis that is emerging in the nonprofit sector makes a similar point. See Kanner and Kania, "Collective Impact."
46. R. Paxcale, J. Sternin, and M. Sternin, *The Power of Positive Deviance: How Unlikely Innovators Solve the World's Toughest Problems*. Cambridge: Harvard Business Press, 2010.
47. Powell, "Targeted Universalism."
48. Michael Paris, *Framing Equal Opportunity: Law and Politics of School Finance Reform*. New York: Bloomsbury Press 2009.
49. S. Sturm, Building the Architecture of Inclusion, note 9.
50. Susan Sturm, et al., Building Pathways of Possibility from Criminal Justice to College: College Initiative as a Catalyst Linking Individual and Systemic Change (2010). Report available at www.changecenter.org.
51. Strive Together, 2012–2013 Strive Partnership Report Card, available at http://reportcard.strivetogether.org/content/2012-13-strive-partnership-report-card.
52. Saru Jayaraman, *Behind the Kitchen Door*, Ithaca: Cornell University Press (2013).
53. S. Sturm, T. Eatman, J. Saltmarsh, and A. Bush, *Architecture for Diversity and Public Engagement in Higher Education* (White paper). Columbia University Law School: Center for Institutional and Social Change (2012).
54. Sturm, supra note 9.
55. Jessica Brown, "CPS Plans African-American Male Initiative," www.strivenetwork.org (2011).

# Commentary on Chapter 4 Susan Sturm's "Reframing the Civil Rights Narrative: From Compliance to Collective Impact"

Steven H. Hobbs

## Introductory Musings

This symposium on civil rights in the American story comes at a time when we are commemorating the fiftieth anniversary of important events of the civil rights movement. In the case of *NAACP v. Button*, in 1963, the U.S. Supreme Court affirmed the practice of civil rights lawyers actively recruiting clients to bring cases designed to enforce the mandate of *Brown v. Board of Education*. In Birmingham, Alabama, under the leadership of Reverend Fred Shuttlesworth and Dr. Martin Luther King, Jr., the foot soldiers marched to integrate the public spaces of Birmingham.[1] Sheriff Bull Connor unleashed dogs and fire hoses on children as they attempted a peaceful protest march from the Sixteenth Street Baptist Church to downtown Birmingham. The horror of that assault was broadcasted nationally and provided the moral impetus for the Civil Rights Act of 1965. On August 28, Dr. King led the 1963 March on Washington where he gave his iconic "I Have a Dream Speech." A few weeks later, he returned to Birmingham to eulogize the four little girls who perished in a Sunday morning bombing of the Sixteenth Street Baptist Church. And, on June 11, 1963, Alabama Governor George Wallace unsuccessfully attempted to block two black students from registering for classes at The University of Alabama in Tuscaloosa.[2]

As Dr. Vincent Harding might declare, 1963 was just one monumental year from that long river of struggle for full equal rights and inclusion in American society, stretching back to the days of the first slave ships and extending up to this present moment.[3] Once the claim for civil rights was formally recognized in law and began to be actualized in fact, the struggle shifted to preserving those rights and extending them to all aspects of civil life in America. It is this part of the struggle that Professor Susan Sturm addresses in Chapter 4 of this volume. If one assumes, as Professor Sturm does, that the equality ideal stated emphatically in the Declaration of Independence is embedded in our Constitution, then the efforts of the last fifty years were designed to ensure compliance with that ideal as articulated in case law, legislation, and regulations. By pursuing this ideal mostly through litigation, the strategic goal was to enforce antidiscrimination norms, reduce disparities in economic and political opportunities, and to establish compliance standards that could be objectively met. Professor Sturm finds that this form of pursuing change in society, although effective in establishing formal equality, still leaves too much systemic inequality and entrenched bias in society and thus calls for a new framework in which to continue the struggle for maximizing the equality ideal.

In many ways, her work echoes the demand Dr. King made to the nation for deep systemic change in order to fulfill the promise of the Declaration of Independence. On the steps of the Lincoln Memorial on August 28, 1963, Dr. King proclaimed:

> So we've come here today to dramatize a shameful condition. In a sense we've come to our nation's capital to cash a check. When the architects of our republic wrote the magnificent words of the Constitution and the Declaration of Independence, they were signing a promissory note to which every American was to fall heir. This note was the promise that all men, yes, black men as well as white men, would be guaranteed the unalienable rights of life, liberty, and the pursuit of happiness.
>
> It is obvious today that America has defaulted on this promissory note in so far as her citizens of color are concerned. Instead of honoring this sacred obligation, America has given the Negro people a bad check; a check which has come back marked "insufficient funds." We refuse to believe that there are insufficient funds in the great vaults of opportunity of this nation. And so, we've come to cash this check, a check that will give us upon demand the riches of freedom and the security of justice.[4]

Like Dr. King, Professor Sturm is deeply committed to that fundamental structural change in our society that will obtain the equality ideal for all segments of society. Although we have surely made spectacular progress toward ending de jure discrimination, much remains to be accomplished to root out systemic inequality. Hence, she recognizes that pursuing a strategy of litigation designed to force compliance with the rights gained in the civil rights movement has not yet met the demand put forward by Dr. King in his speech. Her agenda for action is premised on the inclusion of all individuals into the social fabric of our community and entails race, gender, class, mobility, and any other forms of discrimination that sets us apart from each other. This commentary will focus on several aspects of her proposed call for a comprehensive, collaborative effort to fully cash that check of which Dr. King so eloquently spoke.

## Shaping a Collaborative-Impact Framework

The core of her inquiry is to construct an ideological framework for shaping a strategic plan of action to reduce and eliminate bias, discrimination, and all forms of exclusion based on immutable characteristics. Accordingly, all members of society should be empowered to pursue the opportunity to live a life of dignity and meaning within the ability of each member of our society. The framework she proposes calls for the broadest participation of an array of stakeholders – those individuals and institutions and agencies that can bring creative responses and resources to bear on the problem of persistent inequality. The fundamental aspect of the frame she constructs is thus one of collaborative action featuring all aspects of society, or at least as much of society as can possibly be mustered.

Furthermore, the framework is holistic; not only does it attempt to address the obvious disparities, but she takes a larger perspective and asks why those disparities persist over time, spaces, and places. After 150 years of struggle since President Abraham Lincoln issued the Emancipation Proclamation to formally chip away at the legal institution of slavery, the ideal of universal freedom is elusive for significant segments of our society. Geographically, there are spaces in this country were bias continues to haunt persons of color, immigrants, and those who hold non-majoritarian religious beliefs. Certain areas of the country are openly hostile to citizens who are different than they are. Finally, this lack of full participation in civil society is observed in such places as employment, education, housing, voting, the criminal justice system, and other places where obstacles and barriers to entry inherently exist or are imposed by those in privileged positions.

Professor Sturm uses the example of Rutgers University's efforts to increase diversity in its student body. Even though there were significant numbers of diverse students, far too few came from New Jersey's larger cities such as Camden, Newark, and New Brunswick – places where there are significant numbers of minority students. A deeper, broader look at the issue showed that many students from these school districts where not prepared to pursue higher education. A collection of actors from different segments of the larger community asked why these disparities in the admission of inner-city students existed when Rutgers was affirmatively seeking diverse student bodies. Professor Sturm notes that a group of varied leaders collaborated to address this challenge using an approach aimed at transforming the status quo:

> They asked why is it that people from the community to which Rutgers as a public university is accountable, are not able to enter, thrive in, and graduate from Rutgers University? What can we do to change this situation, and to create higher education institutions that *enable* community members with potential from all backgrounds to enter, succeed, and thrive? (emphasis added)

Asking these forms of questions moves the discussion beyond the linear frame of pursuing compliance through litigation and toward attacking the challenges from a multidisciplinary, multiple-systems approach. It extends beyond a limited time frame, looks at the spaces where student achievement is lacking, and steers students to places that enables success. The result was the Rutgers Future Scholars initiative that went beyond educational remediation to a consideration of anything that would impede success, including "their housing, nutrition, resources, health, access to cultural institutions, and relationship with the criminal justice system."

## The Collaborative-Action Paradigm

From my point of view, I agree with the collaborative, holistic approach pursued in conjunction with the current efforts seeking compliance with basic constitutional and civil rights laws and regulations. Certainly we must be ever vigilant in maintaining the tremendous gains of the civil rights movement. There must be advocates, both legally trained and those who are moved to stand and be a voice for persons who are dispossessed of civil rights owing to circumstances beyond their control. Some action will be on behalf of individuals seeking to vindicate civil wrongs. Other compliance efforts will come in the form of more traditional impact litigation or by grassroots movements that call attention to unfair and disparate treatment. For example, in child welfare, each child should have at least a guardian ad litem to fight for that child's right to a safe, loving, and permanent home. And yet, a state system of foster care can so utterly fail all children in the system that only class action litigation can rectify the systemic harm done to children who linger in an abusive foster care system. As Professor Sturm notes, achieving court victories is essential in this struggle; however, a deeper work is required to truly bring about the principles and ideals of our founding documents.

Moving beyond compliance, the collaborative framework is designed to widen the parameters of achieving a society free of bias, discrimination, and persistent inequality. This is what Professor J. Clay Smith has called, "the doctrine of pure legal existence," where one's possession of civil rights are presumed to exist beyond color, gender, class, or other arbitrary classifications totally unrelated to full participation in our society.[5] What Professor Sturm's work does is call for fresh thinking about strategies that could be deployed to creatively evolve a civil rights narrative that more nearly "bends towards justice," as Dr. King would declare.[6] I will now focus on some of the aspects of Professor Sturm's collaborative framework that speak to me.

First, the framework of a collaborative process is contingent on possessing a *vision* of what freedom looks like. In setting goals that address systemic inequality, there must be a destination that not only reflects the values of our constitutional ideals, but also manifests a real change. What sticks with most people who hear Dr. King's speech at the 1963 March on Washington is the articulation of a new-world *dream*. He gave a broader, truer meaning to the words justice, freedom, and equality by drawing all persons, or as he says, "all God's children,"[7] within the arc of liberty guaranteed at our nation's founding. As he said, this vision is "deeply rooted in the American dream."[8] He wraps that part of the speech around all children and the future where their character will count and not their color or region of the country. Professor Sturm similarly creates a vision that is rooted in the past and projects a future where all have an equal opportunity to thrive as human beings. Another expression of the ideal can be found in the Langston Hughes's poem, "I Dream a World," which in part says:

> I dream a world where all
> Will know sweet freedom's way,
> Where greed no longer saps the soul
> Nor avarice blights our day.
> A world I dream where black or white,
> Whatever race you may be,
> Will share the bounties of the earth
> And every man is free, . . .[9]

As my friend and filmmaker Billie Field has suggested to me, the important fact to remember about the integration of the University of Alabama is not that Governor George Wallace stood in the schoolhouse door at Foster Auditorium; the real remarkable event is that Vivian Malone and James Hood actually *walked* through the schoolhouse doors to obtain an education. It should be noted that behind the scenes, various stakeholders worked to create the conditions necessary for educational success and for others to follow. This is in great contrast to the situation in 1956 when Autherine Lucy successfully sued to gain admission to and enroll in The University of Alabama. She was expelled after several days because of violence that erupted on campus after her attempt to integrate the school.[10] In Professor Sturm's work, she insists that the various stakeholders buy into the vision in order for it to come to pass. We all ultimately are benefited when all can freely participate in the life of the beloved community, as Dr. King so spiritually put it.

Second, it is important to the framework that there be a full and complete identification of all the obstacles to full citizenship participation. Any efforts should recognize large and small barriers that prevent or impede progress toward the ideal. Correspondingly, the effort is beyond what we might perceive as political correctness, where we sprinkle around diverse individuals to showcase an appearance of inclusion. Often, they are not fully incorporated into the community's fabric and given full access to all positions and programs. Thus, one must be vigilant and mindful of the doors that block entrance and stymie progress.

This requires an openness and honesty to listening and expressing both obvious and hidden biases that we all have as human beings. Moreover, the situational analysis that identifies barriers and biases must become an organic part of the strategic-planning process. The ideal of inclusion must be reflected in every decision-making process, including such details as making the literature published by an institution look like America. For example, the Girl Scouts of the United States, in all of their promotional and instructional materials, endeavor to include in pictures and illustrations an array of diverse girls, including race, ethnicity, mobility and so forth, so that any girl who views the material will see someone who looks like her. They do not just talk diversity, they manifest it. The process is never finished, only continually refined, bending always toward justice.

Next, to achieve the vision there must be action – something must happen to change the dynamics of the status quo. Professor Sturm calls these "arenas of action" that can function in multiple places and spaces. Moreover, the action must be accomplished by the fullest collectivity of stakeholders possible. Talent and resources are spread across the spectrum of social, business, and government institutions and no one should be ignored who can address the challenge of inequality. The vision must be so articulated, or marketed if you will, so individuals and their institutions are motivated to respond to that call to achieve the ideal of an inclusive, equalitarian society. Certainly the vision must be rich and inspiring enough that we recognize that the struggle is continuous and requires constant application of thoughtful action.

Professor Sturm borrows from systems theory, which is generally utilized in such fields as social work and therapy. The essence of this theory is that individuals and families tend to address problems and move through life by accessing resources situated in people and institutions that touch their lives. For example, a couple with children might call on extended family or friends to assist with child care. In meeting educational, recreational, and health needs of the children, the parents might reach out to schools, civic organizations, religious institutions, or government agencies to partner with in meeting those needs. Each of these entities constitutes a system that families can access to navigate through the world. A community's livability may be judged by how well these systems function. These systems are also within the arena of action where positive change can occur. Within the collaborative framework, these systems can be creatively mobilized to further the goal of full and equal participation.

And finally, in order to have a holistic, collaborative-impact framework that actually achieves real change, many, many individuals must have the heart, soul, and spirit to work together for the collective good. Fundamentally, change happens when neighbors reach out to neighbors out of care, concern, and love. Love of the other is what fueled Dr. King's nonviolent civil rights movement. It is the essence of his appeal to the conscience of the country. He literally preached that we must see ourselves in our neighbors' faces, both near and far, proclaiming:

Now let me suggest first that if we are to have peace on earth, our loyalties must become ecumenical rather than sectional. Our loyalties must transcend our race, our tribe, our class, and our nation; and this means we must develop a world perspective.[11]

This is not a foreign concept in America. Indeed, we at least subscribe to the ethic of care and love when we must face emergencies and tragedies together. When the nation was struck by terrorists on 9/11, we rallied together to comfort and support each other. When devastating storms such as the tornados that struck Tuscaloosa in April 2011, killing 54 people, or Hurricanes Katrina and Sandy brought death and destruction, we Americans gave of our time, treasure, and talent to aid those whose lives were forever changed. We do well together over the short term of an immediate emergency. However, the systemic change that Professor Sturm seeks recognizes a deeper and longer commitment. And this ultimately will determine if the collaborative framework will have longevity.

## Concluding Thoughts

It is my sense that the flame that generates the energy for action is part and parcel of the American spirit, but it must be continually reclaimed and renewed in each generation in each time. Here is where our country's leaders, nationally and locally, must step up and hold a mirror to our souls as Claude McKay says in his poem, "I Know My Soul."[12] I believe that this is what President Barack Obama does in some of his addresses. He recalls to our memory that we are citizens, an honored title that comes with both blessings and obligations. He so declared it in a speech following his reelection on November 7, 2012:

> What makes America exceptional are the bonds that hold together the most diverse nation on Earth – the belief that our destiny is shared; that this country only works when we accept certain obligations to one another, and to future generations; that the freedom which so many Americans have fought for and died for comes with responsibilities as well as rights, and among those are love and charity and duty and patriotism. That's what makes America great.[13]

I cannot think of a better description of collective impact. I am moved by this verse of poetry by Jelaluddin Rumi:

> Out beyond ideas of wrongdoing and rightdoing,
> there is a field. I'll meet you there.
> When the soul lies down in that grass,
> the world is too full to talk about.
> Ideas, language, even the phrase *each other*
> doesn't make any sense.[14]

That field must be a space where all of our assumptions drop away and we are left with the time to begin again without any preconceived notions of who the other is. Professor Sturm is calling us to that field in which we can place ourselves for a deep collaborative discourse on how we honor the equality ideals of our nation. Far too often we let politics and ideological differences dig trenches between people who otherwise love their country. The challenge is that we have too many visions of what America should be and become. However, within these seemingly competing visions, there are common threads by which we can weave the best of our ideas and motivations. Our care and compassion for each other is a part of being American. Let us lay down our tribal affiliations and meet on that field that was purchased by our collective efforts to make the Declaration of Independence live.

## Notes

1. See generally, Howell Raines, *My Soul is Rested: The Story of the Civil Rights Movement in the Deep South*, Penguin Books, 1977.

2. E. Culpepper Clark, *The Schoolhouse Door: Segregation's Last Stand at the University of Alabama*, Oxford: Oxford University Press, 1993, pp. 223–226 (hereinafter, The School House Door).
3. Vincent Harding, *There Is a River: The Black Struggle for Freedom in America*, Vintage Books, 1981.
4. James M. Washington, ed., *The Essential Writings and Speeches of Marin Luther King, Jr.* Harper, 1986, p. 217 (hereinafter, *The Essential Writings*).
5. J. Clay Smith, "In Memoriam: Professor Frank D. Reeves Towards a Houstonian School of Jurisprudence and the Study of Pure Legal Existence," 18 *Howard Law Journal* 1 (1973).
6. Washington, *The Essential Writings*, at 230.
7. Id., 220.
8. Id., 219.
9. Arnold Rampersad and David Roessel, eds., *The Collected Poems of Langston Hughes*. Vintage Classics, 1994, p. 311.
10. Clark, *The Schoolhouse Door*, pp. 96–98.
11. Washington, *The Essential Writings*, at 253.
12. Claude McKay, "I Know My Soul." Retrieved from http://www.poemhunter.com/poem/i-know-my-soul/.
13. President Barak Obama, *Remarks by the President on Election Night*, November 7, 2012, McCormick Place, Chicago, IL. Retrieved from http://www.whitehouse.gov/the-press-office/2012/11/07/remarks-president-election-night. Last visited 3/6/2013.
14. Coleman Barks with John Moyne, trans., *The Essential Rumi*. HarperCollins, 1995, p. 36.

Professor Steven H. Hobbs graduated magna cum laude from Harvard University in 1975 with a Bachelor of Arts degree and received the juris doctor from the University of Pennsylvania Law School in 1979. Professor Hobbs was a member of the Washington and Lee law faculty for sixteen years before accepting the position of Tom Bevill, Chairholder of Law at Alabama in 1997. He also has visited on the law faculties at Willamette University and Florida State University. Upon graduation from law school, Professor Hobbs practiced in the Department of the Public Advocate in Trenton, New Jersey. Both his professional and scholarly interests demonstrate his commitment to the fair distribution of social and legal benefits to individuals. The classes he has taught, the topics of scholarship on which he has written, and the issues he has addressed at professional conferences deal with entrepreneurship, storytelling, history, family law, legal ethics, and social and economic justice. He has written numerous law review articles on these subjects and was instrumental in drafting the Virginia Human Rights Act. Professor Hobbs teaches professional responsibility, family law, adoption law, children's rights, and a seminar on law and entrepreneurship.

5

# Civil Rights and the Myth of Moral Progress*

Richard Thompson Ford

This country ultimately gets it right. That was my point in that speech [advocating same-sex marriage]. It was about the march of equality. It's not always an easy fight. In fact, it's never been easy. But whether the majority of people like it or not, we get it right.[1]
– San Francisco Mayor Gavin Newsom, 2008

No one was more surprised by the rise of the gay marriage issue than many veterans of earlier forms of gay activism. To them marriage seems both less urgent and less agreed-upon than such issues as HIV and health care, AIDS prevention, the repeal of sodomy laws, antigay violence, job discrimination, immigration.... The campaign for marriage... was launched by a relatively small number of lawyers, not by a consensus among activists. It remains a project of litigation.... If reform of marriage was the goal, the tactics of legal advocacy have not worked, and in some ways have made the problem worse.... [And] for whom would marriage be a victory?... Where does the politics of gay marriage lead?[2]
– Scholar and queer activist Michael Warner, 1996

I don't do not want to focus on the merits of this surprising disagreement; instead, I want to focus on the two very different ideas of how social change occurs. Gavin Newsom suggests that social change is a matter of tapping into an almost impersonal historical process: We will have gay marriage because gay marriage is pProgress and pProgress is inevitable and inexorable; we ultimately get it right. Warner describes social change as a matter of struggle and radical contingency: The "campaign" for gay marriage was a surprise and a departure from the pro-gay activism of the

* Portions of this essay were inspired by my arguments in Rights Gone Wrong: How Law Corrupts the Struggle for Equality (2011), The Race Card: How Bluffing about Bias Makes Race Relations Worse (2008), and Racial Culture: A Critique (2004).

past; it was initially a minority agenda that gained traction because of the unusual features of the legal system – if we have gay marriage, it will be because some powerful members of the gay community succeeded in advancing this. In Warner's view, a conformist agenda is achieved at the expense of the more radical ambitions of sexual liberation that are inconsistent with marriage.

Newsom's idea of change is part of a myth – a very powerful myth – of a nation that is always improving technologically, militarily, economically, socially, and morally – a nation that always ultimately gets it right.

This is a powerful myth and in many ways, a beneficent one. But Nevertheless, it can be a dangerous and misleading myth as well. Warner's account of the gay marriage struggle *within* the gay equality movement shows us that Newsom's Whiggish idea of progress can blind us to the contingency of political strategies and hence to the stakes of political decisions. Warner's point is not that it is hard to decide between marriage equality and the homophobic rejection of marriage equality; his point is that the pursuit of marriage equality foreclosed a critique of the sexual regulation and compulsory domesticity of marriage – a critique he saw as implicit in much of early pro-gay politics. For Warner, gay marriage is certainly better than the status quo without gay marriage. But those are not the only two choices. At least at some earlier point in time (he wrote the passage in 1999, before the gay marriage movement had really hit its stride), there was also a choice to further the agenda of respect and dignity for gay men and lesbians (and many straight people, incidentally) by undermining the hegemony of marriage. From that perspective, gay marriage is not progress – it is not simply "getting it right." It is an improvement in one area achieved at the expense of other potential, foregone improvements. It only looks like progress now that the pursuit of marriage equality has bolstered the prestige of marriage and made the project of undermining its hegemony untenable. It may be that the esteem, dignity, and material benefits of marriage outweigh its costs in terms of sexual surveillance and the sacrifice of a more libertarian sexual ideal. But this is not the way the decision to pursue same-sex marriage is framed. Instead, it is framed as a choice between progress and stagnation and accordingly, no real choice at all.

Incidentally, the evil twin of the progress story is the story of decline: If things go badly from our perspective, then we have suffered a "set back," a "backlash," or, in our more pessimistic moments, we might even lament a long, sad decline in the fortunes of the nation. The optimistic, Whiggish narrative of progress and the pessimistic, conservative narrative of decline are, analytically, mirror images. Both evoke a two- dimensional notion of history: We are either making progress or we are in decline.

The progress myth is especially powerful today in the context of civil rights and that will be the subject of this essay.

Myths can sometimes be perfectly true and they almost always reflect some important truth, even if they are fabricated in many details. There may not have been a round table in the court of a medieval English king or a conjurer named Merlin; Robin Hood might have spent the spoils of his criminal adventures at the brothel and the tavern rather than distributing them to the poor. That's not what matters. What matters is that these legends reflected some ideas about the evolution of England and the relationship between its rulers and ruled – the state and civil society. Both were nation-building myths – they were a part of the working out of the relationship between diverse tribes, between a conquering race and an indigenous people, the injustices done in the name of divine right and the negotiation of political legitimacy that created the now ancient Anglo-Saxon people.

Michel Foucault tells us that history is always a form of political theory: The accounts of a nation's past are also in some way either apology or critique.[3] So it is with more recent history. The American civil rights story is now a central part of the myth of America. The black civil rights movement is now as much a part of American nationalist lore as the Boston Tea Party or Paul Revere's midnight ride. Like the colonists who tipped the East India Company's heavily taxed Orange Pekoe into Boston Harbor, the soon-to-be leaders of the civil rights movement were long-suffering solid citizens, pushed to rebellion by manifest oppression. History (after a scant forty years, already slipping into legend and cliché) has it that Rosa Parks refused to yield her seat on a Montgomery, Alabama public bus simply because she was tired. No political activist, she: just a simple workingwoman demanding her dignity. Both the freedom fighters and the freedom riders had a gift for practical problem solving, an outsider's disdain for conventions, a mavericks' ability to think outside the box – the paradigmatic Yankee virtues of pragmatism and ingenuity.

And perhaps most importantly, both revolutions are stories of progress – examples of American idealism and industry shaping a society where continual improvement can almost be taken for granted. American history is, from this quite widespread perspective, a story of uninterrupted technological, economic, and moral progress. At least since the Jacksonians advanced the doctrine of Manifest Destiny, Americans have taken comfort in the belief that our position in the world and in history is preordained. An indispensable part of this confidence is the belief that we as a nation are getting not only stronger, but also better: wiser, nobler, more beneficent, and more just. Our institutions and customs are superior, not only because they contain timeless principles and reflect unshakable truths, but also because they possess the capacity to adapt and improve. Just as the cotton gin replaced manual cleaning of the raw crop, so, too, American ingenuity eventually developed superior replacements for slavery, sharecropping and Jim Crow segregation. The civil rights movement – once a marginal and suspect political radicalism – has been neatly woven into this tale of inexorable national progress. Now racial justice is among the most touted achievements of American society. Like assembly line production, the tungsten filament, and jazz, it is a source of nationalist pride and a valuable international export; it builds morale at home and helps in the symbolic balance of trade abroad.

Obviously, there's a lot to like here. Antiracist causes acquire authority as a result of their conscription into the vanguard of nationalistic pride and enjoy legitimacy as a result of their induction into the popular cult of psychotherapy. But along with these advantages come the characteristic drawbacks of patriotic nationalism and pop psychology: on the one hand, jingoism and fanaticism; on the other hand, sentimentalism and magical thinking. Like patriotic movements generally, antiracism now attracts yahoos and opportunists: "It's a Black Thing; you wouldn't understand" is as insipid and dangerous a slogan as "My country right or wrong." Just as hack politicians wrap themselves in the flag, they now also seek cover under the mantle of racial justice.

And even politicians of the highest refinement exploit the civil rights progress story in slightly disquieting ways. Barack Obama's first campaign for the presidency unfailingly evoked the civil rights story; from the campaign slogan of "Hope" to Obama's messianic cadence and phrasing, the clear message was that the election of a black president would be a profound moment in – if not the culmination of – the civil rights struggle and hence, vindication for both those who fought for racial justice and for those who defended the nation against the charge of racism. It's little wonder that President Obama could not live up to the expectations created by candidate Obama. Those expectations were not only unrealistic, but contradictory. On the one hand, they fulfilled the promise of the civil rights movement and enacted the ultimate civil rights agenda; on the other hand, to establish by his very presence that the nation had *already* achieved racial justice (and hence, further reform was unnecessary).

The mainstream of American politics is defined by a deep faith in the progress story. Only extremists and cranks resist or dispute it: Reactionaries insist the nation has been in a long, steady decline since some halcyon age – typically sometime before the New Deal – and improvement lies not in progress, but in a retreat whereas radicals think the nation is fundamentally corrupt and hence incapable of progress – improvement can come only from crisis, rupture, and wholesale reconstruction. But everyone else, liberals and conservatives alike, believe in progress: We are getting better – wealthier, more powerful, more productive, more free, more just. Our enemies – whether left or right – are the enemies of progress; they can do damage in the short term, but they cannot win because they are fighting the future. On the right, progress is globalization, free markets, the march of capitalism and democracy; the past is sclerotic big government, the cabal of organized labor, the tepid socialism of Old Europe. For the left, the future is cosmopolitanism, diversity, tolerance, the march of human rights, the democratization of the media, the death of men; the past is bloated and rapacious corporations, reactionary religious zealots, and the flaccid old boys' club.

## Progress versus Improvement

Civil rights are a comfortable part of the American progress story; we now are a better nation than the America of slavery or of Jim Crow, better than the America that won the West, better even than the nation that won World War II. It is a remarkable tale: A society built with captured labor slaves and based on the corrupt morality required to justify the monstrous theft, now models respect for human dignity and equality for much of the world. This is moral progress and we are stewards of this accomplishment and of the momentum that comes with it. The arc of the moral universe is long, but it bends toward justice.

In this essay, I will question this narrative of moral progress. But I won't deny the existence and importance of discrete *improvements*. We benefit from countless improvements, as many in the domains of civil rights and social justice as in any other area. But just as the plural form of anecdote is not data, the plural form of improvement is not progress. Technology offers a good example. No one would deny that technology has resulted in innumerable discrete improvements; the computer I use to compose this essay is superior in every way to the electric roller-ball typewriter and bottle of White-Out I used in college; the iPhone 5 is a stunning improvement over the five-pound brick portable phone carried by flashy Wall Street analysts in the 1980s. Whether or not these impressive gadgets add up to progress is a more complicated question. Is being in touch 24/7 through email, text messaging, and Twitter better than being able to take the rotary-dial phone off the hook, ignore the doorbell, and pretend you were in the bathroom? Are 100 blogs a day on Gawker, Huff Po, and the Drudge Report superior to five or so thoughtful essays a week in the *Saturday Evening Post*?

Similarly, we can point to many discrete improvements in social justice since the 1950s. And it is very tempting to say these improvements are evidence of progress – especially when you are among the people who benefited most from them, as I am. But there is the risk of winner's history: the people lucky enough to weigh in on these questions are almost exclusively the beneficiaries of the social changes of the last fifty years. There is no doubt that the late-twentieth century saw a vast improvement on the whole for people like me – well-educated blacks poised to take advantage of new opportunities in a more racially open society. But daily life for blacks without such advantages – the isolated residents of poor inner cities – is in many ways worse than during the days of Jim Crow segregation. To be sure, race relations are significantly improved with respect to overt racism, conscious racial attitudes, and interactions between white and non-white racial groups of similar class background. But the relations between poor minorities and police, employers, and wealthier people of any race are arguably quite a bit worse, if incarceration rates or unemployment are taken as reliable measures. And the coexistence of improvements for some and worsening fortunes for others raises the disturbing possibility that the former were achieved at the expense of the latter – that the civil rights story is not one of progress, but instead one of trade offs and tragic compromises. This is what I take to be Derrick Bell's main point in his series of critical reactions to *Brown v. Board of Education* and school integration: The undeniable improvements attributable to integration came at the expense of potential improvements that might have reached a greater number of black students.[4]

Similarly, it's hard not to wonder whether we have come so far from the era of the sharecropper when visiting the nation's so-called bread baskets – the vast, corporatized agricultural regions of central California, for instance – where hundreds of men and women labor in the summer heat, bent over harvesting the crops that will make their way into plastic clam shells and cellophane wrap and onto the refrigerated shelves of American supermarkets. Now consider that as these people labor away for starvation wages to bring cheap food to American tables, we now, for the first time in human history, face a nutritional public-health crisis borne, not of scarcity, but of wretched excess.

Certainly there are important differences between slavery and sharecropping on the one hand and the situation of migrant farmworkers today on the other hand – most notably that slaves were forcibly brought to the sites of their toil by sharecroppers and forced to remain there whereas migrant farmworkers typically come voluntarily and often at great risk. Still, one might look at the status distinctions between citizen and noncitizen, or between documented and "illegal" immigrant, as justifications for exploitation and see our current agricultural practices as moral affronts, if not civil rights abuses. So whether, on the whole, the changes of the previous fifty years represent progress – in terms of social justice or in terms of social equality – or instead a reshuffling of winners and losers, is less certain.

## Progress and Law

These are large questions, and I can only pose them. The narrower question is what the idea of progress means for the law. It is very hard to understand our current civil rights law and the thinking that underlies arguments in the civil rights tradition without reference to progress. Civil rights rhetoric and legal argument is saturated with the romance of progress – it determines what we can see as a question of social justice and what is invisible to us, and it influences the direction that reform will take. And for those that not so long ago would have been called liberals, progress has become such an article of faith that we've taken it as a moniker: we're Progressives.

The idea of progress has two major influences on legal thought. Most obviously, it suggests that what we have today is better than what we had in the past – not just different or a mixed bag: better in some ways and worse in others. This can have many implications. At the most programmatic level, it might suggest that desegregation is better than Jim Crow, that voluntary desegregation is better than court-imposed busing, and that the Harvard Plan for affirmative action is better than a quota. At a more institutionally specific level, it might suggest that "we've learned" that the regulatory state is subject to capture or that private enforcement of individual entitlements is better than "social engineering" in the public interest.

Another implication – not necessary, but very tempting – of the progress idea is a sort of stages-of-development notion: Progress is inevitable and progress in one area will take a similar form to progress in another area. If the Romans developed large cities only after they developed aqueducts, then we can't expect another civilization to develop large cities without first developing aqueducts, and the development of aqueducts suggests that large cities can't be far behind. If blacks gain the franchise and later integrated education, then it is "only a matter of time" after granting the franchise to women that we will abolish all-boys and all-girls schools; if blacks gain fuller equality and dignity through interracial marriage, it follows that same-sex marriage is the necessary step on the way to equality for gays and lesbians. Again, my point here is not to oppose any of these specific policy reforms – in fact I've deliberately chosen reforms I support and that I suspect others support in order to focus attention on the idea of progress rather than the wisdom of the discrete reforms – it is only to question the progress idea and, incidentally, the justification that the reforms carry the mandate of destiny.

The movement from slavery through sharecropping and Jim Crow segregation, to civil rights legislation, affirmative action, and diversity looks like moral and intellectual progress. It is certainly a profound improvement in many respects. But the idea of progress demands more than discrete improvements; it demands improvements that are parts of a larger whole, improvements that are the consequences of an inevitable growth or evolution – an inexorable, if perhaps uneven, process of societal or human betterment. The idea of progress allows discrete improvements to serve as evidence of general improvement and gives us confidence that changes in the social body are, on the whole, positive. It also allows the partisans of progress to defend their preferred political positions in the seemingly neutral and uncontroversial terms of an inevitable historical momentum – a momentum that one can either accept and participate in or resist and be swept away by – as opposed to defending them in terms of values, beliefs, and distributive preferences. The progress meme has certain benefits as a matter of rhetoric, but it also presents dangers – particularity when its partisans do not see it as mere rhetoric, but instead actually believe their own press releases. If one favors a specific series of reforms *because* they are progress, it becomes hard to debate whether or not they are good in substantive terms – it's not progress because it is good; rather, it is good because it is progress.

The dangers inherent in the progress notion are clear if one considers some of its earlier, discredited variations in the age of exploration or the Industrial Revolution. Colonial adventures, the genocide or enslavement of "savage" peoples, and the rape of the natural environment were all progress in the not-so-distant past.

But these are not my main themes. Instead, I wish to examine the effect of the progress meme on law and in particular, on civil rights law. I will offer two examples of how the progress meme has shaped the law: (1) in the shift from quotas and the goal of integration to holistic individualized evaluation, and (2) the goal of "diversity" in affirmative action and in the expansion of antidiscrimination law from the short list of forbidden grounds listed in the Civil Rights Act of 1964 to a longer and ever-growing list today. My argument in both instances is that because civil rights law is tightly bound to the Whiggish idea of progress, it is too easy to take the wisdom of developments in the law for granted and to assume that subsequent reform must involve more of the same.

### *From Quotas to Diversity: Progress?*

As the Supreme Court considers, for the third time in less than forty years, whether or not affirmative action in university admissions violates the Constitutional guarantee of equal protection, a few things are settled and widely agreed on. Any acceptable form of affirmative action cannot involve a quota or separate admission track for minority students. Each candidate for admission has a right to be evaluated as an individual. It may (or may not) be permissible to consider the race of an applicant as a part of a holistic evaluation of the candidate as an individual, but race must not confer any automatic or formulaic preference and there can be no fixed numerical goals of minority admissions.

Left, right, and center agree on the superiority of individualized review over quotas; almost no one defends quotas in any form – even the staunchest defenders of race consciousness reject quotas as embarrassingly crude – the policy equivalent of H. Rap Brown denouncing "whitey." Diversity, by contrast, reflects the sophisticated and nuanced racial politics of Barack Obama or Harold Ford. The evolution of affirmative action from quotas to diversity reflects progress in race relations and racial policy.

But does it? To be sure, quotas had their drawbacks, which are well known and regularly rehearsed. But diversity and holistic evaluation eliminated few of those drawbacks – most they simply disguised. And diversity and holistic evaluation have come with their own drawbacks. Holistic evaluation is a less-effective way of integrating selective universities than quotas. It is also more cumbersome and expensive – a serious limitation for larger public universities with proportionally smaller admissions budgets. Diversity has shifted focus away from the reparative justice and social equality goals of affirmative action in favor of a limited and at times dubious pedagogical rationale. Worst of all, diversity has led applicants to tailor their self-presentation to fit a remarkably standard diversity profile. And to some extent, this has changed the self-image of minority students and racial politics on college campuses, often to the detriment of classic integrationist values.

In 1973, Alan Bakke applied and was denied admission to the University of California at Davis medical school. Bakke discovered that racial minorities with lower grades and test scores than his were admitted under an affirmative action program that essentially established separate admission tracks for different racial groups. Bakke sued the university, asserting that his Fourteenth Amendment rights to equal protection had been violated. Bakke prevailed.

Justice Powell, the author of what is widely considered to be the controlling opinion (the Court splintered 4–1–4 and Powell cast the deciding vote), did not find that all affirmative action was unconstitutional. Instead, he found that numerical racial quotas could never be sufficiently narrowly tailored to survive strict scrutiny under the equal protection and that the governmental purpose of remedying past discrimination was sufficiently compelling to survive strict scrutiny only if the university endeavored to rectify and could identify specific instances of institutional discrimination, but not to remedy societal discrimination in general.

But the Powell opinion left one door tantalizingly ajar: A non-quota based affirmative action plan served a compelling interest (and thereby could overcome strict scrutiny) if it was designed to promote "diversity." Hence, colleges and universities could continue to consider the race of applicants as a factor in admissions provided that their purpose was not to remedy societal discrimination, but rather, to attain a diverse student body.

Shortly after *Bakke*, many questioned Justice Powell's sweeping rejection of quotas in favor of the holistic "Harvard Plan." Detractors of the Powell approach pointed out that the Harvard Plan was fine and well for very elite schools with small entering classes and large admissions offices, but cumbersome and costly for universities with large entering classes and limited staff. And how was an individual applicant disfavored because of his or her race less injured because the university buried the racial consideration in a holistic evaluation? Powell's approach emphasized form and aesthetics over substance. Powell constitutionalized an expensive Ivy League refinement that did little to ameliorate the real costs of affirmative action. Like a manicured lawn in front of the dorm or tea and cucumber sandwiches in the Dean's study, the Harvard Plan was a superficial luxury that large public universities could not afford. But it didn't take long for proponents of affirmative action – faced with the alternative of risking the continued viability of affirmative action on the outcome of another round of constitutional litigation – to embrace the *Bakke* diversity rationale like a life preserver.

Today, quotas are now almost universally described as a crude and brutish approach to affirmative action. The rejection of quotas is emblematic of progress, a needed refinement in the use of race that guarantees individual justice and eliminates the risk of a slide into an undignified spoils system in which competing groups squabble over their share of the pie. Parroting Powell in *Bakke* and O'Connor in *Grutter* to a fault, all selective universities boast of their holistic and comprehensive review of applicants, in which race is one of many factors considered in order to get a picture of each individual as a complete person. No school admits that it considers, even informally, the numerical representation of any racial group. We know better than that now, because we *are* better than that now.

### *Diversity and Progress*

Before *Bakke*, diversity was one of many reasons selective universities employed affirmative action. For instance, in 1969, a publication of the Stanford Medical School cited the need to remedy societal discrimination (now an unacceptable reason under *Bakke*): "the Medical College Admission Test . . . may be inaccurate in indicating the basic ability and motivation of a minority student who has been subjected to social . . . barriers." The chairman of the medical school's minority search committee reported that the school sought to increase minority enrollment in order to better serve underserved minority communities (also unacceptable under *Bakke*): "[T]he health problems of the ghetto have become serious. We know from past experience that the [typical white] medical student has failed to meet the challenge . . . [we need minority enrollment] to increase the number of black and brown physicians, not to integrate Stanford with the most qualified minority students in the country." After *Bakke*, selective colleges and universities spoke only of "diversity" when defending affirmative action.

The diversity rationale is benign when understood as one of many possible reasons a university might care about the racial composition of its student body. But it is dangerous when enshrined as the only or primary reason race is significant. The diversity rationale embraced in the Powell opinion silently analogized racial diversity to ethnic diversity: both the Powell opinion and the amici curiae briefs submitted by Columbia, Harvard, Stanford, and the University of Pennsylvania on which Powell relied used the term "racial" and "ethnic" almost interchangeably. The Powell opinion silently institutionalized an ethnicity model of race that, by its very nature, emphasizes the innocent "fact" of cultural difference over the politically imposed wrongs of status hierarchy. In the ethnicity paradigm, the position of blacks is analogous to that of, say, some Italian-Americans – both have distinctive cultural backgrounds and therefore, may contribute a unique perspective to the university environment. What is excluded by this paradigm is any acknowledgment that a very recent history of state-sponsored and institutional subordination distinguishes the two groups. Here the *cultural* identity of racial minority groups is emphasized at the expense of the history of racism.

*Bakke*'s codification of the diversity rationale pushed institutions that wished to engage in affirmative action *and* minority groups themselves to *emphasize* cultural difference. Only by highlighting the stark differences in perspectives, norms, and experiences marked by race could universities justify affirmative action post-*Bakke*. Despite judicial and university disclaimers, this rationale effectively requires universities to incorporate a substantive theory of racial difference into their admission processes – the post-*Bakke* universities and their minority applicants needed not only to assert that racial minorities would bring distinctive ideas and perspectives to the seminar table, they also needed at least a sketchy working account of the distinctive perspectives that racial minorities would bring. And a more subtle and much more pernicious implication hovered over post-*Bakke* university life: *only* by highlighting their own distinctiveness could minority students justify their presence in the universities that had admitted or might admit them.

Applicants to selective universities were not slow to figure out what was expected of them. As admissions literature and get-into-college handbooks harped on the importance of diversity, pretenders to the entering classes made sure to put their most diverse foot forward in the application process. But was all of this focus on diversity making the applicants more and more *alike*? Admissions officers noticed a minor literary genre of "cooking smells" essays, in which the applicant waxed nostalgic about the evocative aroma of a distant relative's ethnic cuisine. Students of every color and hue described their diverse backgrounds and experiences. The bluntly titled *How to Get into Harvard Law School* offered examples of the personal statements of successful applicants; here are some characteristic excerpts:

> "My primary motivation for receiving a law degree surfaces from my personal experiences with the struggles of the Latin American immigrant . . . "
>
> "My experience with other cultures gives me sensitivity to the voices of today's international America."
>
> "[W]hen I supported funding for the Carolina Gay and Lesbian Association . . . "
>
> "My curiosity about foreign cultures . . . began early."
>
> "As the child of Paraguayan immigrants, I too occupy a borderland."

> "I studied American Sign Language and was introduced to Deaf culture . . . "
>
> "By the time I entered college, I had mastered the language of three communities: the Paraguyan Spanish spoken by my mother at home; the profanity-laden slang of our poor, all-Black Washington D.C. neighborhood; and the textbook English enforced in the private schools I attended . . . "
>
> "I am a fourth generation Mexican-American with Cajun ancestry . . . "
>
> "[A]s an expatriate I developed a keen awareness of cultural diversity by actually being a part of different cultures"
>
> "I want to get involved with the law to preserve a state wealthy with culture and diversity."
>
> "If accepted, I will bring to Harvard Law School a very rich and diverse background"[5]

The diversity rationale requires universities and their students to maintain a precarious balance. They must insist on the salience of racial difference – if race is only skin deep, it's implausible that it will affect the educational experience. But some of the effects of racial difference are bad. Minorities *suffer* as a result of racism – they internalize negative stereotypes as a result of widespread bigotry and they adopt dysfunctional behavior patterns as a result of the poverty and isolation of many minority communities. What we might call "black culture" has to include these negative features as well as the many virtues multiculturalists are correct to extol. Education should correct and counteract the unfortunate legacies of racial injustice – not reinforce and encourage them. Liberal multiculturalists get tongue tied when they have to confront this. When condemning bigotry, they want to insist on the deleterious effects of racism, but when describing the "culture" of the victims of the racism, they deny that it has, in fact, had any deleterious effects. What looks like paranoia (understandable after years of deliberate persecution), they insist, is really an "alternative perspective"; what looks like belligerence (again, a predictable response to sustained assault on one's dignity) is, in fact, a culturally unique mode of interaction.

The results are often tragicomic. Consider for instance, a book entitled *Black Children: Their Roots, Culture and Learning Styles* that admonishes educators to adapt to, rather than correct, the following allegedly black cultural traits:

> Afro-American people tend to prefer inferential reasoning to deductive or inductive reasoning . . .
>
> Afro-American people tend to approximate space, numbers, and time rather than stick to accuracy.
>
> Afro-American people in general tend not to be "word" dependent. They tend [instead?] to be very proficient in nonverbal communications.
>
> Black people think in terms of approximation of time, rather than punctuality. An "in house" expression is "C.P.T." – meaning "Colored People's Time"! . . . Meetings that begin on C.P. Time usually begin about twenty minutes after the appointed time.[6]

Is it bigoted or insensitive to point out that these traits are not distinctive to *black* children, but rather are characteristic of children generally? Much of the point of primary education, after all, is to force little homo sapiens – who, if left to their own devices, would certainly choose to do something else – to learn the skills of inductive and deductive reasoning, to internalize the disciplines of mathematical accuracy and punctuality, and to supplement the communication common to all mammals with the "word dependent" language that is unique to humans. One can only hope that those charged with educating minority children reject the advice of this book and work to rid black children of the burden of these characteristics (and of the stereotype that they are distinctively black) before graduation.

Diversity rhetoric is an admirable attempt to make a virtue of racial difference. In so doing, it has offered minority students a source of pride and self-esteem and has made all students rethink reflexive prejudices. But the resulting psychological investment in racial difference can be an impediment to the educational process. One of the practical virtues of an elite education is a subtle but profound form of socialization. For the average occidental Brahmin, this process of socialization begins at home with the nanny and continues at Choate, Exeter, or Andover. If one is not to the manner born, four years at Princeton might be just long enough to pick up some of the subtleties of ruling-class style. Like it or not, this socialization is as valuable a credential as any Ivy League degree. Of course, socialization is a two-way street: It's possible that the mannerisms of the elite will acquire a multicultural accent over time. But it's unrealistic to think that any such exchange of cultural affect will be strictly "equal." There are people who have jobs to offer and people who want those jobs, people who are members of the co-op and those who want to move in – each may influence the other, but the relationship between them will not always be that of peers. The diversity idea reveals a touching naiveté about the world outside academia and a poignant irony as well: diversity emphasizes the value of cultural distinctiveness, yet many of the benefits of elite education flow from what it's fair to call cultural assimilation.

## Diversity Uber Alles

Twenty-five years after *Bakke*, the Supreme Court reaffixed its by then faded imprimatur to "diversity" and only "diversity" in *Grutter v. Bollinger*. *Grutter* upheld the University of Michigan Law School's race-conscious admissions policy – a policy that followed the blueprint drawn by Justice Powell in *Bakke*. The Law School's admissions policy avoided the use of quotas, but did consider race as one factor among others for the purpose of achieving "diversity" in its student body.

Writing for the majority, Justice O'Connor endorsed Powell's opinion in *Bakke* and upheld the Law School's admissions policy. The majority opinion asserts that "Powell approved the university's use of race to further only one interest: 'the attainment of a diverse student body.'" And the opinion emphasizes that "Powell rejected an interest in 'increasing the number of physicians who will practice in communities currently underserved.'" *Grutter* also endorses *Bakke*'s rejection of an interest in "reducing the historic deficit of traditionally disfavored minorities" (described as impermissible "racial balancing") and its rejection of an interest in remedying "societal discrimination."

Yet, as if the majority were aware that "diversity" alone cannot justify race-conscious affirmative action, the *Grutter* opinion notes in passing that "*By virtue of our Nation's Struggle with racial inequality*, [minority] students are both likely to have experiences of particular importance to the Law School's mission, *and less likely to be admitted in meaningful numbers on criteria that ignore those experiences*" (emphases added). This single sentence all-too-subtly acknowledges a point that the diversity rationale obscures: racial minorities are likely to have suffered from a distinctive type disadvantage, which often will depress their grades and performance on standardized tests. This remedial rationale, based on a frank acknowledgment of the persistence of racism, needs not suggest that minority students must exhibit their racial difference in recognizable form in order merit admission. This alternative rationale – less than one sentence buried in thirty-two pages extolling the virtues of diversity and only diversity – offers a compelling rationale for affirmative action, one which offers a more dignified portal of entry to minority students than diversity alone and one that undoubtedly comes closer to accurately describing the sincere motivations of selective universities and professional schools than does diversity alone. Yet the prospects of anyone openly acknowledging this shadow rationale are dim indeed; because the *Bakke* and *Grutter* courts rejected the goal of remedying "societal discrimination," to do so would invite a lawsuit.

Yet, of course, the lawsuits came even though uninvited and today, as the Court considers the constitutionality of affirmative action again, the delicate compromise struck in *Bakke* and *Grutter* looks set to collapse under its own weight. After decades of dissimulation on all sides, lawyers for the University of Texas are faced with the daunting task of defending affirmative action without referring to many of the best reasons for the policy. John Hart Ely noted almost forty years ago that equal protection analysis is designed to make it hard to offer pretextual or incomplete justifications: a policy is likely to be "narrowly tailored" to serve the interests that actually inspired it, but not to justifications cooked up in response to litigation.

So as the University of Texas sought to defend its affirmative action policy, it focused, as *Bakke* and *Grutter* require, on the need for a critical mass of minority students to advance the pedagogical virtues of diversity. At the same time, the university insisted – also as *Bakke* and *Grutter* require – that it evaluates each application as an individual and does not employ any form of racial quota. This led the skeptical Justices to ask what exactly then, the university meant by a "critical mass." The university wisely avoided giving a precise answer, as any precise answer would look dangerously like an unconstitutional quota. But in the absence of a precise answer, it is hard for the university to defend affirmative action as narrowly tailored to serve a compelling governmental interest: after all, how can a policy be tailored to fit a goal that is itself vaguely defined? As *Slate's* legal affairs editor Emily Bazelon put it, "UT is between a quota and a hard place."

So this is progress. Universities should respect individual rights – not look to the numbers. The Supreme Court is keeping the universities honest. We will continue to refine university admissions – perhaps to the point of banning the consideration of race altogether – in service of the greater good of individual rights. But there is another way to look at this. Since the New Deal and the rise of the professional, scientifically driven administrative state, large institutions have set goals and measured performance by looking to statistics. Administration by the numbers has become the norm in fields as diverse as environmental regulation, occupational safety, the control of automobile traffic, the administration of health care, and the management of the economy. In every case, there are people who justifiably complain that a statistically driven approach fails to capture the complexities of the individual case. That is why the word "bureaucracy" has become a general term of opprobrium and why the prestige of the federal courts – the charismatic guardians of individual rights – is dramatically higher than that of the various federal agencies charged with enforcing the mundane comprehensive regulations that make modern civilization possible. But popularity contest aside, there is no other way of managing life in a large and complex society; like it or not, administration by the numbers – disparaged as "quotas" whenever it is under attack – works. Anyone who doubts this need only compare the air and water quality of the 1960s to that of today, after more than forty years of comprehensive environmental regulation enforced largely through the application of numerical goals. Universities – particularly public universities charged with serving large and diverse populations – used numerical goals in crafting their admissions policies because it was the most sensible way to proceed. One can argue that the numbers employed were inappropriate or that the quotas were too rigidly adhered to, but the notion that a quota is somehow inherently offensive is a direct attack on the defining methodology of the administrative state. To deny a large institution the use of numerical methods is to deny it the power to act effectively at all. Therefore, it is no surprise that a numerical approach has reappeared, despite the Court's impractical admonishments, in the guise of what was supposed to be its opposite: "diversity."

The interventions of the Supreme Court in *Bakke* and *Grutter* preempted an honest conversation about the merits of affirmative action in colleges and universities: precisely the institutions we as a society rely on to evaluate difficult policy questions. The Supreme Court ruled out many sensible approaches to affirmative action and many compelling arguments for it. As a result, the public has never had the benefit of a complete and rigorous consideration of affirmative action. Instead, we have come to accept the casually considered judgments of a few judges and their law clerks and limited our evaluations to their preferred policies and rationales. Part of the reason for this is undeserved charisma of the Supreme Court, but I would suggest much of the reason is a vague but powerful sense that the development of civil rights in this area is a symptom of progress. The movement from a remedial rationale and quotas to the diversity rationale and the Harvard Plan is now widely seen – even by supporters of affirmative action – as the natural evolution of university admissions policy and equality jurisprudence, when, in fact, this development is the result of controversial decisions involving deeply problematic compromises and a good deal of dishonesty on all sides.

Like the stages of grief, opposition to the *Bakke* opinion among affirmative action supporters gave way to bargaining, rationalization, resignation, acceptance, and finally, unqualified embrace. Those of us who believe that race consciousness is necessary might have been more effective in presenting the most compelling principles and intuitions underlying our commitment to racial awareness (rooted in a recognition of historical and ongoing subordination based primarily on atavistic prejudice – not cultural difference) when freed from the exclusive and obligatory mantras of "diversity." Now, of course, the ship has sailed and for better or for worse, the fate of race-conscious affirmative action rests in the less-than seaworthy vessel of diversity. The journey from quotas to diversity seems destined to end in the repudiation of affirmative action. A world-weary European might greet this with a resigned, "C'est la vie." For an American, "that's Progress."

### *Antidiscrimination Law: From Social Justice to Individual Entitlement*

Another characteristic of civil rights progress is an assumption that civil rights protections are moral entitlements that should be progressively extended to an ever-growing number of arguably vulnerable groups. If antidiscrimination laws are sensible ways to protect racial minorities and women from hostility and unfair treatment in employment markets, it seems to follow that other groups that suffer from social isolation, constrained upward mobility, or unflattering stereotypes are entitled to similar – indeed, almost identical – protections. The regular expansion of civil rights protections reflects a growing awareness of social injustices and an ever stronger resolve to confront them. In other words, progress.

This idea transforms what should be a detailed policy analysis specific to the unique circumstances of each group into a simple copy and paste: copy what we've done for one group and paste it into a law for the next one.

In 1967, roughly half of all private job openings were explicitly closed to applicants over the age of fifty-five; one-fourth of jobs were limited to those forty-five or younger. Older people were disproportionately unemployed and stayed jobless longer than younger people. Spurred to action by the pathetic image of a jobless older person reduced to eating pet food in his cold-water flat, Congress passed the Age Discrimination in Employment Act of 1967 or ADEA. Naturally, the ADEA was modeled on the Civil Rights Act of 1964 passed three years earlier, which prohibited discrimination on the basis of race, color, national origin, religion, and sex. Unlike the 1964 Act, the ADEA sailed through a Congress made up overwhelmingly of middle-aged and older people, buoyed by a broad consensus that discrimination on the basis of age was cruel, inefficient, and unjust: "[N]obody defends such discrimination, and – it ought to be stopped" declared a labor union representative in his testimony before Congress.

As expected, employers quickly took down the "Elderly Need Not Apply" signs after the ADEA was enacted. But unemployment among the elderly actually *increased* in the ten years after the ADEA was passed.[7] Was the reason lack of enforcement? Did employees not know their rights under the ADEA? To the contrary, there was a "backlog" of age discrimination lawsuits that had grown every year since the ADEA was passed. The problem wasn't enforcement; it was the design of the ADEA. Age discrimination was different than discrimination based on race, sex, and religion. It was oddly lopsided: older people suffered discrimination in hiring, but once hired, they fared as well or better than younger workers. The Department of Labor's Commissioner on Aging found that older employees were "frequently preferred over the younger" for promotions and received favorable treatment on the job.[8] That's still true today: "If you are old and have a job, you are less likely . . . to be fired," said Alicia Munnell of the Center for Retirement Research at Boston College in 2009.[9] There was really no need for a civil rights law to protect older *workers* – it was older *applicants* for jobs who needed protection. This was still true more than forty years after the ADEA was passed; in the recession of 2009, older people were disproportionately laid off and were out of work for an average of 22.2 weeks; by contrast, younger people were unemployed an average of 16.2 weeks.[10]

The ADEA didn't do much for job *applicants* because an unemployed person is unlikely to sue for a job he didn't get. An applicant has very little information about the hiring process, the decision makers, or the qualifications of other people vying for the same job; it's hard to know whether discrimination or legitimate factors made the difference. Moreover, litigation takes time – time that could be better spent continuing the job search. That's why only about 9 percent of all employment discrimination claims challenge hiring decisions.[11] By contrast, once hired, people become invested in their jobs and are much more likely to sue to keep them and to advance in them. Accordingly, almost 80 percent of all employment discrimination claims involve firing and denied promotions. Unsurprisingly, then, the ADEA encouraged current employees to sue over promotions and termination – where age discrimination wasn't much of a problem. The ADEA empowered older workers who, as a group, were already better off than younger employees, but did little to solve the problem of chronic unemployment among the elderly. In fact, because the law gave older people a new weapon to use against employers – a weapon that in practice they would use only once hired – the law probably *encouraged* employers to discriminate against older job applicants, thereby worsening the problem the law was designed to solve.

The civil rights solution didn't fit the problem of unemployment among older workers very well. Even when the ADEA was passed, it was well known that "age discrimination is . . . seldom a matter of blind or arbitrary prejudice which often exists for reasons of race, creed, color, national origin, or sex . . . [it] is a more subtle series of problems . . . a combination of institutional factors and stereotyped thinking."[12] But the civil rights approach focused only on stereotypes, neglecting the subtler institutional factors that are actually the biggest cause of the problem. Congress basically cribbed from the 1964 Civil Rights, extending the same civil rights protections to a new group: the elderly, as if age discrimination was caused by irrational bigotry against the aged and inaccurate stereotypes abut their qualifications. For instance, Secretary of Labor Willard Wirtz argued that age discrimination reflected outdated attitudes: "[A] failure on the part of employers to realize how technology and the life sciences have combined to increase the value of older people's work"[13] and William D. Bechill, Commissioner on Aging, insisted that "stereotyped attitudes about the ability of older people . . . play a major role in barring older workers from fair . . . consideration."[14]

Stereotypes about older people are a problem, but age discrimination is often driven by simple economics. Labor economists describe the typical career path in terms of a "life cycle." The typical employee needs training early in his or her career, becomes a seasoned and efficient worker in mid-career, and then slows down a bit near the end of his or her career. If wages and salary perfectly matched the productivity of each employee, most people would receive very low compensation early in their careers when they are still learning – in fact, in many cases, the costs of training might be greater than the contribution new employees make, suggesting an "apprenticeship" model where the new employee should work for very little. Then pay would rise very quickly after the employee became accomplished. Finally, pay would level off and eventually drop as the older employee slowed down and thoughts turned from work to a well-earned retirement filled with grandchildren and exotic travel.

But of course, this is not how compensation is usually set. Let's take legal practice, where, because partners are not employees covered under the ADEA, mandatory retirement has long been the norm. Starting salaries at the more prestigious law firms in large cities are, as I write, as high as $170,000 a year. With all due admiration for the graduates of our nation's law schools, I'm certain that no student fresh from law school or a clerkship can justify these salaries, especially when the costs of inevitable on-the-job practical training is deducted from the balance sheet. It's `well known that the firm loses money on first and sometimes even second-year attorneys and only begins to break even in the third year. Law partnerships remain lucrative because senior associates earn much more than they take out of the enterprise in salary: salaries rise with seniority, but nowhere near as rapidly as skill and productivity do. Of course, salaries almost *never* go down, so some senior partners continue to earn more even as their productivity levels off and even drops. In effect, the mid-career employees subsidize both the novices and the oldsters.

This type of arrangement involves an implicit bargain between employer and employee: the junior employee builds up a debt while being trained, which she pays off as she gains skill, eventually banking a surplus, which she will collect as she ages and her compensation exceeds her value to the firm. It's a humane and practical model based on a long-term relationship: Younger people receive a decent wage and avoid the indignities of apprenticeship and older workers enjoy compensation that reflects the esteem and respect they have earned throughout a long career. But the deferred compensation and cross subsidy inherent in this approach encourages three types of age discrimination. Two are necessary parts of the implicit bargain and therefore defensible if one accepts its terms; one is an indefensible breach of the implicit bargain by the employer.

First, an employer might refuse to hire older employees because they will enter the pay scale at just the point where compensation exceeds contribution, never having "banked" the surplus by working when their contributions exceeded compensation. If the firm pays according to seniority, or guarantees retirement benefits at a certain age, the newly hired older worker will arrive just in time to collect the subsidy. Even an employer that is happy to retain older workers hired in early or mid-career might not want to *hire* workers already near the end of their careers. Of course, such an employer could hire a senior employee for a wage he or she's worth – even if it is much less than other workers of the same seniority who have contributed to the firm during their most productive and less- well-compensated years. But this would require the firm to be explicit about the implicit cross subsidy involved in the salary structure. The genius of the employment life cycle is that the subsidies are implicit. Making them explicit would be bad for employee morale: mid-career employees would resent subsidizing older and younger employees, and older employees would lose esteem and respect. The ADEA may have made the problem worse, giving employers an *additional* reason to avoid hiring older people. After the ADEA, an older employee who didn't work out could sue for age discrimination when he was fired or passed over for promotion. An employer who wanted to hire a new employee on a trial basis would have to worry about a lawsuit if things didn't work out. It's not surprising that employers responded to the ADEA by eliminating conspicuous discriminatory policies while continuing to discriminate against older job applicants in less obvious ways.

Second, a smoothly and inexorably rising pay scale assumes mandatory retirement: at some point, the surplus banked in mid-career runs out. Before the ADEA was amended to prohibit the practice, most employers discriminated by imposing a mandatory retirement age. The ADEA originally covered only employees between forty and sixty-five,[15] but the upper limit was eliminated in 1986, effectively outlawing most mandatory retirement. Many older workers now had the option of staying on at high compensation long after having recouped any surplus they had contributed during mid-career. But employers adjusted to the new legal regime by replacing "lock-step" compensation based on seniority with bottom-line oriented compensation such as merit pay and low-base salaries supplemented with productivity bonuses. This shift ultimately affected more than compensation: It was part of a change in attitude; the demise of a more collaborative and genteel business relationship and the rise of a more beady-eyed, "eat what you kill" approach. As law professors Samuel Issacharoff and Erica Harris put it, "employees who currently have expectations of wages above marginal output, will appear to be an unaffordable luxury in highly competitive markets."[16] For example, an internal Wal-Mart memo that came to light in 2005 notes unapprovingly that "the cost of an associate with seven years of tenure is almost 55 percent more than an associate with one year of tenure, yet there is no difference in his or her productivity. Moreover, because we pay an associate more in salary and benefits as his or her tenure increases, we are pricing that associate out of the labor market, increasing the likelihood that he or she will stay with Wal-Mart."[17] The atmosphere that Brian Reid encountered at Google reflects this harder-edged employment relationship and the resulting contempt for employees even slightly "past their prime."

Third, an unscrupulous employer may breach the implicit bargain and fire a loyal employee just as he or she is about to recoup the surplus that built up during his or her most productive years: a nasty bait and switch. Ironically, the ADEA does not prevent employers from sacking older employees just before their pensions vest – provided they do so out of greed and not bias. When sixty–two-year-old Walter Biggins was fired just a few weeks before his pension benefits vested, he sued for age discrimination and won a jury trial verdict, which was sustained on appeal. But the Supreme Court held that Biggins hadn't suffered age discrimination. According to the Court, it is the "very essence of age discrimination for an older employee to be fired because the employer believes that productivity declines with old age . . . on the basis of inaccurate and stigmatizing stereotypes. . . ." But in Biggins' case "[t]he decision [was] not the result of an inaccurate and denigrating generalization about age, but . . . rather . . . an accurate judgment . . . that he indeed is 'close to vesting.'"[18] Using the civil rights framework, the Court presumed that age discrimination is primarily a problem of bias and stereotypes. Cheating an employee of his pension doesn't involve anti-elderly bias – just evenhanded greed. As a result, the Court held that age discrimination laws don't prohibit one of the most common tricks employers use to cheat older employees. In fact, the employer's conspicuous avarice was actually a *defense* to the age-discrimination claim: "inferring age discrimination . . . may be problematic in cases where other unsavory motives . . . [are] present," opined Justice O'Connor.

*Biggins* demonstrates how age-discrimination rights have gone badly wrong. But the Court didn't leave Walter Biggins without a remedy. Although his employer didn't discriminate on the basis of age, it did violate the federal Employee Retirement Insurance Security Act, which regulates employee pension plans. *Biggins* doesn't suggest that there's nothing wrong with cheating an employee of his nearly vested pension. Instead, it implies that much of what we call age discrimination may be better dealt with outside the civil rights framework.

Instead of reducing unemployment among the needy elderly, the ADEA benefited those older workers who already had jobs – the group that was already "frequently preferred over . . . younger" employees. The ADEA let employees over forty – and only employees over forty – sue when they were fired or passed over for promotion. Unlike every other civil rights law, the ADEA expressly rules out "reverse discrimination" lawsuits. This in and of itself isn't a reason to condemn the law – if discrimination *against the elderly* is the problem, perhaps it makes sense to limit the law's protection to older plaintiffs. But such an asymmetry does amplify a concern that a law designed to ensure fair treatment will become a boondoggle for a specific, politically connected group. We've all heard this concern voiced loud and long in the context of race-based affirmative action, which former

California Governor Pete Wilson famously condemned as a "racial spoils system." Ironically, the concern is much more valid – albeit less noticed – in the context of age-based civil rights. Although the ADEA is, strictly speaking, an antidiscrimination law and not an affirmative action law, because of its built in asymmetry – age discrimination is unlawful only when it disadvantages older people – one could argue that the law is, effectively, a form of affirmative action. And because older Americans *as a group* are not disadvantaged at all, the remedial purpose of these rights is more dubious than for race- or sex-based civil rights. In fact, people over the age of forty have a vastly disproportionate share of the nation's wealth and political influence and their fortunes were improving dramatically even as Congress continued to expand and strengthen age discrimination laws. Between 1970 and 1984, the median income of people over 65 rose by 35 percent as compared to less than 1 percent for people from 25–64,[19] yet Congress expanded the ADEA to prohibit mandatory retirement in 1986.

The ADEA looks even more like an age-based spoils system when one looks at its effect on retirement benefits. After the ADEA outlawed mandatory retirement, employers were faced with the prospect of having to retain older, overpaid employees long after they had recouped the deferred compensation earned in their more productive and less remunerated mid-career years. Many tried to buy their way out of the problem by offering older employees a "golden handshake" – a one-time cash payment on retirement. Already this was a huge windfall for older employees. The older life-cycle wage arrangement assumed mandatory retirement at a specific age; outlawing mandatory retirement essentially rewrote the deal in favor of older employees. The golden handshake is the amortized cash value of this imposed revision of the employment contract – a direct transfer of wealth from employers (and indirectly, younger employees) to older employees.

Employers typically targeted the golden handshake to employees who were young enough that they were likely to continue working for many years unless bribed to retire, and offered younger employees more than older employees. In other words, the employers discriminated on the basis of age. But this had nothing to do with animus or negative stereotypes – it was a straightforward reflection of the economics that led employers to offer golden handshakes in the first place. The employer was basically buying older employees out of what had become an unprofitable mandatory employment contract from the employer's perspective. The value of the buyout would depend on the expected length of the employees' tenure. Age was a pretty good proxy for expected length of tenure: Older employees would generally retire without inducement earlier than younger employees. The golden handshake had to be enough to allow the employee to live comfortably in retirement and that figure would be higher for younger people who would have to make it stretch over a longer period of time. Adjusting the size of the golden handshake by age made sense, both from a narrow economic perspective and from a more humane perspective.

The American Association of Retired Persons (AARP) had emerged as a powerful lobbyist in favor of expanded and strengthened ADEA provisions in 1986 when Congress revised the ADEA to outlaw mandatory retirement. It continued that role, lobbying Congress in the late 1980s to outlaw age-targeted retirement incentives. Their position was that targeted retirement incentives were age discrimination and therefore violated the ADEA per se. The AARP changed its tune when it realized that a strict prohibition of age discrimination would kill the goose that gave the golden handshakes altogether. Strict application of the ADEA's age discrimination rule would require employers to offer retirement inducements to everyone over the age of forty – or no one at all. As Professors Issacharoff and Harris explain, "no employer could afford to offer retirement inducements to its entire workforce. At this point the AARP did an about-face and began to lobby heavily for the preservation of [age-targeted retirement incentives] . . . so long as they were offered to everyone over a minimum age . . . When it came to benefiting older workers . . . violations of the equal treatment principle proved to be more than just acceptable – they were required."[20]

Issacharoff and Harris describe this and other lobbying for expanded age discrimination laws as "wealth-grabbing self interest" resulting in a "windfall to older workers." But it's important to add that only some older workers benefited, and some benefited much more than others. A common argument against mandatory retirement is that changes in society have made it an anachronism. Advances in public health have allowed people to stay healthy and productive well into what would once have been their golden years, and today many people are psychologically invested in their careers in a way that their parents were not. But in fact, the average age of voluntary retirement from the workforce has *declined* steadily and steeply since the mid-twentieth century, from about age sixty-eight in the early 1950s to age sixty-two in the late 1990s.[21] The abolition of mandatory retirement makes no difference to the many people who choose to retire early. The main exception to the trend toward earlier retirement is highly educated professionals and business managers. Because these careers are not physically demanding, people don't "burn out" as readily as in other jobs. And because performance in such careers can be hard to measure objectively, status and reputation play a large role.

Perhaps older professionals and managers retire later because they are more likely to be productive later in their careers. But productivity may just be harder to measure in the professions and upper management, allowing today's older employees to use their reputations to hang onto coveted positions when an earlier generation would have "passed the baton" to younger protégées. There is no doubt that rigid mandatory retirement deprived businesses and society of talented older employees. But it's easy to exaggerate this loss: after all, nothing *required* employers to have mandatory retirement and nothing prohibited talented older workers who faced mandatory retirement at one firm from working elsewhere. At its best, mandatory retirement was an orderly and humane way of ending the employment relationship on a high note – with a gold watch and party rather than with a bad performance evaluation and a pink slip. It allowed older workers to train and mentor younger replacements without the now-common fear of grooming one's own competition and it gave younger workers some assurance that eventually coveted high-level positions, department chairs, and client portfolios would be open to them.

The ADEA began its life as a modest intervention to correct a flaw in employment markets that locked many older people in unemployment. It failed to correct that flaw, which continues to injure older people looking for work today. Instead, the ADEA morphed into what Isaacharoff and Harris call "a benefits protection regulation for older workers . . . [mandating] open ended obligations to provide older workers lump sum buyouts [and other benefits] without giving any consideration to the economic rationale for these programs."

This has nothing to do with equality or justice for older people. If the real issue here was bias against the elderly or irrational stereotypes, we wouldn't find such ready and compelling economic justifications for so many of the practices the ADEA forbids. If the real issue was the integration of older people into the workforce or the alleviation of material disadvantage, the law would return to its original focus on the *jobless* elderly rather than locking in and increasing advantages for people who are already employed. If the real problem was that discrimination on the basis of age is somehow inherently demeaning or presumptively suspect, then the law would prohibit discrimination against the young as well as against the old rather than limit coverage to people over forty as the ADEA does. After all, unlike stereotypes about race, sex, or disability, which fall almost exclusively on specific maligned groups, every questionable stereotype about the aged is mirrored by a denigrating generalization about the young: If the elderly are "sluggish," youth are "reckless"; if older people are set in their ways, young people lack wisdom; if the aged are complacent, younger people are naïve and inexperienced.

Ironically, civil rights law includes this asymmetry in the context where it is least justified: Title VII prohibits so-called reverse discrimination as a matter of principle, even though there is no evidence of, say, widespread antiwhite or antimale bias. The rationale for prohibiting discrimination on the basis of race, sex, and religion doesn't apply to old age because older people are disproportionately wealthy and powerful and hence can and do take care of themselves quite well in the market and in politics. Fifth Circuit Judge and University of Chicago Law School Professor Richard Posner makes this point well:

> It is as if the vast majority of persons who established employment policies and who made employment decisions were black, federal legislation mandated huge transfer payments from whites to blacks, and blacks occupied most high political offices in the nation. It would be mad in those circumstances to think the nation needed a law that would protect blacks from discrimination in employment. Employers . . . who for the most part are not young themselves – are unlikely to harbor either serious misconceptions about the vocational capacities of the old . . . or a generalized antipathy toward old people.[22]

Today's age discrimination laws are not "mad"; they make perfect sense as interest-group politics. If age discrimination laws just benefited older people at the expense of the young, any inequity they caused would be short lived; after all, with luck we will all be old someday. But age discrimination laws benefit well-off older people – relatively wealthy professionals and business managers – much more than the poor – they are, in effect, a tax on industry levied for the benefit of the rich. That's Progress.

Conventional wisdom has it that a society marks and protects its most cherished values with legal rights. Expanded civil rights are therefore evidence of an expanded commitment to individual welfare and a more generous conception of human needs. That's the role civil rights play in the American story today – an important supporting role in a dramatic myth in which technological advancement and military dominance serve moral progress. But there is an alternative story that is at least as plausible. In this counter narrative, rights are not how we mark our most important commitment, but rather, where a society mothballs ideals that it cannot or will not fulfill. Rights make a show of commitment and seem to promise prompt response and individual control. This mollifies those committed to the ideal and offers a measure of real change for those with the time, sophistication, and resources to seek individual vindication. But rights also let a society avoid a comprehensive policy response that would change the routine of large organizations that control much of social and economic life. Rights – focused on individual cases and privately enforced – can only affect the day-to-day practices of institutions indirectly, by creating incentives for litigation avoidance policies. This mode of enforcement offers no way of determining whether the resulting incentives appropriately balance conflicting interests and no way of ensuring that enforcement resources go where they are most needed. This results in spotty and often perverse enforcement. From this perspective, the rise and expansion of rights is a façade that distracts us from noticing that the more effective and comprehensive policy solutions available to the administrative state have been withheld. As compared to no enforcement at all, private enforcement through rights is an improvement. But as compared to the potential alternatives, rights may not be progress – the one and only way forward – but instead, a questionable trade-off.

If we could get past the idea that rights are the handmaidens of Progress, we might at least be able to make a few discrete improvements. Suppose we limited individual entitlements to cases involving specific evidence of discriminatory intent, and turned over the problems of systemic inequality and bias to comprehensive administrative regulation? Today, private civil rights all too often reward the undeserving, punish the hapless, and leave the truly culpable undeterred. An administrative agency would look at discrimination as a social problem and identify the best means of correcting it. Regulation could improve on the haphazard incentives of civil rights litigation, penalizing violation of the law and rewarding compliance. For instance, an Equal Employment Opportunity Commission (EEOC) with enforcement power could determine whether or not an employer discriminated, identify any offending practices, and issue a cease-and-desist order (similar to a court's injunction) and impose fines for willful noncompliance (similar to a court's award of punitive damages).

This isn't a new idea: The sponsors of the Civil Rights Act of 1964 proposed such an administrative approach, modeled on the National Labor Relations Board. Private enforcement through lawsuits was, for many, a second-best approach. Civil rights leaders worried that private enforcement was a way to weaken the new law, because "many of those discriminated against would be poor and legally unsophisticated."[23] As it's turned out, private enforcement has not led to too little enforcement, as liberal civil rights groups feared, nor has it led to too much, as many conservative accounts would suggest. Instead, it has given us the worst of both: many serious offenses go undetected and uncorrected whereas minor, innocent, and ambiguous transgressions often receive inordinate attention; many people with strong claims involving widespread injustices do not seek relief or can't prove their cases while people with weak or dubious claims can extract undeserved settlements from risk-averse businesses. Worst of all, individual civil rights claims are less and less likely to correct the nation's worst injustices.

State and federal agencies charged with setting guidelines for civil rights enforcement, such as the EEOC, now have decades' worth of experience and information about the nature of inequality. Employers with more than 100 employees are currently required to submit EEO-1 reports that detail the race, national origin, and gender composition of their workforces. Administrative agencies could use this information to develop a set of antidiscrimination goals and identify and eliminate impediments to equal opportunity.

Unlike individual plaintiffs suing in the adversarial legal system, administrative agencies could work with businesses to develop reforms that get results without undermining productivity. The current civil rights model – premised on a struggle between individual victims and callous or belligerent perpetrators – pits business against social justice. But many of today's businesses are not the enemies of equal opportunity; in fact, they could be powerful allies. Today, hundreds of businesses try to recruit minority job applicants, improve job conditions for working women, and provide access to people with disabilities. American businesses devote enough time and money to diversity workshops and sensitivity training that "diversity consultant" is now a common occupation. Most do all of this without judicial coercion or the threat of litigation. Large corporations such as 3M, Coca-Cola, General Electric, Hewlett-Packard, Intel, Johnson & Johnson, Kraft Foods, Microsoft, Nike, Pepsi, Procter & Gamble, Reebok, and Xerox were among the most assertive defenders of affirmative action when the Supreme Court considered it in 2003's *Grutter v. Bollinger*. In an amicus brief they wrote: "[T]oday's global marketplace and the increasing diversity in the American population demand . . . cross-cultural experience and understanding gained from such an education. Many employers sincerely lament their inability to attract and retain a diverse workforce."[24] An empowered EEOC could work together with businesses and other regulated entities; they could assist those that want to improve, offering suggestions based on what has worked elsewhere; and allow them the flexibility to innovate free from the threat of unpredictable litigation.

Similarly, if we suspended the focus on individual rights, we could allow universities to use numerical goals to achieve diversity and do so openly and honestly. Universities could offer the full range of arguments in favor of race-conscious affirmative action instead of limiting themselves to the diversity argument ordained by the Supreme Court and a more honest public and scholarly debate would follow. Crude or ill-considered policies would still be subject to review in the court of public opinion, where voters have shown themselves perfectly capable for overturning affirmative action policies and alumni and donors have made their objections to racial preferences felt.

## Conclusion

I've argued that we should suspend the reflex to describe our history and anticipate our future in terms of progress. This doesn't mean we should deny the possibility of progress; much less should it lead us to adopt the equally reflexive narrative of decline, according to which the present is always corruption and loss – the reactionary mirror image of the progress idea. Perhaps the long arc of human history does reveal moral progress; at any rate, there is as much reason to think that the accomplishments of our own era can improve the lot of the human race as there is to think those of any other era have done so. But from our limited perspective, it is hard to be sure that any given change is progress, and we risk cementing familiar patterns and ways of thinking in place when we assume they are ordained by a teleology. Suspending the progress idea will allow us the flexibility to question existing arrangements, more fully explore new ideas, and change course when approaches that once seemed, well, progressive, lead to dead ends. Ironically, then, abandoning the myth of progress might be the surest way of making it.

## Notes

1. Erin Allday, "Newsom Was Central to Same-Sex Marriage Saga," *San Francisco Chronicle*, 2008. Retrieved from http://www.sfgate.com/news/article/Newsom-was-central-to-same-sex-marriage-saga-3186381.php#ixzz2KttghXGz.
2. Michael Warner, "Beyond Gay Marriage" in *Left Legalism, Left Critique* (Brown and Halley, 2002).
3. Michel Foucault, "Society Must Be Defended," Lectures at the College de France 1975–1978 (2003).
4. Derrick Bell, Silent Covenants: Brown v. Board of Education and the Unfulfilled Hopes for Racial Reform (2004).
5. Willie J. Epps Jr., "How to Get Into Harvard Law School," (1996): 273.
6. Janice E. Hale-Benson, "Black Children, Their Roots, Culture and Learning Styles," (1982): 42.
7. Bureau of Labor Statistics, U.S. Department of Labor, "Unemployment Rate by Sex, Race and Age, 1947–1979" in *Handbook of Labor Statistics* 67 (1980).
8. House Hearings, 154 (William D. Bechill, Commissioner on Aging).
9. Michael Luo, "Longer Unemployment for Those 45 and Older," *New York Times* (2009).
10. Bureau of Labor Statistics, U.S. Department of Labor, (2010) http://www.bls.gov/news.release/pdf/empsit.pdf; Michael Luo, "Longer Unemployment for Those 45 and Older," *New York Times* (2009).
11. Laura Nielsen, Robert Nelson, Ryon Lancaster and Nicholas Pedriana, "Contesting Workplace Discrimination in Court: Characteristics and Outcomes of Federal Employment Discrimination Litigation (1987–2003)," *American Bar Foundation* (2008): 6.

12. House Hearings, 69 (Norman Sprague, Director, Employment and Retirement Program, National Council on Aging).
13. "Age Discrimination in Employment: Hearing on H.R. 2651, H.R. 3768, and H.R. 4221 before the Gen Subcommittee on Labor and the House Comm. on Education and Labor," 90th Congress 7 (1967).
14. House Hearings, 155.
15. Age Discrimination in Employment Act, Sec. 12, 81 Stat. 604.
16. Samuel Issacharoff and Erica Worth Harris, "Is Age Discrimination Really Age Discrimination? The ADEA's Unnatural Solution," 72 *New York University Law Review* (1997): 780, 830.
17. Steven Greenhouse and Michael Barbara, "Wal-Mart Memo Suggests Ways to Cut Employee Costs," *New York Times* (2005).
18. Hazen Paper Co. v. Biggins, 507 U.S. 604 (1993).
19. Issacharoff and Harris, id. 803 (citing Alan Auebach and Laurence Kotikoff, "The Impact of Demographic Transition on Capital Formation, in Demography and Retirement: The Twenty-First Century," in Rappaport and Schieber, eds., (1993), pp. 163, 174.
20. Issacharoff , p.815.
21. Id.
22. Richard Posner, "Ageing and Old Age," (2005), p. 320.
23. Paul Burstein, *Discrimination, Jobs and Politics: The Struggle for Equal Employment Opportunity in the United States since the New Deal,* 1985), pp. 27–28.
24. Brief for Amici Curiae: 65 Leading American Businesses in *Grutter v. Bollinger*, United States Supreme Court (2003).

# Commentary on Chapter 5
# The Best Time of Your Life:

## Reflections on the Myth of Moral Progress and the Continuing Evolution of Civil Rights Law

**Ronald J. Krotoszynski, Jr.**

Now is the time.
Now is the best time.
Now is the best time of your life.
Life is a prize, live every minute.
Open your eyes and watch how you win it!
Yesterday's memories may sparkle and gleam,
tomorrow is still but a dream.
Right here and now,
you've got it made.
The world's forward marching and you're in the parade![1]

### Introduction

Professor Richard Thompson Ford asserts a bold thesis: He invites us to question whether the idea of consistent moral progress serves the law – or minorities – particularly well. He argues that the idea of moral progress "is part of a myth – a very powerful myth – of a nation that is always improving, technologically, militarily, economically, socially, and morally, a nation that always ultimately get[s] it right."[2] Professor Ford invites us to "question this narrative of moral Progress."[3] One cannot seriously dispute Professor Ford's cautionary note against an unbridled, and unconsidered, faith that our own moral understandings, and the legal rules that incorporate and reflect them, are indisputably correct and fully evolved.

We tend to assume reflexively that our moral, legal, and political understandings are superior to those of the generations that preceded us. Professor Ford argues that we maintain "the belief that we as a nation are getting not only stronger, but also better: wiser, nobler, more beneficent, and more just."[4] He adds that, from this vantage point, "[o]ur institutions and customs [appear to be] superior, not only because they contain timeless principles and reflect unshakable truths, but also because they possess the capacity to adapt and improve."[5] He cautions "[t]his is a powerful myth and in many ways a beneficent one" but, at the same time "it can be a dangerous and misleading myth as well."[6]

In this responsive essay, I will consider both the potential costs and benefits of our national faith in the possibility of progress. As Professor Ford posits, real risks certainly arise from a posture of embracing the idea that contemporary social values reflect an end point for moral, political, social, and legal evolution. At the same time, however, we should take care not to throw out the baby with the bath water; even if a reflexive and unthinking narrative of progress can do more harm than good to the project of securing fundamental human rights for all persons living within our polity, a national ethic that promotes the idea of moral evolution and growth, rather than stagnation, surely has something to recommend it.

## I. A Counterexample: The Myth of Moral Progress and Quest for Universal Voting Rights

In some important ways, and in some important contexts, the myth of moral progress bears up reasonably well to sustained scrutiny. Universal suffrage for all citizens who attain the age of eighteen provides an instructive example. When the Declaration of Independence was signed in 1776, the notion of universal white male suffrage would have seemed radically – indeed unacceptably – egalitarian.[7] As Professor Alexander Keysser explains, "[t]he very word *democracy* had pejorative overtones, summoning up images of disorder, government by the unfit, and even mob rule."[8] Simply put, it was not sufficient to be free, white, male, and twenty-one in order to enjoy voting rights.[9] Most of the colonies imposed additional qualifications on voting beyond age, sex, and race, often encompassing personal wealth requirements that commonly included minimum real property holdings (often called "freehold" qualifications).[10] Some colonies even restricted voting rights based on religion. Keysser reports that "in the eighteenth century, Catholics were disenfranchised in five states and Jews in four."[11]

With the advent of Jacksonian Democracy in the 1820s, the notion of universal male suffrage gained broad-based political acceptance.[12] Even then, the notion that wealth should be entirely irrelevant to voting rights did not achieve full acceptance until more than 140 years later, in the 1960s, with the final abolition of poll taxes via a constitutional amendment with respect to poll taxes for federal elections[13] and through judicial invalidation incident to the Equal Protection Clause with respect to poll taxes for state and local elections.[14] Is it unreasonable, or naive, to claim that the expansion of voting rights from a limited class of wealthy, all-white, all-male, Protestant land owners to a model of universal suffrage for all persons who attain the age of eighteen represents moral progress? It seems fairly clear that this consistent movement – or progress – was both real and meaningful.

To be fair, Ford does not reject categorically the idea that things today are, in many important respects, better than in the past. He clearly states that he "will not deny the existence and importance of discrete *improvements*."[15] Ford adds that "[w]e benefit from countless improvements, as many in the domain of civil rights and social justice as in any other area."[16] Even so, however, Ford seeks to "question this narrative of moral progress."[17]

Of course, one should be careful about making totalizing claims to having achieved a state of moral perfection.[18] In the context of securing universal voting rights, one should keep in mind that the project was achieved only incrementally and suffered from more than one false start. For example, the Civil War Amendments plainly sought to secure voting rights for African-American men, but were silent on the question of women's suffrage.[19] Leading women's rights activists of the time, including Elizabeth Cady Stanton and Susan B. Anthony, claimed that a proper understanding of the Equal Protection Clause should encompass voting rights for women.[20] The Supreme Court, however, saw things differently and rejected the claim that the concept of equal protection had any implications whatsoever for the legal status of women.[21]

It took yet another amendment, the Nineteenth Amendment, to correct this constitutional myopia. Even so, however, with time and experience, the Supreme Court came to accept that a just government does not impose burdens or withhold benefits based on sex without an "exceedingly persuasive justification."[22] The expansion of voting rights – of full rights of citizenship – plainly constitutes a kind of progress. And, this progress seems real, substantial, and important.

Does the historical and legal fact of progress mean, however, that we have achieved a state of perfection? Of course not. And, if by questioning the myth of moral progress, Professor Ford is simply cautioning us against the illusion of immanence, Sartre's wonderful turn of phrase for assuming that our ideas and dreams are simply things existing in the mind – things for which we do not bear primary responsibility or control[23] – the warning seems wholly unobjectionable. Surely the fact that things are demonstrably better than they once were does not imply that things could not be made even better.

## II. The Limits and Dangers of the Concept of Moral Progress in the Law

Even though examples exist of more-or-less consistent progress in both our morality and our law, Professor Ford might still be correct to question whether the idea of consistent progress provides a helpful metaphor for the ongoing process of legal and constitutional evolution. In many cases, ideas once considered mainstream and self-evident become anathema over time. Without unduly belaboring the point, a civil rights symposium taking place in 1913 would have a very different agenda and cast of participants from one held in 1813. Without doubt, we sometimes know less than we think we know; moreover, this false certainty can impose tremendous costs on persons whose potential, and agency, are systematically undervalued and denied under color of law.

The early twentieth century was the era of modernism; science would light the way to truth and understanding.[24] After science had unlocked the secret inner workings of the human brain, and we understood precisely how and why our human wiring worked, the solution to virtually all human problems would soon be within our reach.

What is more, most "right thinking" people were modernists. For example, Justice Oliver Wendell Holmes, like many of his contemporaries, subscribed to this world view.[25] Given the remarkable advances that science had made, in such a short span of time, it seemed obvious that a new and glorious period of human flourishing lay just over the next horizon. And, yet, it did not quite work out this way.

Rather than increasing or enhancing the state of moral knowledge, modernism led, by a rather short and direct route, to the death camps at places like Dachau and Auschwitz. For, if we agree to use science to ascertain with absolute precision the potential, and hence worth, of any particular human being, it seems only natural and obvious that the power of the state could be harnessed to "improve" humanity more directly and efficiently.

It would be easy to assume that only Germany erred in taking the lessons of modernism too quickly and too fully to heart – but such an assumption would be quite false. The idea of progress through science led well-educated people in many places, including the United States, to embrace the argument that human flourishing was essentially a question of good genes.[26] As Professor Susan Currell notes, "[b]y the 1920s, eugenic thought permeated modern cultures and societies on a global scale."[27] Today, it is quite easy to look back with abject and unbridled horror on the Nazi death camps and *Lebensborn* program; with time and distance, these historical events take on the sepia tones of the past and we can congratulate ourselves on having transcended these obvious, and glaring, moral failures.

Even though the United States, in concert with its allies, successfully defeated the forces of fascism and Nazism in World War II, modernism made significant legal inroads. For example, the Commonwealth of Virginia's "Act to Protect [White] Racial Integrity," enacted in 1924 and declared unconstitutional in 1967,[28] represented one strand of "progressive" legal thought circa 1924.

To be sure, the Supreme Court invalidated state antimiscegenation laws on both equal protection and substantive due process grounds in its landmark *Loving v. Virginia*[29] decision. But this decision is of relatively recent vintage. For many generations, the state used its power to prevent people of color from intermarrying with whites. In many states, including Virginia, these laws were either created or made stricter in the name of progress.

The Virginia state law at issue in *Loving* provided in relevant part that "[i]t shall hereafter be unlawful for any white person in this State to marry any save a white person."[30] Virginia's antimiscegenation law contained a curious exception for persons with "one-sixteenth or less of the blood of the American Indians," a policy that evidently reflected "the desire of all to recognize as an integral and honored part of the white race the descendants of John Rolfe and Pocahontas."[31] I suspect that this is the kind of "progress" that gives Professor Ford pause about an unflinching and uncritical embrace of the notion of consistent moral progress in the American legal tradition.

Moreover, Virginia's state policy of involuntary sterilization of persons with developmental disabilities provides another example of progress run amok. This policy, like Virginia's antimiscegenation laws, accorded with good science and progressive thinking circa 1924. Unlike *Loving*, however, the Supreme Court sustained Virginia's policy of involuntary sterilization.

Writing for the majority in *Buck v. Bell*,[32] Justice Oliver Wendell Holmes infamously noted that "three generations of imbeciles are enough"[33] and upheld Virginia's involuntary sterilization program against a constitutional attack. For good measure, he shared his personal view that "[i]t is better for all the world, if instead of waiting to execute degenerate offspring for crime or to let them starve for their imbecility, society can prevent those who are manifestly unfit from continuing their kind."[34] To be clear, Holmes was not particularly idiosyncratic for holding these views; they reflect and incorporate the precepts of modernism.[35] Careful adherence to scientific principles, including state-sponsored eugenics programs, would lead to the betterment of humanity – and most contemporary adherents of progress, circa 1924, embraced this viewpoint.[36]

The persistence of public policies rooted in eugenics theory also presents a troubling kind of synecdoche for the larger ideal of progress. Programs of the sort at issue in *Buck* remained quite commonplace well into the 1960s and 1970s.[37] This provides powerful evidence of how the idea of progress can work serious and long-lasting harm.

Professor Ford argues that "[t]he idea of progress has two major influences on legal thought."[38] First, the concept "suggests that what we have today is better than what we had in the past – not just different or a mixed bag: better in some ways and worse in others."[39] Second, the idea of progress "is a sort of stages-of-development notion: Progress is inevitable and progress in one area will take a similar form to progress in another area."[40] Of course, neither of these conditions will always and inevitably prove true. Ford also cautions that "[t]he progress meme has certain benefits as a matter of rhetoric, but it also presents dangers – particularly when its partisans do not see it as mere rhetoric, but instead actually believe their own press releases."[41]

To be sure, we should be cautious not to reflexively assume that moral ideas and values are somehow imposed from beyond rather than chosen in the here and now. As Jean-Paul Sartre puts it, "[f]or if indeed existence precedes essence, one will never be able to explain one's action by reference to a given and specific human nature; in other words, there is no determinism – man is free, man is freedom."[42] Sartre also cautions us strongly against the illusion of immanence, which is the idea that our internal ideas and understandings, our thoughts and dreams, including our present moral understandings, have independent existence and constitute fixed things existing in the world (like other physical objects).[43] He explains that "[w]ithout any doubt, the origin of this illusion [of immanence] must be sought in our habit of thinking in space and in terms of space."[44]

Sartre's existentialist philosophy, including his theory of the imagination, places responsibility for the world in which we live squarely on our own shoulders. As Jonathan Webber explains:

> My situation, then, is partly a result of my imagination. If Sartre is right about all this, then our behaviour is not dictated by our surroundings. Rather, the patterns of salience and significance in our surroundings that motivate our actions result partly from the ways we imagine the world could be. We are masters to our situations, not slaves to them.[45]

Moreover, "[t]he central tenets of Sartrean existentialsim – situation, freedom, and bad faith – are all, then, rooted in his theory of imagination."[46]

What does this have to do with the myth of moral progress? I would suggest a great deal: As obviously true or self-evident as our present moral understandings may seem to us, we should be open to the possibility that the way things are presently ordered could be – and perhaps should be – quite different. As Sartre puts it, "[w]e are condemned to freedom."[47] Accordingly, then, we have the freedom to embrace, or reject, the status quo as represented by the idea of progress.

## III. The Inexorability of Making and Living with Difficult Moral Choices

Sartre admonishes us to reject the folly of living in bad faith; he posits that we all have the burden of choosing our moral path and also of living with the consequences of our choices.[48] The notion that our moral universe has been fixed is no more accurate than the notion that the sun revolves around the Earth or that the Earth is flat. It might give us some comfort to believe that we lack agency, or control, over the scope of our moral universe, but this is a form of false consciousness – what Sartre calls "bad faith" – that simply denies a freedom that we cannot escape.

To make the point a bit more concretely, consider the maintenance of racially segregated schools for the express purpose of maintaining white racial hegemony. Although once commonplace, this practice was categorically rejected as fundamentally incompatible with the baseline notion of constitutional equality. Writing for a unanimous Supreme Court, Chief Justice Earl Warren correctly noted that "[s]eparate educational facilities are inherently unequal."[49] And, accordingly, "in the field of public education, the doctrine of 'separate but equal' has no place."[50] The Supreme Court's resolution of this constitutional question, in the historical context in which the Justices decided it, was and remains entirely unimpeachable.[51]

Yet, suppose that experts in educational theory and practice come to conclude that single-sex, or single-race, K-12 public education represents the most effective means of inculcating basic skills to children?[52] Or, somewhat less radically, that a curriculum expressly designed to foster and instill group pride, esprit de corps, and a sense of shared purpose results in better performance on standardized tests scores, higher graduation rates, and higher levels of success when pursuing higher education? Should our knowledge that single-sex or single-race schools were once used as a principal tool of oppression and subordination prevent states or localities from experimenting with such programs? And, if such experimentation were to occur, would it constitute progress or serious backsliding?

I would argue that such programs would have the potential for *both*. However, the idea of progress should not foreclose a thoughtful debate about whether the noxious history of race- and sex-based exclusion from publicly provided educational opportunities should absolutely preclude the maintenance of such programs when the government's purpose, intent, and effect is to enhance educational achievement – rather than to degrade and demean would-be students. In this respect, I fully agree with Professor Ford's suggestion that "[i]f one favors a specific set of reforms *because* they are progress, it becomes hard to debate whether or not they are good in substantive terms – it is not progress because it is good; rather, it is good because it is progress."[53]

## IV. Building Better Mousetraps and the Myth of Moral Progress: Getting Beyond the Carousel of Progress Meme

In some ways – and for better or worse – Disney World represents a kind of idealized microcosm of the American Dream. When building its new Florida theme park in the 1960s and early 1970s, the Disney Corporation decided to incorporate an attraction that initially debuted at the 1964 World's Fair in New York City. Called "The Carousel of Progress," the attraction took the audience through a series of audio-animatronic vignettes. The theater – a carousel – would spin "forward" from one scene to the next, with each scene set slightly more closely to the present. Essentially, the Carousel of Progress, sponsored by General Electric, took the audience on a trip through time, and across generations.

The point of the exercise was to show the marvel of technology and how it has consistently made life both easier and better. The myth of progress, it would seem, is good for the corporate bottom line. The presentation is actually a fairly powerful endorsement of the American idea of progress; things move in a single direction, and the national destiny, which lies just over the next horizon, is to achieve an ever-better community and standard of living. We live under the illusion that one path forward exists, and that we have a manifest destiny to embrace it with gusto.

There is, of course, some risk that our system of articulating and enforcing civil rights could fall into the trap of the Carousel of Progress. In this respect, Professor Ford contests the concept of progress in the context of civil rights in two substantive areas: voluntary affirmative action by government entities[54] and in combating age discrimination by private employers.[55] With respect to affirmative action, Ford posits that the idea of progress has led some judges to embrace, prematurely, a color-blind model of equal protection and to deny local, state, and federal government entities the needed flexibility to address the present-day effects of past state-sponsored racial discrimination. In particular, he argues that the federal courts' animosity toward numerical metrics is mistaken: "To deny a large institution the use of numerical methods is to deny it the power to act effectively at all."[56] Ford also suggests that a new federal administrative agency might better be able to address racial discrimination than a system based on privately litigated legal grievances.[57]

Professor Ford criticizes the Age Discrimination in Employment Act (ADEA) for simplistically transposing an antidiscrimination model designed to address race and sex discrimination in employment. Ford laments that "[a]nother characteristic of civil rights progress is an assumption that civil rights protections are moral entitlements that should be progressively extended to an ever-growing number of arguably vulnerable groups."[58] In the context of age discrimination against older workers, however, he suggests that this model has worked poorly and both under protected older job applicants and also overprotected incumbent older workers.[59]

Ford recommends rethinking both areas of civil rights law because doing so might lead to significant improvements. In his view, simply resting on our laurels will not constitute a sufficient response to the real-world problems in need of a solution.

I agree with Professor Ford that we should be open to rethinking how we approach fundamental rights. If anything, it seems to me that we should be open to asking even broader, bolder, and more systemic questions about the first principles of civil rights law and practice. For example, our current understanding of free speech privileges speech and press rights over efforts to secure human dignity and personal reputation in ways that the rest of the world categorically rejects.[60] Are we right to place such weight on one set of human rights over another? I do not intend to answer that question now – but I would suggest that it is a question well worth considering.

In the United States, we also tend to conceptualize human rights as inhering in the individual, rather than in groups.[61] There are some normatively attractive reasons for doing this, but other democratic polities, including Canada, take a different view.[62] In these places, the vesting of human rights in both individuals and groups is both natural and obvious. To be clear, I am not arguing that the United States has decided this question wrongly – or that we have a moral or legal duty to copy the Canadian approach. Instead, we should be open to the possibility of a different basic organizational structure in thinking about how best to secure and protect human rights.

The question of whether to conceptualize human rights as running against only the state also presents an important foundational human rights question that probably merits more attention than it usually receives in the contemporary United States. In the United States, we have accepted as settled legal doctrine the idea that constitutional rights apply only against the government; the state-action doctrine limits the scope of constitutional limitations to exclude nongovernment entities from their strictures.[63] In other places, however, such as Germany[64] and in the jurisprudence of the European Court of Human Rights,[65] a different understanding of the role of the state prevails. In these places, the state itself certainly has a duty to refrain from violating human rights, but it also has an obligation to advance and secure these values more broadly within the society. Simply put, it is not enough for the state to refrain from violating fundamental human rights; instead, the state must work to promote these values in all economic, social, and political interactions within the nation.

Whether a strict application of the state-action doctrine better advances collective happiness and human flourishing is a question that lies beyond my ken (and present purpose). However, the fact that other industrial democracies have decided not to limit the application of fundamental rights only to violations committed by the state should give us at least some pause and serve as a basis for considered reflection regarding whether our answer to this important question about the scope of human rights is the best possible answer.

Finally, elections and voting rights also merit mention. To state the question simply, why do we use eighteenth-century methods and technologies in the twenty-first century? Why do voting rights vest only at eighteen, when we permit young people to make important life choices, such as marrying, becoming a parent, pursuing gainful employment, and operating a car at earlier ages?[66] Does becoming a parent and raising a child somehow require less judgment than casting a ballot? On this question, however, we seem to have settled, at least in the United States and in most other Western-style industrial democracies, on the idea that only upon attaining the age of eighteen does a person possess sufficient judgment and experience to take an active role in the project of democratic self-government. And, yet, at earlier points in world history, the idea that anyone under twenty-one was incapable of making reasoned electoral choices was universally accepted.

Professor Vivian Hamilton recently has pointed out that "[m]ore than a dozen nations have recently lowered local, state, or national voting ages to sixteen."[67] The self-evidence of maintaining and enforcing a minimum voting age of eighteen is not quite as inexorable as one might initially have thought it to be; a policy that constituted progress in 1971 no longer appears to be quite as progressive as it once was.

To be clear, I am not suggesting that we should permit infants or toddlers to vote. On the other hand, the complacency with which we accept eighteen as the minimum voting age provides an important, and powerful, cautionary note about how we can come to believe that we have been on the road of moral progress and, happily, have reached its end. We must be open to moving the goal posts, as it were, if we come to understand that our present understanding fails to take into account relevant social facts.

The notion of limiting suffrage to men who own real property would have seemed obvious and self-evident to the framers of the U.S. Constitution.[68] Indeed, voting qualifications were sufficiently off their radar that the original Constitution does not directly vest any person with voting rights save by implication – persons entitled to vote for the most numerous branch of the state legislature must be permitted to vote in the biannual elections for the U.S. House of Representatives.[69] Senate elections were left entirely to the discretion of state legislatures,[70] as was the manner of selecting presidential electors.[71] As Professor Keysser observes, "this new constitution, born in celebration of 'republican government,' did not grant anyone the right to vote."[72]

It was not until 1870, and ratification of the Fifteenth Amendment, that express voting rights were guaranteed under the U.S. Constitution.[73] The Nineteenth Amendment, ratified in 1920, extended these guarantees based on sex.[74] Finally, the Twenty-Fourth Amendment, ratified in 1964, abolishes property qualifications for voting in federal elections,[75] and the Twenty-Sixth Amendment, ratified in 1971, guarantees voting rights to all persons eighteen years of age.[76]

We have not seriously rethought the vesting of voting rights in more than a generation – more than forty years have passed since ratification of the Twenty-Sixth Amendment. Even if no clear moral, legal, or political imperative exists for permitting persons younger than eighteen to vote, it is unfortunate that we do not bother to ask whether we have resolved this important question correctly.

## Conclusion: On the Conflicting Virtues and Vices of Myth of Moral Progress

In the end, to the extent that the myth of moral progress makes us strive to be better than we have been, it constitutes a force for good in society.

To the extent that it makes us complacent about questioning our present legal, political, and moral commitments, it can blind us to possibilities that, if considered and adopted, would enhance our collective utility and happiness. In the end, although we should not churlishly refuse to give credit where credit is due for the real and important advancements in human rights in the United States since the Constitution was drafted in 1787, we also should not assume that we have reached the pinnacle of perfection, either. As Professor Ford suggests, "[s]uspending the progress idea will allow us the flexibility to question existing arrangements, more fully explore new ideas, and change course when approaches that once seemed, well, progressive, lead to dead ends."[77]

The genius of civil rights law in the United States has been the willingness of courts, lawyers, and legal academics to press for better answers when the existing legal structures and doctrines appeared to promote injustice. Starting from a very weak baseline in 1787, we have collectively redrawn the circle of inclusion to incorporate all persons without regard to wealth, religion, race, sex, and, based on recent portents from the Supreme Court, sexual orientation.[78] To deny these important improvements in our self-definition as a community would be both irrational and unpersuasive. But, we also cannot simply declare victory and move on, either.

A real and meaningful commitment to equality – the true heart and soul of the American civil rights story – demands that we always be open to asking whether our present orderings are fundamentally compatible with our stated ideals; ideals perhaps best expressed in the Declaration of Independence:

> We hold these truths to be self-evident, that all men are created equal, that they are endowed by their Creator with certain unalienable Rights, that among these are Life, Liberty and the pursuit of Happiness. – That to secure these rights, Governments are instituted among Men, deriving their just powers from the consent of the governed.[79]

The irony, of course, is that at the time Thomas Jefferson drafted these majestic words, all men were most emphatically not equal under the law, and did not have an equal chance to enjoy "Life, Liberty, and the pursuit of Happiness."

Moreover, the generation that drafted and adopted the Declaration of Independence was well aware of the fundamental contradiction at the heart of the American experiment with democratic self-government – the practice of human chattel slavery. And, yet, with the passage of time, we do seem to have come closer to creating a polity that better reflects the moral sentiment that Jefferson so eloquently articulated. Whether because of, or despite, the myth of moral progress, the United States is a far better place in 2014 than it was in 1776 – or even 1976.

The American civil rights story will always be, I hope, the legal, political, and moral equivalent of a major highway construction zone – with all the tumult, inconvenience, and discord that this implies.[80] The myth of moral progress tends to presume that we have already arrived at our scheduled destination, whereas the reality of moral progress requires us to question whether we will ever really get there. This is undoubtedly why Professor Ford suggests that "abandoning the myth of progress might be the surest way of making it."[81]

Unlike Professor Ford, however, I would not go so far as to advocate the wholesale abandonment of the myth of moral progress. Instead, I would make a more modest proposal: namely, that we must possess both the courage and the willingness to question it – and where it would take us as a people – from time to time. Civil rights in the United States, since the time of the founding, have always been a work in progress. This is precisely why, despite countless fits and starts, we have reached the position where we find ourselves today. Our equality project is neither perfect nor is it complete – but it is quite literally worlds removed from the moral universe of 1787, 1868, or 1954 (all points in time when great leaps forward in our conception and enforcement of civil and political rights took place).[82] Future progress in securing and advancing civil rights will be contingent on being open to asking whether things could be better tomorrow than they are today – and seeking in good faith, with an open mind, the answer to that question.

## Notes

1. Richard M. Sherman and Robert B. Sherman, *The Best Time of Your Life* (General Electric Theater, Walt Disney World, Orlando, FL). Burbank, CA: Walt Disney Productions, Wonderland Music Company, 1973. This was the theme song in use from 1974 to the early 1990s at "The Carousel of Progress," an attraction located in Disneyworld's "Tomorrowland" area. The Carousel of Progress, sponsored by General Electric Company, debuted at the 1964 World's Fair in New York City. In 1973, it was relocated to the Walt Disney Company's Disney World theme park in Orlando, Florida.

2. Richard Thompson Ford, "Civil Rights and the Myth of Moral Progress," in Austin Sarat, ed., *The American Civil Rights Story*, p. 193. Cambridge, UK: Cambridge University Press, 2014.
3. Ford, "Civil Rights and the Myth," p. 197.
4. Id., p. 195.
5. Ibid.
6. Id., p. 193.
7. See Alexander Keysser, *The Right to Vote: The Contested History of Democracy in the United States*. New York: Basic Books, 2000; see also Marchette G. Chute, *The First Liberty: A History of the Right to Vote in America, 1619–1850*. New York: E.P. Dutton and Co., 1969.
8. Keysser, "The Right to Vote," p. 2.
9. Grant M. Hayden, "The False Promise of One Person, One Vote," 102 *Michigan Law Review* (2003), 213, 256. ("At the country's founding, many states limited suffrage to white men who owned a certain amount of property.") For a comprehensive list of state voting requirements during the Revolutionary and Framing eras, see Keysser, "The Right to Vote," pp. 328–390, app. tables 1–3.
10. Keysser, "The Right to Vote," pp. 1–3, 15–21, 24–25.
11. Keysser, "The Right to Vote," p. 6; see Chilton Williamson, *American Suffrage: From Property to Democracy 1760–1860* (Princeton, NJ: Princeton University Press, 1960), pp. 15–16 (discussing pervasive discrimination against Catholics and Jews with respect to voting rights in the British North American colonies and noting that "[t]here we[re] legal discriminations against Catholics in some colonies even where there were no Catholics, or very few"). Even more draconian religious restrictions on voting rights existed in seventeenth-century Massachusetts, a place where "only members of the Congregational church could vote." Keysser, "The Right to Vote," p. 6.
12. Keysser, "The Right to Vote," pp. 29–52; Chute, "The First Liberty," pp. 299–305; see also Williamson, "American Suffrage," pp. 12–19, 138–181, 260–271 (describing the historical diffusion of voting rights in the United States, including the Jacksonian demand for universal white male suffrage); Charles G. Sellers, *The Market Revolution: Jacksonian America, 1815–1846*. New York: Oxford University Press, 1991, pp. 107–115 (discussing that national movement toward universal white male suffrage in the early nineteenth century).
13. U.S. Const. Amend. XXIV, §1.
14. See *Harper v. Virginia State Board of Elections*, 383 U.S. 663 (1966). Cf. Hayden, "The False Promise," p. 256 (noting that after abolishing property ownership requirements as a precondition to voting, many "states replaced property requirements with taxpaying requirements").
15. Ford, "Civil Rights and the Myth," p. 197.
16. Ibid.
17. Ibid.

18. In this context, some recent opinions of the Supreme Court of the United States regarding the use of affirmative action devices strike an oddly evangelical tone and also seem to assume a world that does not yet exist. Although we have made substantial progress in advancing the equality project, it very much remains a work in progress. Accordingly, to thunder that "[t]he way to stop discrimination on the basis of race is to stop discriminating on the basis of race,"sounds an obviously false note. *Parents Involved in Community Schools v. Seattle School Dist. No. 1*, 551 U.S. at 701, 748 (2007) (plurality opinion). Chief Justice Roberts oversimplifies a problem that presents many complexities – to be sure, legal complexities, but also social, political, economic, and moral complexities as well. If we are truly committed to eradicating the present-day effects of past racial discrimination, it will not do to simply say "we have stopped discriminating," because this approach leaves in place the present-day effects of past racial discrimination. See *United States v. Fordice*, 505 U.S. 717 (1992) (requiring Mississippi to undertake remedial efforts to undo the present-day effects of the operation of state-sponsored colleges and universities on a racially discriminatory basis in the past); *United States v. Paradise*, 480 U.S. 149 (1987) (upholding a remedial decree that required race-conscious hiring by the Alabama Department of Public Safety until the workforce resembled the workforce that would have existed but for the department's prior official policy of refusing to hire African-American applicants for most positions within the department). Sometimes, as Justice Harry Blackmun once observed, you must take account of race in order to get beyond it. See *Regents of the University of California v. Bakke*, 438 U.S. 265, 407 (1978) (Justice Blackmun, concurring in part and dissenting in part) ("In order to get beyond racism, we must first take account of race.").
19. See infra text and accompanying notes 66 to 76.
20. Susan Zaeske, *Signatures of Citizenship: Petitions, Antislavery, and Women's Political Identity*. Chapel Hill: University of North Carolina Press, 2003; see also Carrie Chapman Catt and Nettie Rogers Shuler, *Woman Suffrage and Politics: The Inner Story of the Suffrage Movement*. New York: Charles Scribner's Sons, 1926 (discussing the unsuccessful efforts to secure inclusion of women's suffrage in the post-Civil War constitutional amendments).
21. *Minor v. Happersett*, 88 U.S. 162, 168, 173–175 (1875) (holding that the Equal Protection Clause does not secure voting rights for women); *Bradwell v. State of Illinois*, 83 U.S. 130, 142 (1873) (holding that the Equal Protection Clause did not protect against sex discrimination with respect to the ability to practice law, infamously observing that "[t]he natural and proper timidity and delicacy which belongs to the female sex evidently unfits it for many of the occupations of civil life," and positing that "[t]he paramount destiny and mission of women are to fulfill the noble benign offices of wife and mother").
22. *Mississippi University for Women v. Hogan*, 458 U.S. 718, 724–725, 731 (1982).
23. Jean-Paul Sartre, *The Imagination: A Phenomenological Psychology of the Imagination*. London: Routledge Press, 2004. Sartre's *The Imagination* was first published in 1940 as *L'Imaginaire*.

24. See David Bradshaw ed., *A Concise Companion to Modernism*. Malden, MA: Blackwell Publishing, 2003; Susan Currell and Christina Cogdell, eds., *Popular Eugenics: National Efficiency and American Mass Culture in the 1930s*. Athens, Ohio: Ohio University Press, 2006.
25. Michael F. Duggan, "The Municipal Ideal and the Unknown End: A Resolution of Oliver Wendell Holmes," 83 *Notre Dame Law Review* (2007), 463, 469 n.28 (noting that Justice Holmes "lived long enough to straddle the naturalist and modernist traditions" and that "Holmes was also a great believer in the theories of population expressed by Thomas Robert Malthus").
26. Linda L. McCabe and Edward R. B. McCabe, "Are We Entering a 'Perfect Storm' for a Resurgence of Eugenics? Science, Medicine, and Their Social Context," in Paul A. Lombardo, ed., *A Century of Eugenics in America: From the Indiana Experiment to the Human Genome Era*. Bloomington: Indiana University Press, 2011 (noting that advocates of eugenics "argued that science could be harnessed to improve genetic outcomes, and careful management of human breeding would be more efficient for society economically").
27. Currell and Cogdell, "Popular Eugenics," p. 2.
28. *Loving v. Virginia*, 388 U.S. 1, 6 (1967) ("The present statutory scheme dates from the adoption of the Racial Integrity Act of 1924, passed during the period of extreme nativism which followed the end of the First World War"). Chief Justice Warren, writing for the *Loving* majority, went on to note that:

    > The central features of this Act, and current Virginia law, are the absolute prohibition of a "white person" marrying other than another "white person," a prohibition against issuing marriage licenses until the issuing official is satisfied that the applicants' statements as to their race are correct, certificates of "racial composition" to be kept by both local and state registrars, and the carrying forward of earlier prohibitions against racial intermarriage.

    Id., 6–7; see also Va. Code Ann. §§20–50 to 20–54 (1960 Repl. Vol.).
29. *See Loving*, 388 U.S. 11 ("There is patently no legitimate overriding purpose independent of invidious racial discrimination which justifies the classification"); id., 12 ("These statutes also deprive the Lovings of liberty without due process of law in violation of the Due Process Clause of the Fourteenth Amendment").
30. Va. Code Ann. §20–54 (1960 Repl. Vol.).
31. Plecker, "The New Family and Race Improvement," 17 *Virginia Health Bulletin*, Extra No. 12 (New Family Series No. 5, 1925): 25–26, cited in Walter J. Wadlington, "The Loving Case: Virginia's Anti-Miscegenation Statute in Historical Perspective," 52 *Virginia Law Review* (1966): 1189, 1202 n.93.
32. 274 U.S. 200 (1927).
33. Id., 207.
34. Id.
35. See Stephen Jay Gould, "Carrie Buck's Daughter," in Stephen Jay Gould, *The Flamingo's Smile: Reflections in Natural History*. New York: W.W. Norton and

Co., 1985, 306, 310–311 ("Eugenics, touted in its day as the latest in scientific modernism, attracted many liberals and numbered among its most vociferous critics groups often labeled as reactionary and antiscientific").

36. See David Bradshaw, "They Should Certainly Be Killed," in *A Concise Companion to Modernism*, supra note 24, at 34–55.
37. See Paul A. Lombardo, ed., *A Century of Eugenics in America: From the Indiana Experiment to the Human Genome Era*. Bloomington: Indiana University Press, 2011.
38. Ford, "Civil Rights and the Myth," p. 199.
39. Ibid.
40. Ibid.
41. Id., p. 200.
42. Jean-Paul Sartre, *Existentialism is a Humanism*. New Haven, CT: Yale University Press, 2007, 29. Sartre delivered this lecture on October 29, 1945 in Paris, France at a presentation to the Club Maintenant; the text was first published in 1946. Id. at vii.
43. Sartre, "The Imagination," 5–6.
44. Id., p. 5; see also id., 53 ("The illusion of immanence consists in transferring the externality, spatiality, and all the sensible qualities of the thing to the transcendent psychic content. It does not have these qualities: it represents them, but in its own way").
45. Jonathan Webber, "Philosophical Introduction," in Sartre, "Existentialism," p. xxvi.
46. Id.
47. Jean-Paul Sartre, *Being and Nothingness*. Northampton, UK: John Dickens and Co., 1969, 485.
48. Sartre, "Being and Nothingness," 55–70 (discussing the theory of bad faith and its relationship to human freedom); Sartre, "Being and Nothingness," 481–489 (discussing the concept of freedom and the inevitability of freedom for all human beings to make and live with moral choices).
49. *Brown v. Board of Education*, 347 U.S. 483, 495 (1954).
50. Id.
51. See id., 495–496 (holding the segregation of public schools by race violates the Equal Protection Clause); *Bolling v. Sharpe*, 347 U.S. 497, 500 (1954) ("In view of our decision that the Constitution prohibits the states from maintaining racially segregated public schools, it would be unthinkable that the same Constitution would impose a lesser duty on the Federal Government").
52. See, e.g., *Hunter v. Regents of the University of California*, 190 F.3d 1061, 1067 (9th Cir. 2000), cert. denied, 531 U.S. 877 (2000) (upholding, against an equal protection challenge, the use of race and ethnicity classifications as part of a model public school in Los Angeles, California, and holding that "California has a compelling interest in providing effective education to its diverse, multi–ethnic, public school population"); *Wittmer v. Peters*, 87 F.3d 916, 919 (7th Cir. 1996), cert denied, 519 U.S. 1111 (1997) (upholding, against an equal protection challenge, the

use of race-based and gender-based hiring and staffing decisions for a government-sponsored "boot camp" aimed at preventing recidivism by juvenile offenders). The *Hunter* panel squarely found that the experimental public elementary school's "use of race/ethnicity in its admissions process is narrowly tailored to achieve the necessary laboratory environment to produce research results which can be used to improve the education of California's ethnically diverse urban public school population." *Hunter*, 190 F.3d 1067. But see *Parents Involved in Community Schools v. Seattle Public School Dist. No. 1*, 551 U.S. 701, 731–733, 748 (2007) (plurality opinion) (opining that considering race in the assignment of students to particular schools violates the Equal Protection Clause and suggesting that "the way to stop discrimination on the basis of race is to stop discriminating on the basis of race").

53. Ford, "Civil Rights and the Myth," p. 200.
54. Id., pp. 200–210.
55. Id., pp. 210–216.
56. Id., p. 209.
57. See id., pp. 221–223.

Ironically, I found Ford's faith in the ability of a federal agency to effectively address a problem as large and complex as racial discrimination in the workplace an arguable example of undue faith in the idea of progress. Administrative agencies, at the federal level at least, were creatures of Modernism and the idea that if we could simply transcend politics, and find the appropriate experts, we could better achieve wise public policy and good government. See Sidney A. Shapiro, "*United Church of Christ v. FCC*: Private Attorneys General and the Rule of Law," 58 *Administrative Law Review* (2006), 939, 955–956; see also William Funk, "When Smoke Gets in Your Eyes: Regulatory Negotiation and the Public Interest – The EPA's Woodstove Standards," 18 *Environmental Law* (1987), 55, 89–90 (noting that the Progressive and New Deal faith in the ability of administrative agencies to resolve seemingly intractable problems rested squarely on a contestable assumption, namely that these agencies "faced problems capable of [an] objective solution"). Ford argues that "[a]n administrative agency would look at discrimination as a social problem and identify the best means to correct it." Ford, "Civil Rights and the Myth," p. 222. Maybe – but maybe not. It would depend entirely on the powers that Congress vested in the agency, in the persons that the president nominated and the Senate confirmed to serve as the agency's principal officers, and on whether the agency was a well-oiled administrative machine or a poster child for inefficiency, waste, and corruption. For example, the Minerals Management Office (MMO) was designed to operate exactly as Ford suggests this new federal agency would operate, and yet it became mired in mismanagement, dysfunction, and even outright corruption. See Ronald J. Krotoszynski, Jr., "Transparency, Accountability, and Competency: An Essay on the Obama Administration, Google Government, and the Difficulties of Securing Effective Governance," 65 *University of Miami Law Review* (2011), 449, 454–457. The end result was the Deepwater

Horizon oil spill in the Gulf of Mexico. See id. at pp. 455–456. So, although it might well be true that "[r]egulation could improve on the haphazard incentives of civil rights litigation, penalizing violation of the law and rewarding compliance," (Ford, "Civil Rights and the Myth," p. 222), objectively better outcomes might well *not* result from an agency replacing a private litigant model of securing workplace civil rights. See Sam Batkins, American Action Forum, "Red Tape Challenges to America's Veterans," July 2, 2013. Retrieved from http://americanactionforum.org/topic/red-tape-challenges-america%E2%80%99s-veterans (reporting the results of an empirical study that found myriad dysfunctions exist in the processing of claims for disability and medical benefits within the Department of Veterans Affairs, noting that a "logjam" of more than 600,000 long-delayed claims remains to be processed, and observing that "[t]he number of veterans waiting more than a year to receive benefits jumped from 11,000 in 2009 to 245,000 by December 2012"); see also Jerry L. Mashaw, *Bureaucratic Justice: Managing Social Security Disability Claims*. New Haven, CT: Yale University Press, 1983 (providing a comprehensive overview of the theoretical and practical difficulties of an administrative agency designing and operating a mass-claims system, in the specific context of the Social Security Administration's disability program, and positing that we must learn to live with "the impossibility of rational administration" and instead accept "bureaucratic rationality" as good enough for government work).

58. Ford, "Civil Rights and the Myth," pp. 210–211.
59. Id., pp. 211–216. Ford goes so far as to characterize the ADEA as "an age-based spoils system," at least in the context of its effects on the distribution of retirement benefits among younger and older workers. Id., p. 217.
60. See Ronald J. Krotoszynski, Jr., *The First Amendment in Cross-Cultural Perspective: A Comparative Legal Analysis of the Freedom of Speech*. New York: New York University Press, 2006, 104–118 (discussing the priority that German constitutional law places on securing human dignity and personal honor, even when doing so requires placing limits on expressive freedoms).
61. *Adarand Constructors, Inc. v. Pena*, 515 U.S. 200, 226–227 (1995) (explaining that the application of skepticism, congruence, and consistency rules for equal protection review of government race-based classifications "all derive from the basic principle that the Fifth and Fourteenth Amendments to the Constitution protect *persons*, not *groups*"); Ronald J. Krotoszynski, Jr., "The Argot of Equality: On the Importance of Disentangling 'Diversity' and 'Remediation' as Justifications for Race-Conscious Government Action," 87 Washington University Law Review (2010), 907, 917 (noting that the contemporary Supreme Court consistently has held that "equal protection rights belong to individuals and not to groups").
62. See Krotoszynski, "Argot of Equality," 48–51 (discussing the importance of group and community-based rights in Canadian constitutional law).
63. See *NCAA v. Tarkanian*, 488 U.S. 179, 191–199 (1988); see also *Lugar v. Edmonson Oil*, 457 U.S. 922, 936–937 (1982) (holding that "[c]areful adherence to the 'state

action' requirement preserves an area of individual freedom by limiting the reach of federal law" and has the salutary effect of preventing the imposition of constitutional responsibility on a government entity for conduct that it could not control).

64. See Krotoszynski, "The First Amendment," 98–102 (discussing the general applicability of human rights regardless of state action in German constitutional law); see also Dieter Grimm, "Human Rights and Judicial Review in Germany," in David M. Beatty, ed., *Human Rights and Judicial Review: A Comparative Perspective*. Dordrecht, Netherlands: Martinus Nijoff Publishers, 1994 ("In their capacity as objectives, human rights penetrate the whole social and legal order").
65. See *X and Y v. Netherlands*, App. No. 8978/80, 8 European Human Rights Reports, 235, 239–241 (1985) (holding that Article 8 of the European Convention for the Protection of Human Rights and Fundamental Freedoms *requires* signatory states to create and maintain social conditions that pervasively safeguard Convention-protected rights, including privacy).
66. See Joshua Gans, "Why It's Time to Give Voting Rights to Minors," *Forbes*, April 20, 2012. Retrieved from http://www.forbes.com/sites/joshuagans/2012/04/20/its-time-to-give-children-the-vote/ (arguing that minors should enjoy voting rights at an age earlier than eighteen); Vivian E. Hamilton, "Democratic Inclusion, Cognitive Development, and the Age of Electoral Majority," 77 *Brooklyn Law Review* (2012), 1447 (arguing that the United States should follow the lead of several other democratic polities and lower the minimum voting age below eighteen).
67. Hamilton, "Democratic Inclusion," 1447.
68. See Keysser, "The Right to Vote," 2–7.
69. U.S. Const. art. I, §2, cl. 1 ("The House of Representatives shall be composed of Members chosen every second Year by the People of the several States, and the Electors in each State shall have the Qualifications requisite for Electors of the most numerous Branch of the State Legislature").
70. U.S. Const. art. I, §3, cl. 1 ("The Senate of the United States shall be composed of two Senators from each State, chosen by the Legislature thereof for six Years; and each Senator shall have one Vote").
71. U.S. Const. art. II, §1, cl. 2 (providing that "[e]ach State shall appoint, in such Manner as the Legislature thereof may direct, a Number of Electors, equal to the whole Number of Senators and Representatives to which the State may be entitled in the Congress").
72. Keysser, "The Right to Vote," 4.
73. U.S. Const. amend. XV, §1 ("The right of citizens of the United States to vote shall not be denied or abridged by the United States or by any State on account of race, color, or previous condition of servitude") (ratified on February 3, 1870).
74. U.S. Const. amend. XIX, §1 ("The right of citizens of the United States to vote shall not be denied or abridged by the United States or by any State on account of sex") (ratified on August 18, 1920).
75. U.S. Const. amend. XXIV, §1 ("The right of citizens of the United States to vote in any primary or other election for President or Vice President, for electors for

President or Vice President, or for Senator or Representative in Congress, shall not be denied or abridged by the United States or any State by reason of failure to pay any poll tax or other tax") (ratified on January 24, 1964).

76. U.S. Const. amend. XXVI, §1 ("The right of citizens of the United States, who are eighteen years of age or older, to vote shall not be denied or abridged by the United States or by any State on account of age") (ratified on July 1, 1971).
77. Ford, "Civil Rights and the Myth," p. 224.
78. See *U.S. v. Windsor*, 133 S. Ct. 2675 (2013) (invalidating, as a violation of equal protection principles, section 2 of the Defense of Marriage Act, which prohibited federal recognition of state-sanctioned same-sex marriages).
79. The Declaration of Independence, para. 2 (U.S. 1776).
80. See *Cohen v. California*, 403 U.S. 15, 25 (1971) ("That the air may at times seem filled with verbal cacophony is, in this sense not a sign of weakness but of strength").
81. Ford, "Civil Rights and the Myth," p. 224.
82. See, generally, 2 Bruce Ackerman, "We the People: Transformations," 3–31, 132 (1998) (positing the existence of "constitutional moments" during which our accepted understanding of the Constitution's meaning and effect shifts or changes in an important – indeed fundamental – way, but without any recourse to the formal amendment process set forth in Article V); 1 Bruce Ackerman, "We the People: Foundations," 81–87, 116–119, 266–294 (1991) (same).

# Index

CPSIA information can be obtained at www.ICGtesting.com
Printed in the USA
LVOW10*2329020414

379979LV00005B/63/P

9 781107 039292